TRUST IN THE LAW

TRUST IN THE LAW
ENCOURAGING PUBLIC COOPERATION WITH THE POLICE AND COURTS

TOM R. TYLER AND YUEN J. HUO

VOLUME V IN THE RUSSELL SAGE FOUNDATION SERIES ON TRUST

Russell Sage Foundation • New York

The Russell Sage Foundation

Library of Congress Cataloging-in-Publication Data

Tyler, Tom R.
  Trust in the law : encouraging public cooperation with the police and courts / Tom R. Tyler and Yuen J. Huo.
    p. cm. — (Russell Sage Foundation series on trust)
  Includes bibliographical references and index.
  ISBN 0-87154-889-5
    1. Law enforcement—United States—Public opinion. 2. Justice, Administration of—United States—Public opinion. 3. Trust—United States. 4. Social control—United States. I. Huo, Yuen J. II. Title. III. Series.
HV8138 .T95 2002
306.2'8'0973—dc21

                                                                    2002066751

Text design by Suzanne Nichols

RUSSELL SAGE FOUNDATION
112 East 64th Street, New York, New York 10021
10 9 8 7 6 5 4 3 2 1

The Russell Sage Foundation Series on Trust

THE RUSSELL SAGE Foundation Series on Trust examines the conceptual structure and the empirical basis of claims concerning the role of trust and trustworthiness in establishing and maintaining cooperative behavior in a wide variety of social, economic, and political contexts. The focus is on concepts, methods, and findings that will enrich social science and inform public policy.

The books in the series raise questions about how trust can be distinguished from other means of promoting cooperation and explore those analytic and empirical issues that advance our comprehension of the roles and limits of trust in social, political, and economic life. Because trust is at the core of understandings of social order from varied disciplinary perspectives, the series offers the best work of scholars from diverse backgrounds and, through the edited volumes, encourages engagement across disciplines and orientations. The goal of the series is to improve the current state of trust research by providing a clear theoretical account of the causal role of trust within given institutional, organizational, and interpersonal situations, developing sound measures of trust to test theoretical claims within relevant settings, and establishing some common ground among concerned scholars and policymakers.

Karen S. Cook
Russell Hardin
Margaret Levi

SERIES EDITORS

Previous Volumes in the Series

Trust and Governance
Valerie Braithwaite and Margaret Levi, editors

Trust in Society
Karen S. Cook, editor

Evolution and the Capacity for Commitment
Randolph M. Nesse, editor

Trust and Trustworthiness
Russell Hardin

Contents

About the Authors

Tom R. Tyler is University Professor of Psychology at New York University.

Yuen J. Huo is assistant professor of psychology at the University of California at Los Angeles.

Acknowledgments

The argument outlined in this volume is based on a study conducted in Oakland and Los Angeles, California, and is further supported by several survey-based datasets collected as part of our own and others' research. We would like to thank all those who have supported this program of research, whether by assisting us in designing and implementing our own studies or by allowing us to analyze their datasets.

The California study was supported by a grant from the Law and Social Science Program of the National Science Foundation (SBR-95-11719) and supplemented with funding from the American Bar Foundation, under the directorship of Bryant Garth. These grants were jointly awarded to E. Allan Lind. Further funding was provided by the Public Policy Institute of California, under President David W. Lyon. John Ellwood, Andrew Isserman, Robert MacCoun, and Mike Teitz from the Public Policy Institute of California provided valuable help and feedback on the project. Karen Garrett, Yuteh Cheng, Jeff Royal, and Madonna Camel, all from the Survey Research Center of the University of California at Berkeley, helped to design and implement the survey, which was also fielded by the Survey Research Center. The initial findings of the California study were reported in Huo and Tyler (2000) and Tyler (2001e).

The 1997 sample of residents of high-crime areas in Oakland, California, described in chapter 13, was funded by a grant from the National Institute of Justice (NIJ-95-IJ-CX0046) to Jerome Skolnick, Jose Canelo-Cocho, and Tom Tyler. The Chicago panel dataset was supported by a grant from the Law and Social Science Program of the National Science Foundation (SES-83-10199) and by additional funding from the American Bar Foundation when John Heinz was director. The primary findings of that study are reported in Tyler (1990).

The first national sample of the public used to assess views of the courts was funded by a Hearst Foundation grant to the National Center for State Courts. The second national sample of the public was funded by a grant from the National Institute of Justice to the National Center for State Courts. We thank David Rottman of the National Center for State Courts for allowing us access to these datasets. Initial analyses of these data are reported in Tyler (2001e, 2001f).

We would like to thank the Russell Sage Foundation and its director, Eric Wanner, for giving the senior author a visiting scholar appointment, which allowed him to complete an initial draft of this manuscript. During that appointment the project benefited from feedback during presentations to visiting scholars at the Russell Sage Foundation and to the Working Group on Trust (Karen Cook, Russell Hardin, and Margaret Levi).

Finally, many colleagues provided feedback during preliminary presentations of our findings. We made such presentations at the Organizational Psychology Program of Baruch College; the Research in Progress Seminar Series of the National Institute of Justice; the Research Seminar on Organizational Theory and Public Management at the John F. Kennedy School of Government; the MacArthur Foundation Network on Juvenile Justice; the Justice Department Conference on the Police Use of Deadly Force; and the Law Program of the Research School of the Social Sciences at Australian National University. We would also like to thank John Darley, Wayne Kerstetter, Doris Lambertz, and Robert MacCoun, who provided helpful comments and advice throughout this project.

We have discussed some aspects of these findings in earlier papers. The policy implications of the California findings are outlined in Huo and Tyler (2000), a report published by the Public Policy Institute of California. The issue of trust is examined by Tyler (2001e) in a special issue of the *Boston University Law Review*. The question of general support for legal authorities, the topic of chapter 13, is also discussed by Tyler (2001f) in a special issue of *Law and the Behavioral Sciences*. Finally, the issue of superordinate and subgroup identification is addressed in Huo and Tyler (2001).

A number of people provided helpful feedback on this manuscript. We would like to thank Karen Cook, Russell Hardin, Margaret Levi, Stephanie Platz, Bruce Western, and two anonymous reviewers for their suggestions for improvements in earlier drafts.

This material is based in part upon work supported by the National Science Foundation under Grant no. 9996364. Any opinions, findings, and conclusions or recommendations expressed in this material are those of the authors and do not necessarily reflect the views of the National Science Foundation.

Introduction

This book addresses issues of regulation and examines the role of outcomes, procedural justice, and trust in shaping public willingness to defer to legal authorities. We focus on the strategies that legal authorities can use to bring public behavior into compliance with the law and increase the likelihood that members of the public will more willingly accept the directives of police officers and judges, two key points of public contact in our legal system.

Legal authorities have focused on laws and directives because they may restrict people's freedom of behavior or provide them with outcomes that are less than what they desire or feel they deserve. For these reasons, legal authorities are justifiably concerned about their ability to secure public compliance with their decisions, and they view willing cooperation from community members as a desirable, but sometimes elusive, goal.

The problem of regulation is made more difficult by the need to gain compliance with the law that continues over the long term. Judges and police officers do not want people to comply with their orders only when they are present and can readily sanction lawbreaking behaviors. Without ongoing, voluntary compliance, legal authorities must revisit problems and problem people, continually seeking to bring the behavior of lawbreakers into line with the law through the threat or actual use of sanctions.

The desirability of being able to obtain continued compliance suggests that legal authorities benefit when people accept their decisions and become self-regulating. Self-regulating people are law-abiding. They follow legal decisions and rules because they think that they ought to do so, irrespective of whether they believe that legal authorities might sanction them for noncompliance.

In this book, we explore the impact of two factors that shape willing deference to the law: the actions of particular police officers and judges, and people's views about the overall legitimacy of these authorities.

One of our goals is to show that the behavior of the police officers and judges with whom people have personal experiences can encourage voluntary decision acceptance. We argue for the value of a "process-based" approach to encouraging voluntary decision acceptance. This model is based on the argument—empirically tested in this study—that individual legal authorities can behave in ways that encourage the voluntary acceptance of their directives.

We show that people are more willing to consent to the directives of legal authorities when police and court procedures are in accord with people's sense of a fair process for handling a dispute, and when people believe that the motives of the authorities are trustworthy. We demonstrate that strategies of regulation based on the way in which members of the public are treated by legal authorities—process-based policing and process-based problem-solving by the courts—can enhance their willingness to cooperate with and defer to those legal authorities. We focus on two key judgments: assessments of the procedural justice of the actions of the authorities, and evaluations of the trustworthiness of the motives of authorities.

We also examine the influence of the second factor—overall views about the legitimacy of the police and the courts—in shaping an individual's decision acceptance. Legitimacy is the belief that legal authorities are entitled to be obeyed and that the individual ought to defer to their judgments. This belief is distinguished from the view that it is in one's self-interest to accept those judgments. Legitimacy is a value in the sense that it is a feeling of obligation or responsibility that leads to self-regulatory behavior—that is, voluntarily bringing one's behavior into line with the directives of those authorities one feels ought to be obeyed. Individuals with strong beliefs in the legitimacy of the police and the courts are more inclined to self-regulation; they take personal responsibility for following laws, accept the decisions of legal authorities, and are more likely to defer voluntarily to individual police officers and judges.

In part II, we focus on the effects of different views of the legitimacy of the police and the courts. We show that people's views about that legitimacy shape their reactions to the behavior of the particular legal authorities with whom they are interacting. Those who view the police and courts as legitimate authorities defer to particular police officers and judges because they think those individuals are acting fairly or because they trust their motives. Those who do not view the police and the courts as legitimate societal authorities decide how to react to their decisions in terms that are more strongly outcome-based.

In part III, we present findings showing that people generalize from their personal experiences with individual police officers and judges to form an overall view about the legitimacy of the police and the courts.

The degree to which people experience fair procedures and are able to trust the motives of individual legal authorities in personal encounters helps to shape more accepting views of societal authorities.

These results suggest that, by focusing on how they treat the people with whom they interact in the community, legal authorities can engage in a process-based strategy of regulation whose goal is to build their legitimacy in the eyes of the public. By reinforcing their legitimacy, legal authorities would thus both increase voluntary public deference to police and court directives and encourage long-term public acceptance motivated by a sense of personal responsibility to follow the law. We refer to this approach to regulation as the effort to create a law-abiding society. In this effort, the goal is to build supportive public values that encourage voluntary deference to the police and the courts. Thus, not only is the behavior of legal authorities important in the immediate situation, but it is also a form of civic education that shapes people's broader, long-term relationship to law and legal institutions.

In part III, we also explore the role of people's identification with society and their communities in shaping their reactions to the law and legal authorities. We argue that people are affected by their connections to their communities, and that the strength of these connections shapes not only their law-abidingness but their views about the legitimacy of authorities. Those who feel a connection to their community are more deferential to legal authorities. Further, they are more likely to evaluate their personal experiences with those authorities in procedural and trust-based terms than in terms of the outcomes they receive. Therefore, like legitimacy, societal connection facilitates process-based regulation and encourages law-abiding behavior.

Part IV examines the role played by differences in ethnicity or race in people's views of the law and legal authorities. The sample used to study this issue was designed to include large groups of African Americans and Hispanics in addition to a group of white respondents. Consistent with past studies, we find that minority group members are less willing to defer to the decisions of legal authorities. They are also more negative in their assessments of the authorities with whom they have had personal experiences. Our findings suggest that a process-based model explains such ethnic group differences: lower levels of acceptance prevail among minority respondents because they feel that they are treated less fairly and because they are less trusting of the authorities' motives.

Part IV also explores the role of ethnic group identification in shaping reactions to authorities. Minority group members are found to identify more strongly with their ethnic groups than do whites. However, it does not appear that ethnic group identification influences the willingness to accept the decisions made by legal authorities.

In part V, we draw conclusions and discuss the implications of the research presented for strategies of regulation. An analysis of a series of national-level studies of public evaluations of legal authorities suggests that the general public's attitudes toward the law and legal authorities are based on judgments similar to those we find to be important in personal encounters with police officers and judges. People's evaluations are linked to their views about how the police and the courts generally treat citizens. Factors that are more strongly based on outcomes, such as the ability of the police to control crime or the cost or speediness of court processes, are found to be secondary considerations when the public assesses legal institutions. This suggests that policies focusing on providing greater levels of justice to those who deal with legal authorities would resonate strongly with the public.

We conclude by arguing for a process-based model of regulation. Under this model the key to both the short-term and long-term success of a legal authority is rooted in the ability to gain the cooperation and consent of members of the public. In the short term such cooperation and consent are gained by fair decision making and treatment on the part of individual police officers and judges when exercising authority. In the long run cooperation is reinforced by building and maintaining favorable societal orientations toward legal authorities among the members of the community. The societal orientations of value include the public view that legal authorities are legitimate, public trust in others in the community, and identification with that community.

PART I

STRATEGIES OF REGULATION

THE PROBLEM of regulation becomes important whenever society and social authorities are responsible for enforcing rules that limit people's conduct. In our society, this task of regulation is managed by the police and the courts. The range of issues these authorities deal with can vary from stopping bank robberies to monitoring people's drinking, drug use, or sexual behavior. In each case, it is the responsibility of particular police officers or judges to issue directives against particular types of behavior and to effectively enforce those orders.

The arena of acceptable behavior is always a contested one, and people are often defiant and resistant when told by legal authorities to limit or change their behaviors. As a result, public compliance can never be taken for granted, and both the police and the courts are concerned with understanding how to effectively gain the cooperation of particular members of the public within a wide variety of regulatory situations.

Of course, the police and courts are not only agents of regulation. People also go to these authorities for help in resolving their problems. In such situations, the police or courts may be able to solve people's problems and provide them with desirable outcomes. In other cases, however, they cannot effectively deal with the issues involved, and must instead present people with partial solutions, or even failures to resolve the problem at all. With a burglary, for example, the police can seldom recover stolen items, while the courts may have limited success securing money from a "dead-beat dad." Hence, even in the area of providing help, legal authorities are not always able to gain acceptance by providing desirable outcomes.

This book explores the factors that shape public acceptance for decisions made by legal authorities. It advances the argument that acceptance is not primarily a reaction to the favorability or unfavorability of the decisions made. Instead, it is a reaction to the manner in which the police and the courts exercise their authority—for example, the procedures they employ to settle disputes or resolve problems. This argument is tested by exploring the factors shaping people's deference to the police and courts in a variety of types of personal experiences.

Chapter 1

Gaining the Public's Acceptance of the Decisions of Legal Authorities

O UR DISCUSSION of regulation begins with an issue of central concern to police officers and judges: the need to have their decisions accepted during personal encounters with members of the public. (For earlier discussions of this issue, see Tyler 2001e.) The ability to bring public behavior into line with their directives is a key indicator of the effectiveness of police officers and judges. If people do not comply with the decisions made by legal authorities, they cannot discharge their social regulatory role and implement the rule of law. When a judge issues a ruling, for example, those affected by the ruling must be willing to follow it rather than engage in evasion or simply ignore the order. Similarly, when a police officer directs a person to engage in a particular type of behavior, such as stopping to be questioned, that person needs to do as asked (Tyler 1990).

The public's willingness to comply with the directives of police officers or judges can never be taken for granted. As Mastrofski, Snipes, and Supina (1996, 272) suggest, "Although deference to legal authorities is the norm, disobedience occurs with sufficient frequency that skill in handling the rebellious, the disgruntled, and the hard to manage—or those potentially so—has become the street officer's performance litmus test."

The Mastrofski, Snipes, and Supina (1996) study provided some evidence about the frequency of such noncompliance problems, based on observations made of police encounters with residents of Richmond, Virginia. The researchers found an overall noncompliance rate of 22 percent: 19 percent of the people observed failed to comply when told by a police officer to leave another person alone; 33 percent failed to comply when told to cease some form of disorder; and 18 percent failed to comply when told to cease illegal behavior. The study looked at immediate compliance—whether the person did as instructed when the police officer was actually present—not at whether compliance continued after the officer had left the scene. The researchers noted that "citizens who acquiesce at the scene can renege" (283), and that they were more likely to do so if they had initially backed down in the face of superior police or court power but had not willingly accepted the decisions the authorities made about how to enforce rules or resolve disputes.

A replication of this study in Indianapolis, Indiana, and St. Petersburg, Florida, found an overall noncompliance rate of 20 percent: 14 percent of the people observed failed to obey when told by a police officer to leave another person alone; 25 percent failed to cease some form of disorder; and 21 percent failed to cease illegal behavior (McCluskey, Mastrofski, and Parks, 1998). In neither study was noncompliance an issue in the majority of cases. People usually did what legal authorities told them to do. However, both studies found that when people are dealing with the police, problems of noncompliance are not unusual.

Similarly, there have been a number of discussions about the difficulty of securing both immediate and lasting compliance with the directives issued by judges. In situations ranging from small claims courts to custody and child support hearings, judges often have difficulty gaining compliance (Tyler 1997a). This leads to the need for the parties involved in a case to return to court, often repeatedly, or for the courts to engage in sanction-based approaches to securing acceptance of their orders. One of the major motivations for recent increases in the use of mediation and other forms of alternative dispute resolution has been evidence that such procedures increase public compliance with third-party decisions (McEwen and Maiman 1984; Tyler 1989).

In this chapter, we examine how, in the context of personal experiences with the public, police officers and judges can secure the acceptance of their directives and decisions so as to perform their functions effectively. We look at the particular behaviors that police officers and judges engage in that shape individuals' reactions to their decisions. Legal authorities are often not in a position to solve people's problems; moreover, they are usually compelled to give people less than they want or feel they deserve, or they are bound by law to regulate people's behavior by limiting their ability to act as they wish. Since they cannot give people what they want or feel they deserve, the ability of legal authorities to shape public behavior thus depends on their ability to encourage acceptance in other ways.

Of course, we do not want to overstate the case. Outcomes in the majority of encounters with the police and courts are received favorably and accepted without conflict. We are focusing on the minority of situations in which people do not accept the outcomes. Although they do not make up the majority of cases, it is these cases that are of the most concern to legal authorities. Defiance and resistance can cause immediate problems, such as escalation in the use of force by police, and lead to long-term declines in respect for the law and legal authorities. When people comply unwillingly, they become long-term problems for the legal system, since they are likely both to stop complying with the particular decision after they are out of the presence of legal authorities and to be less willing to obey the law in the future.

Factors Shaping Public Perception of Legal Authorities

In recent years the perception has grown that the relationship between the public and legal authorities is becoming more negative. In particular, the quality of the relationship between the public and the police has become a highly salient public issue, as evidenced by high-profile media coverage of recent incidents involving police abuse of power in New York City, Los Angeles, and elsewhere. The degree of public outrage and level of media coverage precipitated by these and other events are clear indicators of a troubled relationship between the public and the police. Nor is public unhappiness with authorities limited to the police.

The courts, another agent of social control, have also been the target of recent public dissatisfaction with the administration of criminal and civil justice (Tyler 1997a, 1998, 2001c; Tyler and Darley 2000). Interviews with members of the public reveal a wide and varied set of concerns and complaints about the manner in which the courts handle problems and treat people when they are enforcing the law (Ewick and Silbey 1998; Finkel 1995; Hamilton and Sanders 1992; Merry 1990; Flanagan 1996; Robinson and Darley 1995; Sarat 1977).

Unfortunately, legal authorities of all types are in a structural position that makes it difficult for them to generate satisfaction, encourage deference, and create trust and confidence among the members of the public. The police are often called into difficult situations where they are unable to resolve people's problems. This happens because the police are the agency that has the responsibility for managing our society's most immediate, difficult, and intractable problems. For example, when someone is abusing his spouse at 11:00 P.M. on a Saturday night, or even at 10:00 A.M. on a Monday morning, it is a police officer, not a social services agency, that is called in to resolve the immediate problem. Similarly, when a burglary or a traffic accident occurs, the police are the authorities immediately responsible for controlling the situation, meeting the needs of the victims, and, if possible, beginning the process of identifying and apprehending those responsible for breaking the law.

Although they are responsible for taking immediate actions to deal with disputes, the police are rarely in a position to influence the underlying causes of these disputes. For example, there is little a police officer can do to create a long-term solution to the problems that have developed from the relationship between a physically abusive husband and his wife. The officer can only stop specific incidents of spousal abuse as they occur and may be called on to do so repeatedly. The police cannot change the social and psychological conditions that contribute to spousal abuse, high rates of burglary, or the number of auto accidents. Instead, they clean up after each crime or mishap. The police are also often unable to solve people's short-term problems. Many of the actions of the police are thus temporary accommodations to larger problems that legal authorities can neither control nor change, but that they are responsible for mitigating.

Similarly, people come to the courts with a wide array of personal problems, from family or neighborhood disputes to grievances against spouses, ex-spouses, landlords, merchants, or others. Like the police, the courts are often unable to resolve disputes in ways that are satisfactory to all the parties, and they may not be able to recognize or uphold the entitlements that led people to press their grievances against others. So the courts, like the police, can often provide no more than partial and potentially unsatisfactory responses to people's concerns.

Further, when the police stop people for lawbreaking behavior, they must often warn, threaten, cite, or even arrest them. The outcomes of these actions—lectures, fines, arrests—are usually undesirable to those concerned. The courts must also make decisions that result in undesired outcomes, such as orders to pay damages or go to prison.

Because legal authorities must often deliver unsatisfactory outcomes, they cannot be confident that they will always secure public compliance with their decisions and directives. Not being able to rely on the cooperation of the people with whom they interact, in turn, diminishes the ability of regulatory authorities to be effective in their roles. Of course, the scope of this problem should not be exaggerated, since the majority of people are satisfied both with how their problems are handled and with how they are treated when they deal with the police and the courts. This book focuses, however, on the persistent minority of dissatisfied people who create problems for the legal system through defiance or simple noncompliance.

Given that legal authorities cannot consistently provide people with favorable or desired outcomes, many would argue that discontent is an inevitable result of some people's experiences with regulators. They suggest that there are always "losers" when people deal with legal authorities, and that the losers are inevitably dissatisfied with and resistant to accepting the decisions and directives of police officers and judges.[1]

Strategies for Securing Decision Acceptance

How can legal authorities respond to the inevitability that at least some people will be dissatisfied with their decisions? How can they turn dissatisfaction with their decisions into acceptance? In this book, we compare two strategies that the police and the courts could use to implement their decisions. One strategy—social control or deterrence—dominates current thinking about how to manage encounters between the police or the courts and members of the public. In implementing this strategy, police officers and judges use the threat or application of sanctions to pressure people to follow their orders and accept their decisions.

A second strategy, which we advocate in this book, is a process-based model of regulation that encourages voluntary deference to the decisions of legal authorities. We argue that gaining voluntary acceptance is based on encouraging members of the public to make two interrelated judgments about legal authorities: that they are using fair procedures in exercising their authority, and that their motives are trustworthy.

The goal of this second strategy is to facilitate cooperation, consent, and the voluntary acceptance of decisions through behavior that is linked to acting fairly and showing good faith. We refer to the applications of this strategy as *process-based policing* and *process-based problem-solving by the courts.*

The key feature of the process-based approach is its focus on gaining the *voluntary* acceptance of decisions that represent an undesirable outcome for the affected individual. The process-based approach seeks to identify the specific attitudes and behaviors of legal authorities that can enhance their ability to gain public cooperation.

There is considerable evidence that when people regard the particular agents of the legal system whom they personally encounter as acting in a way they perceive to be fair and guided by motives that they infer to be trustworthy, they are more willing to defer to their directives and decisions. Further, they do so voluntarily, taking on personal responsibility for adhering to those decisions and doing so even when legal authorities are unlikely to still be watching or sanctioning them.

We suggest that the process-based approach to regulation has several advantages. First, it increases people's willingness to cooperate with and consent to the decisions of police officers and judges. Second, it lessens the likelihood of either open defiance of these authorities or secret noncompliance with their decisions. Finally, it decreases the likelihood of hostility toward legal authorities by lowering the risk that individuals will act aggressively (Tyler 2001e).

Beyond the specific experience, a process-based approach encourages individuals to believe that the law and legal authorities are legitimate and to trust other members of their community and identify with society. Such general societal orientations, in turn, facilitate the exercise of legal authority in people's future encounters with legal authorities because when they enter into an experience with more favorable views about law, legal authority, and their communities, they are more likely to consent to and cooperate with legal authorities.

Although we focus on the police and the courts, the issues we discuss have broader application to all "street-level bureaucrats"—that is, all public officials who work directly with the public and have "substantial discretion" about how they make decisions and interact with the public (Lipsky 1980). This larger group includes teachers, public welfare workers, and other local, state, and national government employees who exercise constraint (for example, tax collecting) or provide services (including job training, unemployment compensation, and medical and hospital benefits) (Katz et al. 1975). These various authorities are all engaged to some degree in regulation. They seek to bring people's everyday behavior into line with laws (Tyler 1990, 1997b, 1997c, 2001d), including those governing payment of taxes (Levi 1988; Scholz 1998; Scholz and Lubell 1998; Scholz and Pinney 1995) and those regulating institutions as diverse as nursing homes (Makkai and Braithwaite 1996) and prisons (Sparks, Bottoms, and Hay 1996). Even teachers and welfare workers enforce rules about appropriate social conduct (Lipsky 1980).

In other words, although we focus on the police and the courts, these legal authorities are only one aspect of the broader system of regulation that is central to an organized society. We mean for our comments to address the broader issues involved in shaping people's behavior in their interactions with all regulatory authorities, because each instance of regulation involves a key question: How can people be motivated to follow the laws and rules that define appropriate conduct?

Underlying this discussion of the difficulties in securing consent when delivering regulatory decisions is a psychological model that seems self-evident: people are more willing to accept favorable decisions, and they resist decisions that they view as undesirable or unfavorable. Such a model is supported by both common sense and empirical research. Although many factors shape people's reactions to decisions, even favorable ones, it is certainly clear that they are more inclined to accept and follow decisions that give them what they want. Thus, the key challenge for legal authorities is dealing with the situations in which they cannot provide everyone with what they want or feel they deserve, an issue that has also been the focus of most of the regulatory literature. In their efforts to gain people's acceptance of decisions without providing them with favorable or desired outcomes, legal authorities must activate other motivations that will counteract people's resistance to deferring to unfavorable decisions.

The Deterrence Approach to Regulation

One way to motivate people to comply with decisions is to persuade them that they risk being punished if they fail to do so. This strategy is based on the expectation that people will react to the costs and benefits associated with accepting a particular decision, and it seeks to gain their compliance by significantly increasing the cost of noncompliance. This strategy depends on creating potential additional costs to the person that overwhelm any potential gains associated with not accepting police or court decisions. The additional costs change the "coercive balance of power" (Tedeschi and Felson 1994). This power may come from intimidating physical size (Muir 1977), the presence of many officers (Lanza-Kaduce and Greenleaf 1994), or the prominent display of instruments of force—clubs, guns, and so on.[2]

This social control–based view of a strategy for the implementation of legal authority suggests that the police need to be sufficiently empowered to secure public compliance with unsatisfactory or restrictive decisions. They can bring considerable credibility to their threats of immediate or long-term sanctions for failure to comply when their efforts are reinforced by nightsticks and guns and the looming shadow of the courts, which can impose fines or imprisonment.

Operating from a deterrence framework, legal authorities approach interactions intending to "assert authority and gain deference" (Lipsky 1980, 32). "In most threatening situations, the officer attempts to maintain his edge by managing his appearance such that others will believe he is ready, if not anxious, for action. The policeman's famous swagger, the loud barking of his voice, the unsnapped holster or the hand clasped to his nightstick are all attributes necessary to convey this impression" (Van Maanen 1974, 117). And studies do in fact suggest that, as predicted by the deterrence model, the presence of greater coercive force increases compliance (Mastrofski, Snipes, and Supina 1996).

Disorder and Neighborhood Decline

It is important to acknowledge the connection between the deterrence approach to regulation and the widely cited "broken windows" approach to combating neighborhood disorder (Wilson and Kelling 1982; Kelling and Coles 1996). The broken windows model provides a rationale for the application of coercion and advocates the use of arrest as the dominant police response to even minor crimes.

In the broken windows model crime is caused by the disorderly appearance of the environment, which encourages the belief among neighborhood residents that the community is out of control (Skogan 1990a, 1990b). This collectively held view leads to a spiral of increasingly severe crime as community residents make fewer and fewer efforts to exercise informal crime control and public officials stop trying to enforce minor legal rules, such as those regarding building codes and public drunkenness (Kelling and Coles 1996). This "crime contagion" approach suggests that when criminals notice one crime opportunity, they often see others as well, and crime spreads.

Like the deterrence model, this model views the need to enforce rules as a key police activity, supported by the courts. By enforcing even minor laws and making arrests for petty crimes, such as public drinking, authorities are preventing the spiral toward more serious crimes. The police are trying to control particular individuals in troubled communities, not to establish their authority and gain compliance but rather to restore the collective feeling that there is order in the public place. In this view, we need to fix broken windows and control minor crimes because these efforts lessen the likelihood that a neighborhood will decline further into disorder. Evidence supports the argument that the zero-tolerance strategy advocated by the broken windows model can help reduce serious crime (Sherman et al. 1997).

The zero-tolerance policy is associated not only with policing activities but with the courts as well. The implementation of a zero-tolerance policy in New York City in the late 1990s led to massive changes in people's experiences with the courts. Prior to implementation of this policy, 50 to 70 percent of those arrested for misdemeanors were immediately released and told to show up for a court hearing; more than one-third of those so ordered did not appear at their hearing (Jacobson 2000). After the policy was implemented, approximately 90 percent of those arrested for misdemeanors were held in jail for twenty-four to forty-eight hours until they were arraigned in the courts. As a consequence, one hundred thousand additional people per year had personal contact with the jail system and with the court-based arraignment process (Jacobson 2000).

The risk of a zero-tolerance policy is that police and court tactics, whether picking up loitering teenagers, arresting and jailing people for minor crimes, or otherwise intervening in people's lives, will create long-term public ill will toward legal authorities. As Jacobson (2000, 4) suggests: "The current centerpiece of the New York Police Department enforcement strategy, i.e., utilizing high volume arrests of low level offenders and short term pre-trial detention and remands to jail instead of prison, has brought mistrust and open hostility between the New York Police Department and the City's minority communities." Greater hostility toward the police and the courts might have the negative effect of discouraging law-abiding behavior in everyday life (Tyler 1990), thus undermining effective law enforcement in the long term.

Due Process Versus Crime Control   Packer's (1968) famous differentiation between the "due process" and "crime control" strategies of regulation is similar to the one we are making here. Packer notes that people have an interest in controlling crime and maintaining public order (158), and he equates this interest with aggressive efforts to control crime and punish criminals, often through shortcut legal procedures such as plea bargaining rather than having a trial. To this end, he views the police as the primary agents of social control and grants them considerable leeway in how they treat people.

Packer argues that people's interest in crime control conflicts with their concern about due process and the protection of citizen rights. Therefore, he views efforts to control crime as an inevitable trade-off between the need to intrude upon people's lives and the desire to protect their due process rights. To protect people's rights, it is necessary to impose restraints on the police that hamper their ability to control crime. One clear example of such a restraint is the exclusionary rule, which does not allow illegally obtained evidence to be used in the legal system (Roach 1999). This rule protects individual rights at the possible expense of the effort to fight crime.

Process-Based Regulation

The Limits of Social Control   The picture we have presented suggests that the police and the courts should have considerable success in their efforts to secure compliance. After all, we would expect most people to stop behaving illegally rather than risk being sanctioned by the police. However, our argument is that the deterrence approach to social control, while effective and necessary to some degree, especially in the immediate situation, has inherent limitations that make it less desirable as an approach to regulation than a strategy that builds on willing citizen cooperation with the police.

The limits of sanction-based strategies are not well illustrated by highly visible and public behaviors, since people have little opportunity to hide either their illegal behavior or themselves from the police. In many settings, however, behavior is less public and less visible. In those situations, the difficulties of detecting illegal behavior or finding rule-breakers are so great that applying sanctions becomes prohibitively expensive or even impossible. For example, the police cannot monitor the behavior of most people, most of the time. They cannot be on every street, at all hours of the day. A person who is interested in lawbreaking can do so with considerable impunity simply by monitoring the social environment.[3]

Our alternative view suggests that, in the long term, effective regulation by the police and the courts depends on their ability to gain consent and cooperation (Levi 1997; Tyler 1990). Although authorities have power that they can use to regulate people by applying sanctions, or threatening to do so, their ability to regulate people is actually better served by gaining willing deference from them. As we will show, people voluntarily defer when they view authorities as acting fairly and trust their motives.

Under this model, police can control crime in most situations without acting in ways that people experience negatively. Police and court activities, such as field interrogations and court hearings, need not alienate the public if those activities are conducted in ways that people experience as fair—that is, as polite, respectful, and unbiased. The data presented here provide evidence that fair regulatory practices—in particular, process-oriented policing and process-oriented problem-solving by the courts—are viable means of encouraging people to defer to authorities. This conclusion is supported by other studies of police field practices (Boydstun 1975; Reiss 1985), as well as by studies examining the general impact of community policing (Skogan 1994).

Process-based regulation, we suggest, has the additional long-term advantages of encouraging support for legal authorities, enhancing the view that the police are legitimate and ought to be obeyed, and increasing voluntary deference and law-abiding behavior. Through a process-based approach to regulation, we seek to build and maintain the legitimacy of the police and the courts to encourage people to accept willingly the decisions of individual police officers and judges. When people are self-regulating in these ways, the result is a law-abiding society in which the need to use force and coercion to achieve compliance with the law is minimized.

In other words, maintaining respect for people and their rights need not be antithetical to legal authorities' crime-fighting efforts. Instead, it supports long-term efforts to control crime by encouraging the public's deference to authority. In contrast, force-based crime control efforts may lead to defiance in the immediate situation and to alienation and greater levels of criminal behavior among the population in the long term (Roach 1999).

These arguments are supported by studies suggesting that coercion is not an adequate strategy of regulation, even in extreme circumstances, since "to do their work smoothly police officers must obtain the consent of suspects they apprehend" (Lipsky 1980, 57). Even in highly coercive environments, such as prisons, the authorities need and depend on the cooperation of those they seek to control (Muir 1977; Sykes 1958), and prisoners' views about the legitimacy of rules and authorities are central to gaining compliance with prison rules (Sparks, Bottoms, and Hay 1996). It is the goal of a process-based approach to regulation to find ways to encourage willing public cooperation with legal authorities. Rather than maximize compliance motivated by sanction-based risk estimates, the process-based model is directed toward obtaining the consent to the decisions of legal authorities that develops from people's judgment that they are in a cooperative relationship with those authorities.

Again, how much voluntary acceptance might reasonably be obtained when authorities are unable to solve people's problems or they have to punish people's behavior? If people are treated fairly and respectfully by legal authorities and they trust the motives of those authorities, how much more likely will they be to accept voluntarily the decisions and directives of those authorities? What are the consequences of public judgments about two related social motives: procedural justice in the actions of police officers and judges, and trust in the motives of legal authorities?

Our concern with the issue of securing public deference is not a new one. In an earlier examination of public compliance with the law (Tyler 1990), the senior author emphasized the importance of legitimacy as an antecedent to voluntary compliance with the law in everyday life. That study found that the roots of legitimacy lie in "procedurally just" treatment by legal authorities. Here our concern is similar: In an encounter with legal authorities, is an individual more likely to accept their decisions voluntarily if they act fairly?

Although we emphasize the potential of procedural justice and trust to supplement the role of coercion in regulation, we do not want to overstate the argument. It needs to be acknowledged that while authorities are encouraging voluntary acceptance as part of their efforts to engage in effective regulation, elements of coercion are always in the background. On one level, knowing that authorities will apply coercive force if necessary assures all community members that others will cooperate; their cooperation thus prevents others from being "free riders" (Levi 1997). Second, through sanctioning, society must control the behavior of those people who lack social values (Ayres and Braithwaite 1992; Scholz and Lubell 1998). The self-regulatory model outlined here is intended to supplement, not replace, the appropriate role of sanctions in regulation.

We suggest, however, that a society benefits to the degree that it can rely on self-regulatory motives rather than fear of punishment. Although they may be necessary, sanctioning mechanisms are a less efficient and effective model of regulation than the regulation created when authorities can rely on the values and attitudes of the members of the public as a basis for regulation.[4]

Providing Aid to the Community   Our approach is directed toward issues of regulation involving the general public. That is, it focuses on a general sample of the population, with an oversample of minority respondents, that we have studied, not a sample of hard-core criminals, or even those people with a high risk of offending. This is not, in other words, a study of criminals and criminology, but a study that focuses on strategies of regulation within the general population.

In that vein, it is important to note that the police and the courts not only engage in regulation but also help people. In fact, people go to the police and the courts for help more often than for any other purpose, and that function should be recognized as an important aspect of police-community relations. The aspect of help-seeking that is analogous to crime-fighting and prevention is the willingness to accept failures to solve problems. People may be told when they seek help from the police and the courts that nothing further can be done to help them, even when they do feel that their problems have not been adequately dealt with. In this situation, people must also be willing to defer to the police and the courts.

Procedural Justice and Motive-Based Trust   The argument for process-based regulation as a viable alternative to sanction-based strategies is based on two interrelated ideas. The first is procedural justice: deference develops, we argue, when people are treated fairly by legal authorities, and people's willingness to consent and cooperate with legal authorities is rooted in their judgments about the degree to which those authorities are using fair procedures. Past research has highlighted the central role that procedural justice plays in gaining acceptance of the decisions of authorities—legal, political, and managerial (Lind and Tyler 1988; Tyler 2000; Tyler et al. 1997; Tyler and Lind 1992). The key finding of prior studies is that procedural justice judgments have a strong influence on decision acceptance when people are dealing with societal authorities (Tyler 2000).

Procedural justice judgments can be contrasted to judgments about the favorability or fairness of the outcomes of people's experiences. Outcome-based judgments are central to social exchange theories, such as the investment model (Rusbult and Van Lange 1996). An important issue for justice research has been establishing the degree to which people accept decisions because of how they are made rather than because of their content (Thibaut and Walker 1975).

The second idea supporting process-based regulation is motive-based trust: that is, trust in the benevolence of the motives and intentions of the person with whom one is dealing. Such trust is an inference about the *character* of the other person and the *motivations* that shape his or her behavior. If we believe that someone is honest and acts morally, for example, we believe that he or she is motivated by those character traits. Consequently, we interpret that person's decisions and actions in the light of our belief about his or her character, which we see as motivated by moral values.

We contrast such inferences with our expectations about that person's future behavior. One reason we trust people is that we think we can accurately predict what they will do in the future. We can then adjust our level of risk-taking to fit our expectations about what they will do. We refer to such trust as instrumental, because it is linked to our ability to obtain desired outcomes in interactions with others.

In this book, we will show that these two judgments about social motives—that police officers and judges are exercising authority fairly and that their motives can be trusted—are central to the public's willingness to accept their decisions. Our results suggest that experiencing fair procedures and trusting the motives of authorities are connected inferences that people make about their personal experiences. The individual who experiences fair procedures is encouraged to trust the authorities. Conversely, when an individual trusts the authorities, he or she is more likely to see their actions as fair. Despite this connection, our results suggest that each of these two judgments has a distinct, separate influence on the willingness to defer to authorities.

Although our empirical analysis suggests that these two ideas are interdependent, in this analysis we distinguish conceptually between procedural justice and motive-based trust. Further, we explore the connection of both judgments to both outcome favorability and outcome fairness.

Can Public Behavior Be Shaped by the Actions of Legal Authorities?

Demonstrating the facilitative value of procedural justice and motive-based trust is only the first step toward making the case for the viability of a process-based model of regulation. It is also necessary to demonstrate that legal authorities can engage in actions that create and sustain public belief in their fairness and the trustworthiness of their motives. Furthermore, this must be done in the context of regulatory roles in which authorities are often unable to solve people's problems and must deliver undesirable outcomes, such as arrest or incarceration.

As we have noted, our model of procedural justice and motive-based trust is a model of "social" motivations, and it brings to the analysis a basis for judging authorities other than people's evaluations of the outcomes of their personal experiences with authorities. If this model is correct, the inability of authorities to deliver desired outcomes does not necessarily undermine their ability to gain acceptance of their decisions. Legal authorities can facilitate acceptance if they act in procedurally fair and trustworthy ways.

The issues of procedural justice and motive-based trust can never be completely distinct from the favorability of people's outcomes, since people are most likely to think about whether the decisions of authorities are procedurally fair and trustworthy when their personal outcomes are negative or unfavorable. Evidence that authority is being exercised fairly and willingness to trust in the good intentions of the authorities provide a cushion against possible resistance to accepting negative outcomes.

The connection between outcome favorability and concerns about the fairness and trustworthiness of authorities should not be overstated. The fact that the police provide a favorable outcome in a particular situation does not, in and of itself, show that they are fair or trustworthy. Even favorable outcomes can be viewed with suspicion. Moreover, authorities can engage in actions that have favorable outcomes in the short term even when their long-term motives are not benevolent or caring.

We argue that the influence of procedural fairness and trust in the motives of the legal authorities during a personal encounter transcends the outcome obtained. If people feel that the authorities with whom they are dealing have acted fairly and are motivated by a desire to solve problems, then we expect that people will be reciprocally motivated to cooperate with those authorities by voluntarily accepting their decisions or directions. Further, we expect people to be more satisfied with the authorities following their experiences under those circumstances, even in the face of negative outcomes, compared to people dealing with authorities whom they do not think are acting fairly and do not trust.

The Behavior of the Authorities

We will further explore the way in which people define procedural fairness and infer the trustworthiness of others' motives. To enact process-oriented approaches to policing and the operation of the courts, it is necessary to understand the inferences about fairness and trust that people draw from the behavior of legal authorities, and the changes in behavior to which people will respond.

We predict that people will consider two aspects of the behavior of authorities when evaluating procedural fairness and trustworthiness

Figure 1.1   Conceptual Model for Process-Based Regulation

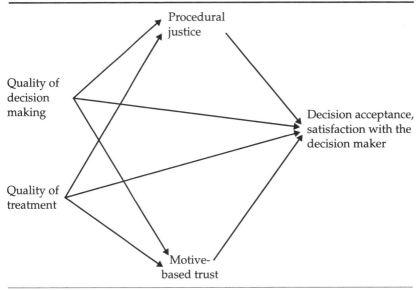

Source: Authors' configuration.

during a personal encounter: the quality of the decision making procedures used by the authority, and the quality of the treatment they receive from the authority. These two elements have also been identified as important within the group engagement model (Tyler and Blader 2000). We expect that these two aspects of people's experiences shape their overall judgments about the fairness of the procedures used by the authority. We predict that judgments about the quality of decision making procedures and the quality of treatment also shape people's views about the trustworthiness of the authorities with whom they are dealing.

Testing the Process-Based Model of Regulation

Figure 1.1 shows the conceptual model for our new perspective on the relationship between members of the public and police officers and judges. In the process-based model of regulation, a central goal of legal authorities is to encourage the reciprocal trust and cooperation of the public by behaving in ways that most people perceive as procedurally fair and based on trustworthy motives.

Our study was conducted in Oakland and Los Angeles, California, to test empirically the argument that experiencing procedural justice and trusting the motives of police officers and judges facilitates public acceptance of the decisions and directives of these legal authorities. If the results of our study confirm this prediction, then they will also suggest that our process-based model of regulation is a viable alternative to the deterrence-based social control model.

The argument that process-based strategies might be a viable approach to regulation is problematic when applied to members of minority groups because of the long history of troubled relationships between minority groups and the police; furthermore, minorities are widely perceived as more likely to encounter negative outcomes from legal authorities than whites are. Therefore, this study focused directly on the experiences of two important minority groups, African Americans and Hispanics, whose experiences are compared to those of whites.

Before we explore the findings of the California study, we need to consider the broader question that this study is designed to address. That issue is effective regulation. The goal of this study is to contrast two styles of regulation. One relies on sanctions and is the "social control" or "command and control" model of regulation. This approach to regulation is concerned with achieving compliance. The other style of regulation relies on gaining voluntary acceptance. This is the core goal of process-based regulatory styles.

Chapter 2

Theories and Strategies
of Regulation

REGARDLESS of whether legal authorities are providing help or regulating behavior, we can ask what it is they need from members of the public to be effective in their role. As we have noted, one critical need is to have people comply with their decisions and directives (Tyler 1990). For example, when summoned to control a crowd during a fire, the police may direct people to move away from the burning building. For the police officers to be effective in their role, all the people surrounding the building need to follow the order and move away. Similarly, a judge seeking to settle a dispute needs to have all of the parties to the dispute comply with his or her settlement. In both of these situations, the ability to exercise authority is diminished if each person involved must be persuaded to accept the directive without being able to draw upon a collective presumption of an obligation to defer.

As discussed, one way for legal authorities to gain compliance is through using the mechanisms of social control. Those mechanisms develop from the role of reward and cost considerations in motivating human behavior. This general model suggests that people tend to engage in actions for which they think there is some likelihood that they will be rewarded, and that they tend not to engage in actions for which they think there is some likelihood that they will be caught and punished (Nagin 2000). In the context of social control, authorities seek to gain compliance by increasing the possibility of punishment for noncompliance. Their belief is that sufficient increases in the likelihood of punishment (certainty) and in the magnitude of the expected punishment (severity) lead people to choose compliance as the most rational behavior.

Police officers carry nightsticks and guns because they need to be able to increase the threat of punishment. Those instruments allow them to gain compliance through the threat or application of force. They can alter the cost that people assign to engaging in different illegal behaviors by increasing the costs associated with conflict with the police. Judges use similar mechanisms of coercion, from fines and imprisonment, to shape people's behavior. The roles played by police officers and judges are, of course, mutually reinforcing. The force exercised by the police ensures that people will appear in court and that punishments ordered by judges will be carried out, while the possibility of courtroom sanctions imposed by judges backs up police efforts on the street.

This social control system is a framework within which the police and the courts gain the public compliance needed to perform their functions of conflict management, problem-solving, and regulation. This approach has been variously labeled a system of social control, a command and control system, a deterrence-based system, and a sanction-based system. But how effective is social control as a mechanism for regulation?

The Effectiveness of Sanctioning Systems

From the deterrence perspective, two issues are relevant to people's decisions about whether to comply with the law in a particular situation: the degree to which they expect to *gain* from engaging in a particular behavior, and the degree to which they expect to *lose* from engaging in a particular behavior.

When calculating an expectation of gain, a person estimates the probable benefits from engaging in lawbreaking behavior by combining the estimated likelihood of gain with the expected amount to be gained. For example, the estimated gain of a person contemplating a bank robbery includes both the likelihood of success and the total amount of money that he or she expects to realize from the robbery. Together these estimates create an expectation of gain.

One way to lessen the frequency of lawbreaking behavior is to minimize the possibility of gain associated with particular situations. Thus, taxi drivers put their profits in a floor safe, and people carry only small amounts of pocket money when they go out at night. In what is sometimes called "target hardening," society generally has many ways of making lawbreaking behavior less potentially profitable by making it more difficult to obtain high rewards.

However, since the potential gain from engaging in lawbreaking behavior is often beyond the direct control of legal authorities, studies of deterrence usually focus on how expectations of loss—the possibility of being caught and punished—influence criminal behavior. Like the expectation of gain, the expectation of loss can be broken down into two components: estimates of the likelihood of being caught and punished for lawbreaking (the probability of punishment), and estimates of the expected magnitude of such punishment (the severity of punishment). The person contemplating a particular lawbreaking behavior combines these two estimates to obtain a subjective estimate of the risk.

The likelihood of being caught and punished for breaking the law can be increased in many ways: police departments increase the number of police officers assigned to solve crimes, thereby increasing the risk of arrest; courts encourage the prosecution of charges rather than their dismissal, increasing the risk of punishment; or legislative bodies alter legal procedures to facilitate convictions, again increasing the risk of punishment.

Although we tend to think that the frequency of illegal behavior is affected by the actions of the police, the courts also shape deterrence. Both the move toward a non-unanimous jury decision rule and the use of a smaller jury, for example, increase the likelihood that an individual will be found guilty and, therefore, punished for a crime. Courts can also alter the severity of the punishment by increasing the penalties for various crimes or limiting or eliminating parole. The recent increase in the number of crimes for which criminals may receive the death penalty is a clear example of heightening the potential severity of punishment. Another example is the use of "three strikes" laws, which mandate life in prison after conviction for a specified number of crimes. More simply, legislative bodies can raise the statutory penalty for crimes.

When legal authorities increase either the likelihood of being caught and punished for wrongdoing or the severity of punishment for wrongdoing, they are increasing the objective risks of the loss associated with rule-breaking. Their assumption is that these changes alter people's subjective estimates of the likelihood and severity of punishment and as a consequence lead to lower levels of rule-breaking behavior. Studies suggest that sanctions do have such deterrence effects (see Nagin 1998).

Nevertheless, studies also find evidence that the magnitude of these deterrence effects is typically small. For example, MacCoun (1993) examined the results of deterrence studies in the area of drug use and estimated that about 5 percent of the variance in drug users' behavior could be explained by variations in the expected likelihood or severity of punishment. Other studies using panel designs have often failed to find evidence of any significant independent deterrence effects, or they found that when those effects exist, they are small in magnitude (Paternoster et al. 1983; Tyler 1990). These findings suggest that social control strategies can have some effect but cannot be expected to have a strong impact on criminal behavior.

The deterrence effects identified in research are found to be more strongly associated with people's estimates of the likelihood of being caught and punished for lawbreaking than with the anticipated severity of punishment (Nagin and Paternoster 1991; Paternoster 1987, 1989; Paternoster and Iovanni 1986). This suggests that efforts to increase compliance with the law need to focus on increasing the presence of the police, encouraging apprehension, and raising the likelihood of conviction in the courts. Efforts to lower the crime rate by intensifying penalties—for example, making more offenses subject to the death penalty—will be relatively less effective, these studies suggest.

Deterrence effects are found in the specific context under study here: the willingness to comply with the decisions and directives of authorities in personal encounters. In a study of 346 police encounters with people observed in Richmond, Virginia, Mastrofski, Snipes, and Supina (1996) found that the coercive balance of power between the police and members of the public shaped compliance.[1] In a further study of additional cities, McCluskey, Mastrofski, and Parks (1998) also found that the legitimacy of the police in the eyes of the public with whom they were interacting also shaped compliance with police requests.[2]

Why are risk judgments not more strongly related to lawbreaking behavior? One reason is that people have to find the risk of being caught and punished for wrongdoing to be reasonably high before that judgment influences their behavior; the risk has to exceed some threshold level to be psychologically meaningful (Ross 1982). However, in the real world the objective risks of being caught and punished are usually quite low. For example, the objective risk of being caught, convicted, and imprisoned for rape is 12 percent, for robbery 4 percent, and for assault, burglary, larceny, and motor vehicle theft around 1 percent (Robinson and Darley 1997). Of course, the psychological or subjective estimate of risk is the key to people's behavior, not the objective risk. Research suggests, however, that subjective risks are not appreciably higher than objective risks. As a consequence, subjective estimates of risk are quite low.

Ross (1982) illustrates some of the problems associated with implementing social control strategies by applying the psychology of deterrence to the problem of lowering the rate of drunk driving. He suggests that raising people's risk estimates enough to decrease the rate of drunk driving behavior, though not impossible, would usually be prohibitively expensive in terms of police manpower and people's willingness to accept state intrusions into their personal lives (for example, setting up random roadblocks).

Ross argues that it is difficult to use deterrence approaches within democratic societies because of these implementation problems. Interestingly, Ross notes that even the more intensive efforts of Scandinavian authorities to create high estimates of risk for drunk driving using random roadblocks and other expensive and intrusive law enforcement measures have been insufficient to create and sustain subjective risk estimates that are high enough to actually deter drunk driving.

Many of the problems associated with deterrence-based strategies are structural and involve finding ways to monitor people's opportunities to break laws. Thus, there are situations in which deterrence strategies will be more or less effective in discouraging illegal behavior. Two key variables that make a situation more or less amenable to a deterrence approach are the ease of behavioral surveillance and the level of resources the community is willing to devote to the task of surveillance. The influence of surveillance on the rate of lawbreaking behavior is illustrated by tax payments. When wage earners' income is recorded, the opportunities to hide cheating are low and the opportunities for effective deterrence of lawbreaking behavior are high.

The relationship between the level of community resources devoted to deterrence and the rate of lawbreaking behavior is illustrated by the case of murder. The objective risk of being caught and punished for murder is high, around 45 percent (Robinson and Darley 1997) for many reasons; one of them is that society has committed considerable resources to solving this type of crime.[3] Since society is willing to devote sufficient resources to investigating murders, the likelihood of being caught for committing a murder is high enough where deterrence should be effective in lowering the murder rate.

However, the case of murder illustrates an important limit to deterrence strategies in general. Such strategies are more effective in lowering the crime rate for crimes that are committed for instrumental reasons. For example, car theft, burglary, and crimes of this type are typically motivated by calculations about the costs and benefits expected from lawbreaking. However, other crimes, such as murder, are expressive—they are more strongly shaped by the perpetrator's emotional state and the events of the moment. Crimes of this type occur "on the spur of the moment" and "in the heat of passion." These crimes are not as strongly influenced by deterrence strategies, regardless of the risk of being caught and punished for wrongdoing, since they are not instrumentally motivated. Thus, even though murderers are apprehended at a very high rate, deterrence strategies are most likely to deter those who murder while committing economic crimes rather than those who murder "in the heat of passion."

The problem faced by those responsible for the everyday enforcement of law in democratic societies is that for many crimes the resources devoted to law enforcement are low and the opportunities for cheating are high. Although deterrence can form the foundation of efforts to maintain the legal order and is always in the background when issues of regulation are considered (Levi 1997), it cannot by itself be a complete strategy for gaining compliance. An effective strategy of public compliance necessarily includes other mechanisms for encouraging people to obey rules and directives.

The difficulties of shaping behavior through the threat or use of force notwithstanding, there are two reasons why legal authorities typically regard sanction-based strategies as the primary mechanism for exercising social control: they recognize the limits of their ability to shape behavior by delivering desired outcomes, and all the factors that make deterrence effective are strongest in the immediate presence of legal authorities. In the presence of a police officer or a judge, an individual is very likely to comply with these authorities' decisions. That is when the force of these authorities is strongest and sanctioning is most likely to be highly effective. Hence, the personal experience of legal authorities tells them that the threat or use of force changes behavior. This changed behavior, however, may occur only at that time and in that setting, a possibility that legal authorities may have had little opportunity to observe personally.

The situation of legal authorities can be contrasted to that of other authorities who have a broader range of ways to exercise social control. Consider managers in work organizations (Tyler 1999b; Tyler and Blader 2000). Those authorities can use threats of demotion or firing to shape behavior in the workplace. To the degree that they exercise social control this way, they are using sanction-based models similar to those used by the police and the courts. However, managers can also use incentive-based models of social control—that is, promising employees certain gains, such as raises, bonuses, and promotions for following the rules.

Studies suggest that incentive-based social control strategies are more effective in shaping behavior (Tyler and Blader 2000), and that approximately 10 percent of people's rule-related behavior is shaped by a combination of incentives and sanctions. As this distinction suggests, we need to separate the general discussion of the psychology of regulation from the more specific question of the effectiveness of deterrence approaches to regulation.

Legal authorities primarily influence only the deterrence aspect of people's gain-loss estimates, that is, their estimates of the potential loss associated with being caught and punished for wrongdoing. Although the options available to the police and the courts are particularly limited, other regulatory authorities are also faced with a narrow range of social control options. Federal environmental regulators struggle with developing effective strategies to ensure compliance with environmental standards, and authorities in private companies seeking to limit the theft of office supplies or the use of the company Internet connection to download pornography are also faced with limited options for shaping behavior.

Compensating for the Limits of Social Control

One way to respond to the problems associated with exercising legal authority through social control is to try to change the situation in ways that make deterrence a more effective approach to gaining public compliance—that is, to target deterrence. This strategy might include trying to deploy the resources of legal authorities more effectively: when police are concentrated in the highest-crime areas, they are more available to catch the right people (Sherman 1998); targeting people who lack other motivations for following the law is another more effective use of police resources (Ayres and Braithwaite 1992).

We advocate a second way of responding to the limits of social control strategies so as to gain public acceptance of the decisions and directives of legal authorities. As we have noted, the viability of our alternative model is based on two assumptions, both of which were empirically tested in the California study. The first assumption is that people's judgments about procedural justice and the motives of legal authorities are a factor in their decisions to cooperate with legal authorities, even when they are not receiving favorable or desired outcomes. To test this assumption, we must show that there are motivational evaluations to which authorities can appeal when seeking to obtain cooperation from individuals. The key motivational evaluations we examine are procedural justice and trust in the intentions of the authorities.

The second assumption is that there are actions that legal authorities can take that influence individuals' judgments of procedural justice and the trustworthiness of the authorities, again, even when those authorities cannot give them favorable or desired outcomes. That is, legal authorities need to have a way to create and sustain the judgments that facilitate cooperation—in this case, the judgment that they follow fair procedures and are trustworthy. We argue that these two judgments about social motives—procedural justice and motive-based trust—can be influenced by treating people in ways that they experience as fair. Two types of fair behavior are emphasized: fair decision making and fair treatment.

The Social Psychology of Human Motivation

Our focus on judgments about procedural justice and on people's trust in the motives of the legal authorities they encounter arises out of a broader effort to demonstrate the viability of non-instrumental strategies for the effective exercise of legal authority. That effort began in earlier studies that demonstrated the ability of legal authorities to gain compliance with the law by activating people's general feelings of obligation and responsibility to obey the law (see Tyler 1990).

To understand the range of possible motivations that might lead people to follow the decisions and directives of legal authorities, either publicly or privately, we can draw upon the extensive social-psychological literature that examines the factors that shape people's behavior. Based on the field theory model originally developed by Kurt Lewin (Gold 1999; Lewin 1997), social psychologists usually assume that behavior is generated from two core types of human motivation: the forces exerted on an individual by the external contingencies in his or her environment, and the motivational forces of his or her own attitudes and values. In Lewin's motivational equation, behavior is viewed as a function of the motivational force of the environment and the motivational force of the person ($B = f(P, E)$).

We have already examined the role of environmental contingencies (that is, assessments of possible gains and losses) in shaping behavior. Lewin's expanded model of motivation suggests that a second motivational factor plays a role in shaping behavior: the individual's intrinsic desires (his or her attitudes and values). These intrinsic factors shape the individual's feelings about what he or she wants or feels would be the right thing to do in a given situation, and they are the powerful motivators on which the alternative model of social control that we advocate is based—the process-based model of regulation.

The process-based model builds on the recognition by social psychologists that people develop intrinsic reasons for the actions they take. These are distinct, or functionally autonomous, from concurrent judgments about environmental contingencies. Of course, we do not mean to suggest that intrinsic and extrinsic reasons for action can be completely separated from each other; there is always some overlap between them. There are always extrinsic aspects to motivation, even when intrinsic motivations are in play. Our goal is to emphasize the distinct contribution of intrinsic motivations, beyond the influence of the extrinsic factors shaping people's actions.

Through their own actions, police officers and judges can shape people's behavior by tapping into their intrinsic motivations. If the authorities exercise their power fairly, they are more likely to encourage people to be intrinsically motivated to cooperate with them and defer to their decisions, to the degree that such motivation shapes behavior (and the results of the California study suggest that intrinsic motivations do play a major role).

From the perspective of legal authorities, behavior based on intrinsic motivations has an important advantage over behavior motivated by environmental contingencies: intrinsically motivated behavior is voluntary. That is, people are personally motivated to engage in appropriate behavior and do it without consideration for the possibility of being caught and punished for wrongdoing. If people consent to and cooperate with regulation by legal authorities, then they want to follow the directives of those authorities, or they at least feel that following those directives is something that they should take personal responsibility for doing because they feel that it is the correct behavior in a given situation.

The California study found that the desire to take actions consistent with their own intrinsic values leads people to defer voluntarily to authorities; thus, society can put fewer of its resources into supporting agents of social control. This finding is good news, because even when social control strategies are effective, they are expensive. For intrinsic motivations to be an important factor in people's relationship with legal authorities, they need to have an influence on decision making that not only is distinct from the influence of environmental contingencies but plays an important role in shaping people's behaviors. Our goal in analyzing the California study data is to demonstrate compellingly that intrinsic motivations do shape the willingness of individuals to accept legal authorities' decisions in personal encounters with them, and that those motivations are activated by the judgment that legal authorities are acting fairly and that their motives can be trusted.

Chapter 3

The California Study of Personal Experiences with the Police and the Courts

TO EXAMINE the role of procedural justice and motive-based trust in activating intrinsic motivations, we focus in this chapter on the results of a study conducted in 1998 in which we interviewed 1,656 residents of two California cities—Oakland and Los Angeles. (For details about the design of this study, see Huo and Tyler 2000.) These individuals were chosen because they indicated during the interviewer's initial telephone contact that they had had at least one recent personal experience with the legal authorities in their community.

Each respondent was interviewed about his or her most recent personal experience with a police officer or a judge; about the procedural justice he or she experienced during that encounter; about his or her trust in the motives of the particular authority; about his or her willingness to accept voluntarily the decisions made or directives issued by that authority; and about his or her satisfaction with the authority. The respondents were also asked about their more general attitudes about the legitimacy of legal authorities and about their trust in and identification with others in their community.

In the California study, we focused heavily on the members of two minority groups—African Americans and Hispanics. Both ethnic-racial groups are more economically deprived and socially marginalized than whites in this country (Schlesinger 1992). As a consequence, each group has a long history of difficult relationships with the police and the courts.

Although African Americans and Hispanics share minority status, a variety of factors clearly differentiate the two groups. African Americans are a traditionally disadvantaged group with a long history of oppression and discrimination in American society. Most Hispanics, in contrast, are relatively recent immigrants, and many Hispanics retain strong emotional, economic, and family ties with their country of origin. It has also been suggested that the two groups differ in their relationships with legal authorities (Lasley 1994): Hispanics have a more positive relationship to legal authorities than do African Americans, but a less positive relationship to them than do whites.

Our study considered each of these minority groups separately and compared the experiences of their members to the experiences of whites, traditionally the majority group. (For a discussion of which groups may actually be the true minority groups, now or in the future, see Unz 1999.)

Although the California study disproportionately sampled minority group members, it is important to note that our procedures were such that we did not target high-risk community residents—the young, minority males who are the focus of much concern among legal authorities and criminologists. We did include young, minority males in the sample, and we discuss this group separately; however, that subgroup is likely to be underrepresented in the study, since these young men are less likely to have residences and telephones. In addition, they are less likely to be at home to answer their telephones, and less likely to be willing to cooperate with interviewers.

The two cities in which we conducted the study, Oakland and Los Angeles, have large minority populations. Of the two cities, police-community relations have recently been most visibly troubled in Los Angeles, where there have been several highly publicized instances of police brutality toward minority group members (the case of Rodney King, for example). After we conducted this survey, the enduring nature of the problems in the police-community relationship in Los Angeles was further illustrated by a new police scandal—the Rampart Division scandal, which involved issues of police corruption in minority neighborhoods. Police-community relations are a recurring issue within the community of disadvantaged minority group members in Oakland as well, although police-community relations are generally better in that city.

The primary focus of the California study was on the factors that shape the public's willingness to accept the decisions made by legal authorities. We explored the factors shaping both the satisfaction that people feel with particular legal authorities and their willingness during personal encounters to defer to the decisions of those authorities.

The Design of the Survey

As psychologists, our primary concern is with people's attitudes, judgments, and feelings, and with the role of these subjective elements in shaping behavior. In this study we interviewed people by telephone to understand their attitudes, judgments, and feelings about a recent personal experience with a legal authority.

We asked each respondent to indicate the nature of his or her recent personal experience with a legal authority—that is, to explain what happened during the experience and to report on subsequent attitudes, judgments, and feelings. We also asked respondents to self-report on their resulting willingness to accept the decisions made by the legal authority.

Sample

This study was based on telephone interviews with 1,656 residents of Oakland and Los Angeles. The interviews were conducted by the Survey Research Center of the University of California at Berkeley.

The people interviewed were drawn from a stratified sample of the population of each city. The study was designed to oversample minority group members within each community. (For sampling details, see Huo and Tyler 2000.) Our goal was to create a sample containing approximately the same number of people from three different ethnic groups: whites, African Americans, and Hispanics-Latinos. Since the members of each group are not equally represented within the overall population, it was necessary to oversample minority respondents. Among those interviewed, 586 were white, 561 were African American, and 509 were Hispanic.

Each person who was identified in the sampling frame and contacted over the telephone was first screened for recent personal contact with legal authorities. Only those who said they had had at least one personal contact with a legal authority during the year prior to the interview were included in the sample. As a result of this sampling procedure, those interviewed were not a random sample of the members of their community, and the percentages reported here do not reflect the views of a complete random sample of the population of either city.

Because of the sampling procedure we used, the percentages reported here do not reflect the views of a representative sample of the population of any of the three ethnic groups living in the cities we studied. If, for example, 20 percent of the African Americans we interviewed in Los Angeles indicate a particular view, that does not indicate that 20 percent of the African Americans in Los Angeles have this view.[1]

The goal of this study was to test a theoretical model of the factors that shape people's reactions to the decisions of legal authorities. As a consequence, we did not weight the interviews to reconstitute a true random sample. We were not concerned with estimating population parameters, and the numbers shown in this book do not reflect the "true" proportions of public views in Los Angeles and Oakland. However, the relationships

Table 3.1   **Study of Intrinsic Motivations, Oakland and Los Angeles, 1998: Demographics**

Respondents	Overall	Whites	African Americans	Hispanics
Number	1,656	586 (35%)	561 (34%)	509 (31%)
Age (mean)	38.2	41.0	39.6	33.6
Sex (percentage male)	49.7	48.3	41.2	56.2
Education level (percentage with high school degree or less)	40	17	38	69
Income level (percentage with annual household income of $35,000 or less)	51	32	57	64

Source: California study data.

shown reflect the true strength of the connections between the variables measured in this study. In other words, our study is about the relationships between variables rather than about their mean levels.

The practical consequence of weighting our sample to represent the population would be to diminish the influence of the minority respondents relative to whites. Whites were underrepresented in our sample relative to their population percentage, while minorities were overrepresented. Using the actual interviews leads to the consideration of three ethnic groups of approximately equal size.

Classifying People into Ethnic Groups

We classified respondents into particular racial-ethnic groups through their self-reports. The classification "African American" is a racial category. The classification "Hispanic" is an umbrella term for a group that includes people from a wide variety of cultural and ethnic backgrounds, including those of Mexican, Latin American, Caribbean, European, and other origins. These groups are united through their common use of Spanish as a language and by some sense of being part of a group variously self-labeled as "Hispanic" or "Latino."

The demographic characteristics of the respondents in the study are shown in table 3.1. As the overall population characteristics of Oakland and Los Angeles would lead us to expect, the minority respondents we interviewed had a lower average income and lower average level of education than the white respondents. This mirrors the general situation of minority group members not only in these California cities but in all American cities.

People's Personal Experiences with Legal Authorities

Legal authorities perform two social functions: assistance and regulation. In this study assistance was the most frequent form of personal interaction that respondents had had with legal authorities, and the encounter was initiated when the respondent called the police to report a crime or an accident or to get help with some problem in his or her life. People's interactions with the courts also frequently resulted from efforts to gain assistance with a problem—for example, in handling a dispute with a neighbor, a merchant, or a family member. Although the police and the courts are sometimes able to help people by completely or partially solving their problems, sometimes there is little they can do to resolve a situation. Further, the solutions these authorities issue may not be satisfactory to the individuals involved. Sometimes people feel that they have gained something by seeking out help from legal authorities, and sometimes they do not.

Legal authorities perform their second function, regulation, by enforcing laws and rules. The police deal with people who are breaking the law and seek compliance with the law by warning, threatening, citing, or even arresting them. The courts seek to gain compliance by enforcing the laws in the decisions they make about criminal and civil cases. Judicial authorities sentence people to pay fines or serve prison terms, and they issue orders to resolve disputes between individuals. In their efforts at regulation, legal authorities are typically unable to do anything that people would think of as a gain. They can provide "positive" outcomes when they do not impose sanctions—that is, to the extent that they do not punish people. A police officer may decide to warn a motorist rather than cite him or her; a judge may decide to dismiss a case. To the person thus avoiding punishment, these are favorable outcomes. However, such outcomes bring no real material gains to people's lives. Thus, in the regulatory context, the possible outcomes of personal experiences with legal authorities range from negative to neutral.

This study identified four types of contact that people have with legal authorities: making calls to the police for assistance of some type; being stopped by the police for questioning or for engaging in lawbreaking activity; going to court to pursue a claim; and going to court to respond to a legal claim (by another person or by legal authorities). These four types of contact involve self-initiated and imposed contact with two types of authorities—the police and the courts.

Table 3.2   Type of Contact with Legal Authorities

	Overall	Whites	African Americans	Hispanics
"Have you called the police?"	76%	79%	76%	72%
"Were you stopped by the police?"	38	45	48	52
"Did you go to court?" (plaintiff or defendant)	27	20	30	31
"What was your most recent contact?"				
Called	54	60	53	49
Stopped	32	28	33	34
Went to court for help (plaintiff)	4	4	6	3
Went to court as defendant	10	8	9	14

Source: California study data.

Individuals were first asked to indicate separately whether they had had any of these four types of contact with legal authorities. Their responses are shown in table 3.2. The most frequent form of contact with police was a self-initiated call to the police (76 percent). Thirty-eight percent said that they had been stopped by the police in their car or on the street. Finally, 27 percent indicated that they had been to court as either a plaintiff (pressing a claim) or a defendant (responding to a claim).

Respondents were asked to think about their most recent personal contact with legal authorities. The nature of those contacts is also shown in table 3.2. These figures suggest that most people's experiences with legal authorities come primarily through their contacts with the police. Of those we interviewed, 86 percent reported contacts with the police (54 percent through calls, 32 percent through being stopped) as their most recent contact with legal authorities, and 14 percent reported contacts with the courts. Interestingly, the majority of the contacts reported were initiated by individuals looking for help in resolving some type of dispute or problem. Of those, the majority said that they went to the police.

Of the people who called the police, 40 percent called to report a crime, 8 percent to report an accident, and 52 percent to report other problems. Those respondents who were stopped by the police were usually pulled over for traffic violations. Almost all of those stops occurred when the respondent was driving; very few respondents were stopped while walking on the street. Those who went to court reported that their appearance was due to a traffic violation (46 percent), a conflict with someone (36 percent), a criminal charge (14 percent), or another reason (4 percent).

The 896 respondents who indicated that their most recent experience with the police involved calling the police for help were asked to indicate whether the police had solved the problem. Forty-seven percent indicated that the police did solve the problem; 45 percent said they did not; and 8 percent said they did not know the outcome. Irrespective of whether the police were able to solve the problem, each person was asked whether the police gave the problem the attention that it deserved. Thirty-four percent indicated that their problem received too little attention; 59 percent said that it received the attention it deserved; and 7 percent said that it received too much attention.

These findings suggest that many people who call the police do not receive favorable outcomes. Almost half of those who called the police for help indicated that their problem was not solved, while 34 percent felt that their problem received too little police attention. As would be expected, those whose problems were not solved were more likely to indicate that their problem received too little attention ($r = 0.54$, $p < .001$).

Separate analyses by ethnicity indicate that whites were the most likely to say that their problem was solved (59 percent). Among Hispanics, 54 percent indicated that the problem was solved, and 51 percent of African Americans reported this result. Similarly, only 29 percent of whites said that their problem received too little attention; 34 percent of Hispanics and 41 percent of African Americans said that their problem received too little attention. Overall, then, whites reported receiving better outcomes from the police.

Among the 521 people whose most recent experience with legal authorities involved being stopped by the police, 51 percent said that the police cited them for a violation of the law, and another 6 percent said that the police arrested them. Another 7 percent said that they were with someone else who was cited and were not cited themselves. Thus, over half of the experiences that involved being stopped by the police ended with a penalty for the respondent (57 percent) or others with him or her (7 percent).

This study relied on self-reports from people who had had personal experiences with the police or the courts. We assessed outcome favorability using a variety of approaches, including self-reports of the objective character of experience ("I was arrested"; "I received a ticket"). Nonetheless, it is important to keep in mind that the validity of these outcome favorability assessments depends on the statements made by respondents. We did not, for example, have independent observers watching the interactions to code their outcomes. Although self-report has been linked in prior research to objective indices of behavior (for discussions of this issue, see Moss and Goldstein 1979; Penick and Owens 1976; Sparks, Genn, and Dodd 1977), it is important to remember the limits of our approach when considering our discussion of outcome effects.

Ethnic Differences in Outcomes

Separate analyses by ethnicity reveal a complex pattern. Whites (53 percent) and Hispanics (54 percent) were more likely to report being cited than were African Americans (45 percent). On the other hand, minorities were more likely to report being arrested: 12 percent for Hispanics, 5 percent for African Americans, 1 percent for whites. Analysis of an overall index that reflects whether the respondent experienced any sanction (citation or arrest) indicates that 54 percent of Hispanics and 53 percent of whites reported experiencing some form of personal sanction, but that only 45 percent of African Americans reported such a sanction. Relative to the other two ethnic groups, African Americans were less likely to experience a sanction when stopped by the police.

Finally, 239 respondents reported that their most recent experience with legal authorities was in court. Of those individuals, 79 percent indicated that there was a resolution of their case: 34 percent pled guilty, 20 percent reached an informal settlement, 16 percent had a trial, 23 percent had their case dismissed, and 7 percent experienced some other resolution. Of those interviewed, 29 percent were plaintiffs and 71 percent were defendants required to be there in response to a complaint from another person or from a police officer or court official. The cases were primarily civil (74 percent); only 26 percent were criminal.

Each person with a court experience was asked to make an overall assessment of his or her satisfaction with the experience: 56 percent indicated overall satisfaction. Sixty-six of the respondents interviewed went to court owing to a dispute. Of those people, 69 percent indicated that the case was settled in their favor. Of the plaintiff respondents, 54 percent were satisfied with their experience, and 61 percent of the defendant respondents indicated satisfaction.

Fifty-seven percent of whites said they were satisfied with their experience in court, as did 57 percent of Hispanics and 54 percent of African Americans. As these findings suggest, there are only small ethnicity-based differences in people's overall evaluations of their experiences in court.

In addition, among those involved in disputes, 50 percent of whites said that their case was settled in their favor; 45 percent of Hispanics and 57 percent of African Americans made the same assessment. Thus, in disputes African Americans were especially likely to feel that the settlements favored them.

Minority Respondents'
Experiences with Legal Authorities

These results make it clear that minorities are more likely to deal with legal authorities because they are stopped more often by the police than whites are. Conversely, whites are more likely to deal with the police because they call the police for help. This does not necessarily mean that whites receive better outcomes, since their problems may not be solved by the police. But it does mean that the experiences that minority respondents have with the police are more likely to occur in the context of regulation—police officers seeking to enforce rules. In this study the experience of whites, by contrast, was more likely to have been initiated by a person's need for help from the police.

The distinction between calling the police for help and being stopped by the police is an important one from the perspective of the outcomes that people receive. If the police are called for help, the outcome may be positive or negative. The police may gain goodwill by solving the problem or helping in the emergency. If, on the other hand, the police stop a person for questioning, the best outcome the person usually receives is neutral—not being ticketed. Outcomes in this case range from neutral to negative. Thus, there is substantially more possibility of building support for the police through the delivery of favorable outcomes for those who call the police for help (assuming that the police can in fact solve some people's problems).

The courts also deliver outcomes ranging from negative to neutral or positive. For many, the courts are imposing sentences or fines, in which case the best possible outcome is neutral (a sanction not being applied). In other cases, people bring their disputes or problems to court and then receive either a favorable or an unfavorable outcome. Thus, the potential for gain exists in some interactions with the courts, but not in others.

The argument that whites are more likely to have contacts with legal authorities that they initiated themselves in an effort to obtain help in solving their problems is further supported by the data on people's experiences with the courts. Within the range of possible experiences with the courts, we can distinguish between those who go to court voluntarily to have their problems solved (plaintiffs or victims) and those who are in court because they are charged by other community residents or by legal authorities with breaking laws (civil or criminal defendants). We find that 29 percent of whites went to court because they were plaintiffs. Among minorities, 29 percent of African Americans were in court as plaintiffs, while 17 percent of Hispanics were in court as plaintiffs. Overall, minorities were less likely to be in court to pursue a legal claim against others, and more likely to be there to defend themselves against such a claim by another person or legal authority.

The findings of the California study show a clear difference in the experiences that minorities and whites have with legal authorities. Whites interact with the police and the courts more often because they are seeking assistance than because they are being stopped by the police or brought into court to respond to complaints. The experiences of minorities are more likely to occur in the context of law enforcement—the police or the courts are seeking to sanction or correct their conduct.

Constructing Indices of Outcome Favorability

Within each type of experience the objective indicators we have outlined can be used to construct an index reflecting the objective quality of the respondent's outcome. For example, a favorable outcome of a call to the police is one in which the respondent indicates that his or her problem was solved.

Since the indicators of objective outcome quality involve different criteria for each type of experience, we standardized the objective outcome favorability scale within each of the three types of experiences. Because of the manner in which the scale is constructed, respondents received a score reflecting the objective favorability of their outcome that is not uniform across all types of experience. However, in each case we created the objective favorability score using the most objective information available about what actually happened to the person during his or her experience.

One inherent limitation of this study is that it relies on self-reports about what happened in each personal encounter with legal authorities. An alternative method is to observe the encounter directly. An example of a study based on such a methodology is Mastrofski, Snipes, and Supina (1996). In that study observers accompanied police officers in their vehicles and directly observed their encounters with members of the public. This approach has the advantage of allowing an independent observer to code the outcome of each experience, free from the biases that occur when this information is reported by the party actually involved in the experience. In relying on self-reports, the California study lacks such an independent perspective on people's personal experiences.

In addition to the previously described index reflecting the objective quality of people's outcomes, as coded by the researchers, respondents were asked five more subjective questions to determine the favorability of their outcome. First, respondents were asked to rate their satisfaction with the favorability of their outcome on a scale ranging from "very

Table 3.3   Relationships Between Indices of Outcome Favorability: Mean/Standard Deviation

	A	B	C	D	E	F	G
Objective outcome (A) (coded from facts about experience)*	−.33/1.21	—					
How much gained? (B)	2.23/1.23	.27	—				
How much lost? (reversed) (C)	3.08/1.17	.33	.29	—			
Judgment about the favorability of the outcome (good-bad) (D)	2.92/1.00	.35	.50	.54	—		
Relative to expectations (E)	2.61/0.98	.25	.45	.42	.59	—	
Relative to others (F)	2.79/0.80	.09	.17	.18	.31	.35	—
Overall index (G)*	0.00/0.55	.52	.18	.28	.72	.63	.57

Source: California study data.
Note: High scores indicate better outcomes. The means reported for the starred indicators (*) are for standardized scales. The objective outcome scale is the summary of four standardized scores, one computed separately for each type of experience.

good" to "very bad" (outcome satisfaction). They were also asked to indicate how much they felt they had gained from the experience (gain) and, separately, how much they felt they had lost during the experience (loss). Finally, people were asked to compare their outcome to two standards: what they had expected prior to the experience (expectation), and what they thought others would receive in a similar situation (others).

Altogether, we created six indices of outcome favorability. Their average correlation is r = 0.34. The relationships among these indices is shown in table 3.3. We combined standardized versions of each scale to form an overall index of outcome favorability.[2]

How Favorable Are People's Outcomes?

Do people generally receive favorable outcomes when they deal with legal authorities? To address this obvious question, we constructed overall indices of outcome favorability using each of the dimensions of outcome favorability already outlined. One approach is to code the quality of the outcome using the objective information provided by respondents. For example, among people who said that they had been arrested, we found that the outcome was favorable 52 percent of the time, neutral 9 percent of the time, and unfavorable 38 percent of the time. We also assessed the quality of the outcome by asking respondents for their subjective opinions. Forty-three percent said that they had gained something during the experience, and 30 percent that they had lost something. Thirty-seven percent said that their outcome was unfavorable; 18 percent said that it was worse than they had expected (25 percent said it was better than they had expected; 57 percent said the outcome was what they had expected). Six percent reported that their outcome was worse than others would have received in a similar situation, 26 percent that it was better than others would have received, and 68 percent that it was the same.

These results suggest that, regardless of the type of contact people have with legal authorities, they report unfavorable or unsatisfactory outcomes during many, but not the majority, of their experiences—about 30 percent of the time. This suggests that in the majority of cases outcomes are favorable. Why, then, do we focus so heavily in our discussion on unfavorable situations? Because it is in such situations that the police and the courts encounter the greatest difficulty. Police officers rarely shoot citizens, for example, but such incidents loom large in discussions of policing. The importance of negative outcomes stems from their dramatic and influential nature, not from their frequency. It is the minority of cases with negative outcomes that consume police and court attention. In the immediate situation, spirals of conflict require the allocation of additional police and court staff. These outcomes also lead to the most serious injuries to both members of the public and the police. In the long run they are damaging because they undermine police legitimacy and increase resistance to the law.

Given that most experiences are favorable, it would seem that public views about the police should be gradually moving in a more positive direction. There is a reason why this has not occurred. Psychological studies suggest that people are more strongly influenced by negative experiences than by positive experiences (Kanouse and Hanson 1972). Interestingly, field studies support this finding by suggesting that attitudes become more negative following unfavorable experiences but remain the same following positive experiences (Katz et al. 1975). In other words, even though smaller in number, negative experiences may have more influence because the typical negative experience has an unfavorable impact on a person that is greater than the favorable impact of the typical positive experience.

The Favorability of the Outcome in Different Types of Personal Experience

People's levels of outcome satisfaction can be further understood by examining a two-by-two matrix of outcomes within different types of personal experiences. This framework has two dimensions: the authority

Table 3.4   Determinants of Outcome Favorability

Determinants	Equation 1: Objective Outcome Favorability (H = Good)	Equation 2: Overall Index of Outcome Favorability (H = Good)
Beta weights		
Hispanic (H = yes)	−.04	−.07
African American (H = yes)	−.03	−.05
Voluntary? (H = yes)	.32***	.03
Authority dealt with (police-courts) (H = police)	−.18***	−.10***
City (H = Los Angeles)	.03	−.03
Gender (H = female)	−.02	−.03
Age (H = old)	.01	−.04
Education (H = high)	.03	.03
Income (H = high)	.01	.01
Party (H = Democratic)	−.03	−.03
Liberalism (H = conservative)	.02	−.04
Total adjusted R-squared	11%***	1%**

Source: California study data.
**p < .01.
***p < .001.

(police and courts) with whom the person dealt, and the voluntary or involuntary nature of the contact, that is, whether it was initiated by the person seeking help or by legal authorities enforcing rules.

A regression analysis, shown in table 3.4, indicates that both dimensions of experience with legal authorities—the particular authority and the voluntary or involuntary nature of the experience—shape the favorability of the outcome. The objective favorability of outcomes is shaped by both dimensions. Respondents were found to receive more favorable outcomes if their experience was voluntary and if they dealt with the courts. Further, total outcome favorability (objective and subjective) was higher when people dealt with the courts.

Looking at the objective index of outcome favorability that we coded, we could find no ethnic group differences in outcome favorability for either African Americans or Hispanics. Both ethnic groups reported more negative outcomes, but in neither case was the difference significant. Similarly, there was no ethnic group difference in subjective outcome favorability.

A second aspect of the findings is the relative lack of background effects on judgments of outcome favorability. Looking at the index of objective outcome favorability, we found no differences for sex, age, education, or income. Further, we found no differences based on political party or ideology. In general, therefore, we did not find that different types of people received better or worse outcomes from the police and the courts. If we look at the overall summary index, we find basically the same result. All of these results suggest that the experiences of different types of people with the police and the courts did not lead to outcomes of differential favorability. Therefore, at least among our respondents, the background and ethnicity of the person involved in the interaction was not a good predictor of the favorability of the outcome.

This finding is surprising and contrary to what we might have anticipated. We typically think that the disadvantaged and minorities are more likely to be cited or jailed when they deal with the police and the courts. To some extent the finding is overstated, since we also found that minority respondents were more likely to have nonvoluntary experiences with legal authorities, and that the direct influence of that factor was strong. Hence, there were some indirect effects associated with minority status. Nonetheless, for whatever reason, we did not find direct effects of ethnicity on outcome favorability.

In our earlier discussion, we differentiated between four types of experiences with legal authorities. It is possible that negative outcomes occur more frequently with some types of experiences than with others. One obvious possibility is that positive outcomes occur most frequently when people have voluntary experiences with the police or the courts. To test this possibility, we divided respondents into four groups, depending on the type of experience they reported. We then looked at the proportion of positive outcomes respondents received within each of the four types of experiences. When they voluntarily sought help, objective coding suggests that they received a favorable outcome 52 percent of the time when interacting with the police and 63 percent of the time when interacting with the courts. When authorities were enforcing rules, respondents received an objectively favorable outcome 50 percent of the time from either the police or the courts. In self-reports about their personal experiences respondents who voluntarily sought help claimed that they had received a satisfactory outcome 70 percent of the time from the police and 61 percent of the time from the courts. When rules were being enforced, they reported receiving a satisfactory outcome 53 percent of the time from the police and 63 percent of the time from the courts.

The general conclusion of this analysis of four types of personal experiences with legal authorities is that, regardless of whether their experiences were voluntary or involuntary, and regardless of whether they were dealing with the police or the courts, our respondents usually received satisfactory outcomes, but that they also received negative or unsatisfactory outcomes in a nontrivial minority of cases. Our assumption that people receive negative outcomes from legal authorities during a subset of their experiences is supported by the results of this study.

If people's reactions to their personal experiences are driven exclusively by the favorability of their outcomes, then we can ask whether the police and the courts experience widespread resistance to the acceptance of their decisions.

Do People Accept the Decisions of Legal Authorities?

For the process-based model of regulation to be an effective way to gain acceptance of the decisions made by legal authorities, people's behavioral responses to these authorities must be shaped by assessments of factors other than their outcomes. In the California study we focused on one type of behavioral response: the voluntary acceptance of the decisions made by legal authorities. We examined the factors that shape the willingness of people to defer voluntarily in their interactions with police officers and judges to the decisions made by those authorities.

We have already noted that, in prior studies based on observations of police encounters with members of the public, people initially failed to comply with police directives about the law 15 to 30 percent of the time. These numbers support the suggestion that gaining compliance, and particularly willing cooperation, is a difficult problem for the police.

As previously discussed, legal authorities must secure compliance to be effective, and they clearly benefit from voluntary acceptance of their decisions and directives by the public. To assess the degree to which acceptance was voluntary among the California study respondents, each person was asked how willingly he or she had deferred to the decisions or directives of the police officer or judge.

Respondents were also asked about their satisfaction with the decision maker. This second measure, which involved an evaluation of the legal authority with whom the respondent was dealing, was relevant to the broader impact of the personal encounter on the respondent's views about legal authorities. Ideally, legal authorities can gain acceptance in ways that maintain or even enhance the evaluations they receive from people with whom they interact.

One useful way to think about individuals' experiences with the police and the courts is the "customer service" perspective, which is integral to how private businesses interact with the public. From that perspective, the experience that a customer has with a company is successful if it leaves the customer satisfied about both the specific outcome of their interaction (did they receive the product or service they wanted?) and the people with whom they dealt in making a transaction (were they treated well by the service personnel they encountered in the store?). A customer service model seeks to provide a satisfactory product in ways that enhance customers' feelings about both the people with whom they interact and the company itself.

Can we apply a customer service perspective to people's experiences with legal authorities? We must begin by acknowledging that legal authorities are limited as service deliverers in two ways. First, they are constrained in their ability to deliver desired products. For example, a robbery victim wants his or her stolen items recovered and the perpetrator punished. The police may not be able to deliver these outcomes. Similarly, both parties to a dispute want the judge to rule in their favor, and the judge cannot satisfy both at once. Second, legal authorities are in the business of responsibility and obligation management. As they enforce rules, they must restrict and limit people's ability to do as they wish. Like those who collect taxes (Scholz 1998) or conscript citizens to fight in wars (Levi 1997), the police and the courts are providing a product that people are not necessarily interested in having.[3]

However, legal authorities can utilize a customer service perspective in one important respect: they can handle problems in ways that show a concern for how people are treated and that reflect a good-faith effort to deal with people's needs. If, as a result, people view authorities as fair and feel that they are trying to act in good faith, we expect that the authorities will both gain acceptance for their decisions and build support for themselves as authorities. We detail more fully in later chapters how authorities might act to encourage people to view them as acting fairly and to trust their intentions.

The Measurement of Acceptance

Respondents' judgments about their responses to the directives of legal authorities are shown in table 3.5. Almost all of them said that they did what they were asked to do by legal authorities: 98 percent agreed or agreed strongly that "I did what I was asked to do." This very high level of compliance reinforces the point made earlier. In the moment, with legal authorities present, people usually comply. However, they may do so reluctantly, complaining and resisting to some degree. And, in fact, previously outlined studies suggest actual compliance rates may be lower. Certainly, people are less willing to say that they accept the decisions. Faced with someone carrying a gun and acting like he or she would be willing to use it, most people follow instructions, however reluctantly, in the immediate situation. However, our main concern is not people's simple compliance but their willing acceptance of the directives they are given.

Table 3.5   Willing Acceptance of the Decisions of Legal Authorities

Responses	Total	Authority		Voluntary?	
		Police	Court	Yes	No
		86%	14%	58%	42%
Compliance					
"I did what I was asked to do."					
Agree or agree strongly	98%	98	97	98	98
Agree strongly	86	86	86	85	87
Acceptance (alpha = 0.80)					
"I willingly accepted the decision."	87	86	83	87	84
"In a similar situation in the future, I would like to see the situation handled in the same way."	59	60	57	65	51
"I considered going to someone else to try to change the decision."*	23	22	27	19	28
"The situation could have been handled better."*	49	48	52	41	60
Satisfaction (alpha = 0.92)					
"The person generally did a good job dealing with my situation."	72	72	70	78	63
"I was generally satisfied with the way he/she handled the situation."	68	68	64	76	57

Source: California study data.
*These items are reversed when the scale is created.

We assessed willing deference to the directives of legal authorities using a four-item scale. These items (also shown in table 3.5) illustrate the difference between compliance and the willing acceptance of decisions. As we would expect, people willingly accept decisions at a lower rate than they comply with them. Although 87 percent of the respondents said that they willingly accepted the decision of the legal authority, 41 percent said that they would *not* like to see future situations handled in the same way; 49 percent said that the situation could have been handled better; and 23 percent said that they had thought about trying to go to another authority to change the decision. These items are combined into an index of acceptance (alpha = 0.80).

A judgment closely related to the willing acceptance of the decisions of legal authorities is satisfaction with the decision maker. Respondents were also asked to indicate how satisfied they were with the decisionmaker. They generally indicated that the authority handled their situation well (72 percent) and that they were satisfied with the way their situation was handled (68 percent). We combined these two items into an overall index of satisfaction with the decision maker (alpha = 0.92).

Summary

Overall, the findings of the California study suggest that, in the majority of cases, the police and the courts provide people with outcomes that are both favorable and satisfactory, regardless of whether those outcomes are evaluated by an objective or subjective standard. When outcomes are favorable, problems with gaining compliance should be minimal, and cooperation between the police or the courts and members of the public should be easy to obtain. In a minority of situations, however, the police and the courts deliver undesirable, unsatisfactory outcomes. In those cases, obtaining consent and cooperation becomes more difficult. It is in such settings that the strategies evaluated in this study become important, since they are designed to facilitate the acceptance of outcomes that people view as undesirable or unfair.

PART II

THE PSYCHOLOGY
OF DECISION ACCEPTANCE

W E HAVE set out two interrelated social motives—procedural justice and motive-based trust—as the foundation for our model
of process-based regulation. For this model to be viable, it is
necessary that these two mechanisms actually play an important role in
shaping people's reactions to their personal experiences with the police
and the courts.

The goal of the analyses in part II is to test the importance of each of
these social motives in encouraging people to accept willingly the decisions made by police officers and judges, particularly those leading to
undesirable outcomes. In chapter 4, we directly address this issue by
examining the degree to which procedural justice influences decision
acceptance and satisfaction with the decision maker. Chapter 5 examines the same issue, but with a focus on motive-based trust, and chapter 6 brings these two issues together to create a unified model of the
influence of social motives.

Chapter 4

Procedural Justice and Decision Acceptance

THE SOCIAL-PSYCHOLOGICAL literature on justice suggests another reason besides desirability that people accept third-party decisions: the fairness of the process of coming to those decisions. To understand the importance of procedural justice, we need to consider whether people are in fact motivated by ethical judgments about what is right and wrong when those judgments suggest that they behave in ways that depart from their self-interest.

For justice to be a real factor in decision acceptance, people's behavior must be shaped by their judgments about what is right or wrong, just or unjust, apart from their judgments about what is personally beneficial. Justice must be able to motivate the acceptance of rules and decisions that depart from individual self-interest. In terms of regulation, justice has little importance if it does not influence how people feel about their personal experiences with police officers and judges and what they do in response to the decisions of these legal authorities. In particular, people's feelings about justice should encourage them to accept unfavorable decisions.[1]

Studies that explore people's behavior in situations in which their feelings about what is just depart from their evaluations of self-interest suggest that people's attitudes, feelings, and behaviors are independently influenced by their sense of what is right and wrong (Tyler 2001a; Tyler et al. 1997; Tyler and Smith 1997). Because of the general importance of justice-based judgments in shaping people's attitudes and behaviors, it seems reasonable to suggest that one basis for gaining deference is by providing people with justice.

In this analysis such ideas about social justice are central to our understanding of how we might secure cooperation from the public. We argue that feelings about justice shape people's behavior during their encounters with legal authorities, and that this justice-based influence on behavior provides a way in which legal authorities can manage conflict and influence people to accept decisions more willingly.

Equity-Based Approaches:
The Distributive Justice Theory

The importance of this issue is first demonstrated in the literature on distributive, rather than procedural, justice. The literature on distributive justice developed as a response to a problem much like the one we are addressing in this book. The managers in work organizations are often required to make decisions about pay or promotion that give employees less than what they want. Social psychologists argue that employees will be more accepting of these decisions and their outcomes if they feel that the outcomes are fair (Adams 1965). Research in work settings establishes that employees typically believe that outcomes are fair when they are distributed equitably, with rewards based on productivity.

Social psychologists further tested, and found wide support for, the argument that employees will in fact be more accepting of outcome distributions that provide them with lower levels of pay than they desire or that deny them desired promotions if they feel that those outcomes are fair.

Although this basic argument of distributive justice theory is now widely supported, equity-based approaches are not found to be as successful in maintaining satisfaction among employees as was originally anticipated. One problem with applying equity concepts comes from people's tendency to exaggerate the importance or value of their contributions to their work groups. Because of this tendency, it is difficult to provide people with the level of rewards that they regard as fair relative to their subjective estimate of the value of their contributions.

Further, equity research finds that issues such as pay and promotion opportunities are often not the key concerns that shape happiness or unhappiness in work settings. For example, Messick, Bloom, Boldizar, and Samuelson (1985) asked people to list the unfair behaviors of others toward them. They found that people seldom mention unfair allocations. Instead, they focus on issues such as being treated with consideration and politeness. Similarly, Mikula, Petri, and Tanzer (1990, 133) found that "a considerable proportion of the injustices which are reported . . . refer to the manner in which people are treated in interpersonal interactions and encounters." These findings suggest that outcomes are less central to the feelings and actions of the individuals who receive those outcomes than is supposed by theories of distributive justice.

Because of the limits of distributive justice models, recent research has turned its focus to issues of procedural justice. The basic procedural justice argument is that people defer to decisions because those decisions are made through processes that they view as fair. The procedural justice effect is believed to be distinct from the influence of concerns about either outcome favorability or outcome fairness. As such, it provides a way for acceptable decisions to be made in situations in which not all participants can be given what they want or feel they deserve.

Recent research on procedural justice is much more optimistic than the distributive justice research on the utility of social justice as a mechanism for resolving social conflicts and the ability of societal authorities to bridge differences in interests and values and make decisions that all parties will accept. Further, the findings of procedural justice research suggest how authorities can act to encourage such results.

Thibaut and Walker (1975) performed the first systematic set of experiments designed to show the impact of procedural justice. Their studies demonstrated that people's assessments of the fairness of third-party decision making procedures shape their satisfaction with the outcomes. This finding has been widely confirmed in subsequent laboratory studies of procedural justice (Lind and Tyler 1988; Tyler et al. 1997).

Thibaut and Walker originally hoped that the willingness of all parties to accept decisions that they view as fairly arrived at would provide a mechanism through which social conflicts could be resolved. Subsequent studies have found that, when third-party decisions are fairly made, people are more willing to accept them voluntarily (Kitzmann and Emery 1993; Lind et al. 2000; Lind et al. 1993; MacCoun et al. 1988; Wissler 1995). What is striking about these studies is that clear procedural justice effects are found in real disputes, in real settings, confirming the earlier experimental findings of Thibaut and Walker.

Procedural justice judgments have been found to have an especially important role in shaping adherence to agreements over time (Pruitt et al. 1993; Pruitt et al. 1990). Pruitt and his colleagues have studied the factors that lead those involved in disputes to adhere to mediation agreements. They found that procedural fairness judgments about the initial mediation session are a central determinant of whether people are still adhering to a mediation agreement six months later.

Antecedents of the Procedural Justice Model

The procedural justice model used in the California study evolved from the relational model of authority (Tyler and Lind 1992) and the group engagement model (Tyler and Blader 2000). These models distinguish between two issues. Are people who experience procedural justice when dealing with authorities encouraged to defer to the decisions made by those authorities? And what criteria do people use to define fairness in procedures? As noted earlier, a large literature suggests that procedural justice does indeed facilitate both immediate and long-term deference to the decisions made by authorities in legal, political, managerial, and other organizational settings. The relational model articulated by Tyler and Lind (1992) identifies three interrelated elements that define procedural fairness: motive-based trust, the quality of decision making procedures (neutrality), and the quality of treatment (status recognition). The role of these elements in shaping procedural justice judgments was more recently reviewed by Tyler and Blader (2000), who argued that two key issues underlie an individual's judgments about procedural justice: a judgment about the quality of the decision making and a judgment about the quality of his or her own treatment. In their discussion of these issues, they included motive-based trust judgments within the overall framework of quality of treatment.

As noted, Tyler and Lind (1992) treated trust as one of three antecedents of procedural justice, while Tyler and Blader (2000) treated motive-based trust as an aspect of quality of treatment, one of two antecedents of procedural justice. The relational model does not suggest that there is a causal relationship between the three relational elements. However, it is easy to make such connections. Judgments about the quality of decision making and the quality of the treatment that people receive are judgments about what authorities do—that is, about their behavior. Judgments about motive-based trust are inferences about the motives of the authorities. Like procedural justice judgments, judgments about the motives of the authorities are inferences based on the behavior of those authorities.

Our approach in this book is different from the approaches of these prior efforts. We distinguish motive-based trust from experience-based judgments about the quality of decision making and the quality of treatment. Our approach treats motive-based trust as similar to procedural justice—that is, as an inference based on the behavior of the authorities. Hence, we view both procedural justice and motive-based trust as the consequences of the quality of decision making and the quality of treatment. The overall model used in this study is shown in figure 1.1.

The Basis of People's Reactions to Authorities: Is Procedural Justice Important?

In the California study we tested the argument that when people perceive that the police and the courts are acting with procedural fairness, they are encouraged to accept these authorities' decisions voluntarily. If people are motivated by simple self-interest, they react to authorities by evaluating the favorability of the decisions made by those authorities, the policies they pursue, and the outcomes they generate. As we have noted, if this psychology of the person is correct, it makes the situation of legal authorities a difficult one, since they are often unable to provide desired outcomes and often must restrict people's behavior or otherwise sanction them.

For the model of process-based regulation proposed here to be sustainable, there must be other ways for legal authorities to gain acceptance from the people with whom they have personal encounters. Further, these other mechanisms must be distinct from those that provide people with the outcomes they want or feel that they deserve and those that threaten people with sanctions for noncompliance.

Measuring Procedural Justice Effects in the California Study

The research reviewed earlier in this chapter supports the argument that procedural justice judgments dominate people's reactions to their personal experiences with police officers and judges. We test that hypothesis here, using data from the California study. The procedural justice model suggests one manner in which the police and the courts could sustain cooperation, since procedures can be evaluated as fair in ways that are distinct from the favorability of the outcomes they produce. Thus, if we demonstrate that the authorities can create and sustain people's judgments that they are participating in a fair procedure, without providing them with the outcomes they want, then we can make the case that the police and the courts have a viable way in which to implement process-based strategies of regulation.

Each respondent in the California study was asked to assess two justice-related aspects of his or her personal experience with the police or the courts: the fairness of the outcome he or she received, and the fairness of the procedures the authorities used to achieve that outcome. The items used to make those fairness assessments are shown in table 4.1. Each item uses a four-point response scale: "agree strongly," "agree somewhat," "disagree somewhat," or "disagree strongly."

The percentages shown in table 4.1 suggest that the respondents generally felt that the authorities with whom they dealt used fair procedures (74 percent agreed) and that they treated people fairly (77 percent agreed). They were more likely to feel that the procedures used by the authorities were fair than they were to think that those procedures provided them with fair outcomes. Only 62 percent felt that they received the outcome they deserved, while only 71 percent felt that the outcome they received was fair. Finally, 66 percent received the outcome that they deserved under the law.

Table 4.1   Procedural and Distributive Justice

Questions	Fair	Agree	Mean (Standard Deviation)
Procedural justice[a]	—	—	1.83 (1.00)
"How fair are the procedures he/she used to make decisions about how to handle the situation?"	74%	—	—
"Overall, how fairly were you treated?"	77	—	—
Distributive justice[b]	—	—	2.15 (1.07)
"According to the law, I received the outcome I deserved."	66	66%	—
"I received the outcome I feel I deserved."	62	62	—
"The outcome I received was fair."	71	71	—

Source: California study data.
Note: Low means indicate high levels of justice.
[a] alpha = 0.91.
[b] alpha = 0.92.

Procedural justice and distributive justice are correlated ($r = .37$, $p < .001$); procedural justice is correlated with outcome favorability ($r = 0.47$, $p < .001$); and distributive justice is correlated with outcome favorability ($r = 0.31$, $p < .001$). Hence, procedural justice is distinct from, but not independent of, outcome concerns. We used regression analysis in this study to look at the independent contribution of each of these judgments in explaining decision acceptance.

Procedural Justice and Decision Acceptance

Does the procedural justice that people think they experience during their encounter with legal authorities shape their willingness to accept decisions? Finding a substantial procedural justice influence is in fact one key to our argument in favor of a process-based model of regulation. To test the strength of the procedural justice influences within our study we looked at the influence of procedural justice on the willingness to accept voluntarily the decisions of police officers and judges.

Table 4.2   **Procedural Justice**

	Trust	Acceptance of Decisions	Satisfaction with Decision Maker
Beta weights for regression analysis			
Procedural justice	.77***	.69***	.76***
Distributive justice	.07***	.12***	.10***
Outcome favorability	.06***	.09***	.11***
Adjusted R-squared for regression analysis Procedural justice beyond distributive justice and outcome favorability	43%	34%	41%
Distributive justice beyond procedural justice and outcome favorability	1	1	0
Outcome favorability beyond procedural and distributive justice	1	1	1
Total adjusted R-squared	69%	62%	74%

Source: California study data.
***p < .001.

The results of regression analyses exploring the role of procedural justice are shown in table 4.2. They indicate that both procedural and distributive justice shape voluntary decision acceptance. Procedural justice is in fact the primary factor that shapes acceptance (beta = 0.69, p < .001), and it has more influence than does outcome fairness (beta = 0.12, p < .001) or outcome favorability (beta = 0.09, p < .001). It is also central to satisfaction with decision makers. The primary influence on satisfaction with decision makers is procedural justice (beta = 0.76, p < .001); the influence of distributive justice (beta = 0.10, p < .001) and outcome favorability (beta = 0.11, p < .001) is somewhat less.

There are also influences from distributive justice and outcome favorability. To estimate the relative magnitude of these influences, we performed a uniqueness analysis. A uniqueness analysis identifies the variance in some dependent variable that is explained by a group of variables after all other variables have already been considered. This analysis indicates the amount of variance that is explained by that group of variables uniquely, or beyond what could be explained without those variables.[2]

In the case of inferences about the trustworthiness of authorities, procedural justice explained 43 percent of the unique variance, distributive justice 1 percent, and outcome favorability 1 percent. With influence on decision acceptance, procedural justice explained 34 percent of the variance, distributive justice 1 percent, and outcome favorability 1 percent. Finally, for satisfaction with the decision maker, procedural justice uniquely explained 41 percent of the variance, distributive justice 0 percent, and outcome favorability 1 percent.

These findings demonstrate that procedural justice was the dominant factor in shaping people's reactions to authorities in personal encounters with them, compared to the favorability or fairness of outcomes. Although there are small outcome-based effects that always need to be considered, these findings suggest that there is substantial reason for legal authorities to encourage the acceptance of their decisions through the manner in which they make those decisions.

We can test the range of procedural justice effects by conducting these analyses separately for the four different types of contact with legal authorities experienced by people in the California study. As outlined earlier, we divided those experiences along two crucial dimensions: whether the experience was voluntary or involuntary, and whether the person interacted with a police officer or with a judge.

An analysis of procedural justice effects within each of the four types of experiences indicated that procedural justice mattered more than did the other factors—distributive justice and outcome favorability—regardless of the type of personal experience involved.[3] Procedural justice was especially key to people's reactions to their involuntary experiences. On the other hand, distributive justice mattered less with involuntary contact. When people go to the authorities for help, in other words, they focus more heavily on distributive justice, and less heavily on procedural justice, than they do when the authorities, in their role as regulators, impose decisions on them.

We conducted a similar analysis across levels of outcome favorability. This allowed us to test the argument that people cease to care about procedural justice issues when their outcomes become highly negative. An analysis that divided people into groups based on the favorability of their outcomes and then examined the relationship between procedural justice and decision acceptance suggested that there was a relationship between an individual's perception that a procedure was fair and his or her willingness to accept the outcome regardless of whether a favorable and unfavorable outcome was being delivered. In both cases, the perceived fairness of the procedure was more important to people than the value of the outcome they were receiving when they were deciding whether to accept that outcome.

Summary

Procedural justice is the first social motive considered in our analysis. The results strongly support the argument that people are significantly more focused on the procedural justice of authorities' actions than they are on either the favorability or fairness of their own outcomes during personal encounters with police officers or court officials. This is true both when people voluntarily seek help from legal authorities and when they are being regulated by those authorities.

The results also strongly support the argument that police officers and court officials can gain consent and cooperation from the public by behaving in ways that are perceived as procedurally fair. The strength of the findings is particularly striking, with procedural justice effects dominating outcome favorability and outcome fairness across a wide variety of settings.[4]

Chapter 5

Motive-Based Trust and Decision Acceptance

THE SECOND social factor that may shape individuals' willing acceptance of the decisions of legal authorities is motive-based trust. Trust in a person's motives or character refers to his or her internal, unobservable characteristics that are inferred from his or her observable actions. Psychologists have long recognized that one of our central goals in dealing with another person, regardless of whether that person is in a position of authority, is making inferences about the motivations shaping his or her actions. Our focus in this chapter on people's inferences about the trustworthiness of other people's motives flows from that recognition.

When we deal with other people, we observe their actions, but their overt actions usually do not directly communicate their motivations. Instead, we must infer the motivations that are causing other people's actions. We cannot directly observe the motivations of others. As a result, motive attributions are inferences that one person makes about another using the behavior observed in a given situation, the behavior observed on previous occasions, the other person's statements explaining his or her behavior, and general social knowledge. The field of attribution theory within social psychology seeks to identify the rules people use to make such motive attributions (Fiske and Taylor 1991; Heider 1958).

Attribution theory emphasizes the ambiguities inherent in understanding the motivations that lead to observed behaviors. It is seldom obvious or completely clear why people are doing what they are doing. Instead, there are usually several possible motivations that could explain why they are engaged in a particular action. For example, in the context of social interaction even a simple act of seeming kindness—for example, helping someone up from a chair—could be a calculated effort to mislead and exploit by creating trust that will later be betrayed to the helper's advantage. Hence, people devote considerable effort to understanding the character of other people in social settings by discerning "true" character and motivation from a complex set of social cues.

One central motive attribution that people seek to make is whether the person they are dealing with is "trustworthy." In interactions with police officers and judges, people make inferences about the degree to which the authority can be trusted to act in ways that are responsive to their own needs and concerns. We refer to this assessment of trustworthiness as a form of "motive-based" trust to suggest that it is linked to views about the character of the other person.

One level of trust is the ability to trust that people will behave as expected, based on their promises or our knowledge of their past behavior. We refer to this as instrumental trust because it is linked to the ability that we believe we have to predict what other people will do in the future. For example, if the police say that they will respond to a call from a member of the public and then fail to respond, this is a clear and simple failure to follow through on a commitment to act. People who fail in this way strike us as not trustworthy in the sense that they may not act as they agreed to act—their behavior cannot be predicted in advance based on what they say they will do. Trust as predictability due to a willingness to keep promises—instrumental trust—is one level on which trust is studied. For example, Burt and Knez (1996, 70) define trust as "anticipated cooperation."

Approaches that link trust assessments to one's perceived ability to estimate others' future actions have been labeled "cognitive" approaches to trust by Kramer (1999). Attention to such future actions illustrates a key element of social interaction—the element of risk. When people interact with others, their outcomes become intertwined with the outcomes of others. This creates the possibility that one person's failure to act as agreed will hurt the interests of another person within a relationship. On some level, each person must make estimates of the likelihood that others will keep their agreements and not act opportunistically (Bradach and Eccles 1989). Those estimates of how others are likely to act in the future are cognitive estimates of their trustworthiness.

This cognitive model of trust is consistent with the image of trust that emerges from the large literature on rational choice (Coleman 1990; Williamson 1993). In this literature, trust is based on the view that people are rational actors who judge the probable actions of others so that they can include those estimates in an overall model of the probable costs and gains of possible future actions. From this perspective, "when we say we trust someone or that someone is trustworthy, we implicitly mean that the probability that he [or she] will perform an action that is beneficial or at least not detrimental to us is high enough for us to consider engaging in some form of cooperation" (Williamson 1993, 463). Trust is thus linked to a heuristic judgment about "the likelihood that the trustee will undertake expected actions if trusted" (Scholz 1998, 137).

A calculative or instrumental view of trust can also be found within the social-psychological literature on social dilemmas, such as groups and communities being faced with scarcities in shared, communal resources. Much of the literature on social dilemmas explores people's willingness to trust others in their community who also consume these resources. One reason people behave cooperatively in such settings is that they trust other community members to reciprocate cooperation. If I cooperate, I expect that others will cooperate in return. I think I know how others will behave in the future and can therefore shape my own behavior in response to my anticipation of the actions of others (Brewer and Kramer 1986; Komorita, Chan, and Parks 1993; Komorita and Parks 1994; Kramer, McClintock, and Messick 1986).

If people are collectively drawing resources from a common but dwindling resource pool, they might all limit their yield so as not to destroy the pool. Fishermen face this problem and sometimes cooperate in not overfishing certain areas. When resources are dwindling, people must estimate what others will do. Everyone has a desire to take as many of the few remaining resources as possible, but if everyone did so, the pool would be destroyed for the future. Each person must therefore base his or her own decision on whether to conserve or overuse resources on an estimate of the likelihood that others will overuse, leaving no long-term gain from the pool and no short-term gain from overuse. In such settings one motivation shaping people's behavior is their trust—that is, their expectations about how others will behave.

Within social relations, people engage in a variety of approaches to make the future behavior of others more predictable. Laws are one example of a social device designed to regularize social interactions by attaching penalties to failures to keep promises. We have more confidence that others will not fail to live up to the terms of a contract because society has established rules about such actions and assigned authorities to sanction those who engage in them. As a consequence, we can more willingly trust, in the instrumental sense that we think that others will do as they promise. More generally, people seek conditions that encourage "credible commitments" (Williamson 1993)—commitments that we can believe will be honored because those who make them would be harmed by failing to keep them.

Hardin (2002) makes the distinction between trustworthiness and trust. Trustworthiness is something that authorities or institutions do that leads people to trust them. From the instrumental perspective, the key behavior that leads to trustworthiness is predictability. People feel that they can predict how others will act, so they know how to calibrate their own cooperative behavior. That predictability can involve the expectations that others will consider or "encapsulate" our interests in their own decisions about cooperation.[1]

However we define this instrumental model of trust, the underlying premise is that people want to know that the situation is one that will lead the other person to act in ways that will benefit them. They can create such a situation by adjusting their own level of risk-taking to their estimates of the likelihood that the other person will reciprocate any cooperative efforts they make. As a result, people feel that they are acting in their self-interest no matter how much they cooperate with others. They cooperate only as much as is reasonable given their estimate of how the other person is likely to behave in response.

Motive-Based Trust

Motive-based trust involves more complex social inferences than are represented by instrumental judgments about whether a person will keep specific promises or commitments. Instead, motive-based trust involves inferences about the intentions behind actions, intentions that flow from a person's unobservable motivations and character. A core argument of social psychologists is that people seek to understand the motives and character of others (Heider 1958). Since character and motives are not observable, people use the actions of others to make inferences about those hidden and unobservable motives. People want to understand the character and motives of others because they feel that people's future behavior as well as their behavior when they are not being observed are both motivated by character. If we understand another person's character, therefore, we can infer whether his or her future actions will be benevolent or malevolent.

Consider the example of a burglary. If the police respond when called, they have kept their commitment—they have behaved as expected and earned trust in the instrumental sense. This behavior is observable, so we do not need to think about the motivations or character of the police officers involved. In situations involving another person's specific and observable behaviors, issues of underlying motivation are less relevant to the perceiver of those actions. However, even when specific commitments are kept, the more complex issue of motive inferences plays a role. If the police take a report after a burglary, but the stolen items are never recovered and the criminal is never identified and arrested, the person who called the police to report the problem must consider whether the police tried to solve the problem. *Did they do everything they could to try to find my stolen property? Were they concerned about my problem? Did they try to do what was right? Did they care about whether the crime was solved?* These are all inferences about the motivations of the police that the person gleans from what the officers say and do in response to the problem.

Motive-based trust is linked to a state of perceived vulnerability or risk that is derived from individuals' uncertainty about the motives and intentions underlying the actions of those others on whom they depend. In this sense, motive-based trust is an estimate of the character and motives of others. It is based on the assumption that knowing the character and motives of another person tells us whether he or she will act reasonably toward us in the future. Hence, our expectation is not that the person will engage in particular actions that he or she has agreed to perform. Instead, we expect that the person will act out of goodwill and do those things that he or she thinks would benefit us (see Heimer 2001; Messick and Kramer 2001).

In this case, we are not concerned with predicting what people will do. We are concerned with understanding the motivations underlying their actions. If we believe that a person is motivated by goodwill, we need not seek to anticipate his or her particular actions. Whatever that person does will be a good-faith effort to help us.

In the case of the burglary, for example, suppose that the police fill out a formal report. They might then question people in the neighborhood, interviewing hundreds of people, canvassing known fences, and interrogating known burglars. They might search local pawnshops or examine the stock of sidewalk vendors in an effort to find the items taken in the burglary. On the other hand, they might walk out of the apartment, file the report, and do nothing to try to solve the crime. We cannot always know what actions are taken, and we may not even know what actions are reasonable and should be taken by the police. We can infer that the officers involved were benevolently motivated or they were not, and therefore that they either tried very hard or did not try at all to take the best actions they could.

Similarly, when the police stop a person on the street for questioning, the person is not always in a position to know whether the police have just cause to stop and question him or her. The police may be in legitimate pursuit of a criminal, or they may be harassing the individual. He or she does not know whether a crime has recently been committed, does not know whether he or she matches the description of the perpetrator, and does not know whether the police have stopped and searched others. As with a burglary, the individual does not have knowledge that allows him to judge whether the police are acting reasonably.

The problem of motive-based trust has recently emerged in the context of racial profiling (see Tyler 2001g). When the police stop a person on the street, that person must make an inference about why he or she was stopped. The police seldom directly explain their actions as being motivated by race ("I stopped you because you are black"), so people make inferences about whether they were stopped for that reason, and about the motives of the authorities who stopped them, based on more subtle cues. Problems of motive-based trust are not confined to the police. When dealing with judges, for example, people receive a legal ruling determining the outcome of their case. However, the judge is in possession of legal knowledge that the litigants do not have, as well as knowledge about how other cases are typically resolved. Litigants cannot very effectively determine whether they have received an appropriate outcome. It is clear that repeat offenders who spend time in jail or prison are better able to do so, since they exchange information with others (Casper, Tyler, and Fisher 1988). Nonetheless, even repeat offenders lack the knowledge held by an experienced judge or lawyer.

One reason we might trust that legal authorities have acted in good faith in these various situations is that we tend to view as trustworthy those who act as agents of society, fulfilling certain social roles—for example, police officers, judges, and doctors (Barber 1983). Part of that role is a set of responsibilities and obligations mandating that the authority act in the interests of those whom they represent. These responsibilities are created and reinforced through training in a specialized role and through various accounting mechanisms (Dawes 1994; Meyerson, Weick, and Kramer 1996). One aspect of trust involves issues of technical competence. The other—the focus here—involves the expectation of moral responsibility, that is, that authorities will act in the best interests of others.

The concept of a fiduciary relationship is key to all situations in which an authority has power over the lives or property of others. Central to such relationships is the expectation that the authority will act in the interests of those for whom he or she exercises authority. That person is trusted. Trust in these cases refers to a judgment about the intentions or motives of the fiduciary agent, that is, a reliance on the goodwill of that person (Baier 1986).

This focus on the intentions or motives of the authority can be clearly distinguished from a focus on the "truth" or "correctness" of their decisions. Well-intentioned authorities can act in good faith and make mistakes—as we learn from weather forecasters every day. But failure to make a correct prediction or decision does not destroy motive-based trust if we believe that authorities have good intentions. In their similar recognition of the distinction between intention and result (Bok 1978) philosophers view intention as reflecting a person's motivations. The law makes this distinction as well. The "business judgment rule" used by the courts to evaluate corporate authorities recognizes that "decisions made

by a board in good faith, with due care, and with regard to the best interests of the corporation" should not be evaluated by courts based on
whether they lead to good or bad results (Mitchell 1995, 192).

One does not need to be a philosopher or a judge to make the distinction between intention and result. For example, Tyler and Degoey
(1996, 334) found that

> some people interviewed indicated that police officers and judges are act-
> ing in a non-neutral, biased way, yet nonetheless evaluated those author-
> ities to be fair. People seemed willing to forgive surface features of racism
> and sexism, for example, if they felt that the authorities involved are basi-
> cally motivated to act in a benevolent manner. It was the trustworthiness
> of the intentions of the authorities that shaped reactions to the procedures
> they employed, not surface features of those procedures (e.g., neutrality).

Unlike instrumental or expectation-based trust, motive-based trust is
a trust in the intentions or motives of another. We do not know what that
other person will do, but we trust that he or she will act in ways that benefit us. Consider the already noted distinction between trust and trustworthiness (Hardin 2002). In the case of motive-based trust, an authority
is not made trustworthy to us by our belief that we can predict the
actions that he or she will take. Rather, we trust an authority when we
believe that we can predict that, whatever the authority does, he or she
will be motivated by a concern for our personal welfare.[2]

When we entrust the police and the courts with power over social regulation, just as when we entrust elected officials with the power to gov-
ern, we take a risk. Both legal and political authorities sometimes become
involved in scandals over influence-peddling and bribery. This illustrates the constant temptation experienced by such officials to put their
own personal interests above the interests of the public, which is not in a
position to know about or control their actions. On the other hand, the
public sees vivid reminders that feelings of duty and responsibility often
motivate authorities to put aside their personal interests and act in the
interests of the public whom they serve. The actions of firefighters and
police officers responding to the attack on New York City's World Trade
Center in September 2001, several hundred of whom died while attempt-
ing to save others, powerfully demonstrate that kind of motivation.

An inference of trustworthiness, in the motive-based sense we are
using the term here, is thus based on a complex set of inputs that is
unique to each person but always reflects the belief that a particular
authority in a particular situation is not using his or her authority for
personal gain. Authorities' actions, we infer, are motivated by the desire
to do what is right for the people with whom they are dealing and whose
interests they represent.

Why Do People Need to Trust Authorities?

There are two reasons people rely on inferences linked to motive-based trust even when the situation is sufficiently uncertain that it is not possible to evaluate fully whether instrumental trust is justified: a lack of knowledge about the actions that an authority has taken, and a lack of expertise in evaluating the actions of the authority.

First, consider lack of knowledge about an authority's actions. People are seldom in a position to know all that has or has not been done in response to their problem, or to understand whether the police or the courts are doing everything possible to try to solve the problem in a reasonable way. In fact, the public's lack of knowledge about what authorities are up to is an integral characteristic of their role. As a result, we cannot exercise control by constantly monitoring authorities' behavior (Luhmann 1979).

Consider the recent example of the Amadou Diallo trial in New York State. Amadou Diallo, a resident of the Bronx, was killed in 1999, while unarmed, by four police officers, who fired forty-one shots at him. The fact that the officers fired the fatal shots is undisputed, and their subsequent trial revolved in part around the issue of the "good faith" of their motivations. Did they make a mistake while acting in good faith and while trying to do their jobs well? The jury trusted the officers' statements about their intentions, aided by the lack of evidence of bias and by the remorse they displayed during their testimony, and acquitted them. In our terms, the jury made a judgment that people make in their everyday encounters with legal authorities—an inference about what they thought the motives of the authorities had been in the situation. When outcomes are bad, what led to those outcomes? Did the authorities act in good faith, although a negative outcome occurred nonetheless? Or are negative outcomes the result of indifference, bias, or malfeasance?

We can contrast the Diallo case with another recent case in New York—the attack by police officers on Abner Louima. A police officer, Justin Volpe, perhaps aided by other officers, brutalized Louima in the stationhouse after his arrest. The jury convicted Volpe. An inference about motives (in this case, "bad-faith" motives) was supported by Volpe's behavior—inflicting injury on the handcuffed Abner Louima, for no legitimate reason—and by the brutal nature of the crime itself. It was difficult to see that the acts of brutality were serving any valid policing function, such as self-defense or maintaining control over the suspect . The jury inferred that the actions of the officer did not involve a legitimate good-faith effort at policing, and they convicted him of a crime. Again, from our perspective, the central point is that the jury, like people in their everyday encounters with the police, inferred the motives underlying the behavior of the police officer when evaluating his actions.

The second reason trust involves inferences about the motives and character of authorities is that to carry out their roles they must have expertise that is not shared by members of the public.[3] Authorities often possess special knowledge and training that allow them to make better professional decisions. Judges and police officers, like doctors, lawyers, and teachers, spend significant time learning their roles and responsibilities, and this training allows them to make decisions that cannot easily be explained to an untrained member of the public. We expect a doctor to know, for example, about the appropriate way to treat an illness. Not having spent our own time going to medical school, we must to some degree trust that the doctor is acting in good faith.[4]

Our argument is that if people trust the motives of the police officers or judges with whom they interact, they are more likely to believe that those authorities have indeed sincerely tried to solve their problem. Consequently, they are also more likely to be satisfied with the decisions and directives of those authorities, and more willing to voluntarily accept them, even when those decisions do not provide them with desired or favorable outcomes.

Why would people focus on the motives of the authorities? Because they recognize that the nature of their problems often combines with the structural factors that are beyond police control to create situations in which the authorities are unable to give them what they want. Accepting the inevitability of unsatisfactory outcomes is part of participating in society.

The problem for people is to distinguish between situations in which their cooperation with authorities is reasonable and situations in which they are being exploited. For example, we should cooperate with our doctor when he or she is motivated by an interest in protecting our health. However, if our doctor is taking kickbacks from a drug company to prescribe ineffective or harmful drugs, our trust is being exploited and we should not cooperate. The difficulty lies in determining which situation we are in when we lack not only the expertise to evaluate independently the appropriateness of the drug but the knowledge that the doctor prescribes the same drug to all patients, regardless of their illness.

Making a judgment about the trustworthiness of legal authorities is often particularly difficult because there is an inherent conflict of interest in the relationship between the public and legal authorities: members of the public must cooperate with the authorities while simultaneously protecting their own interests. Of course, to some degree the conflict of interest in this relationship mirrors that in the relationship people have with society and with others in their private lives. The key judgment that shapes how people balance the opposing factors in their relationship with the police and the courts is their trust in the motives of the authorities.

Police officers may have authority because they develop a personal relationship with people who come to know them through personal experience. In the past "beat cops" patrolled particular geographical areas, often the same area where they lived. This allowed police officers to exercise authority by establishing personal relationships with community residents. Residents could learn to trust a particular police officer by developing judgments about his or her character and motives through repeated personal interactions, as well as through the experiences of other people in their community. A police officer could thus develop a personal reputation that allowed him or her to exercise authority. The goal of recent efforts to encourage community policing is to develop personal connections between police officers and members of the community within which those officers are exercising legal authority.

Motive-based trust is linked first to the single individual with whom one has had or is having a personal experience. Of course, trust builds across time and over encounters, so it is never the result of just one experience. It is also possible to trust an individual with whom one has had no personal experience—for example, the president of the United States—but such impersonal trust is not our focus in this discussion. We emphasize the trust in particular individuals that develops by virtue of their actions, which lead to inferences that the decisions of the authorities should be accepted.

Trust as an Empirical Issue

The alternative regulatory model that we have proposed depends in part on the possibility that voluntary decision acceptance may be enhanced by trust in the motives of authorities rather than in the outcomes they provide. Tyler and Degoey (1996) tested the argument that people's trust in the motives of particular authorities shapes their willingness to accept the decisions of those authorities. By studying decisionmakers in three settings—management, politics, and the family—they found that people are more willing to accept voluntarily the conflict resolution decisions made by third parties when they trust the motives of those authorized to make such decisions. Trust also had an important influence on people's feelings of obligation to follow organizational rules.

Tyler and Degoey's analysis ranges across the boundary between personal and institutional trust. Managers and parents, for example, make trust inferences about the people with whom they have everyday contact. In the case of political trust, people make inferences about a local political authority with whom most of them have had no personal contact. In both contexts, motive-based trust is shown to have a strong influence on decision acceptance.

Tyler and Mitchell (1994) also examined the influence of motive inferences, but in the context of people's judgments about a legal institution with which they have probably had no personal experience: the U.S. Supreme Court. They examined the factors shaping people's willingness to defer to the Court's decisions in a controversial area of public policy: abortion rights. Their study found that people's inferences about the trustworthiness of the motives of the Supreme Court justices shaped their willingness to empower the Court to make abortion policy, and that these inferences also shaped their feelings of obligation to accept and obey court policies on issues such as abortion.

These studies suggest that motive inferences are important both in people's responses to their personal experiences with particular authorities and in their reactions to local and national-level legal authorities, with whom they have had no personal contact. In both cases people are more willing to defer voluntarily to authorities whose motives they trust. Further, in all of these cases the influence of trust is independent of the favorability or desirability of the decisions the authority makes. These findings suggest that trust can be a basis for effective governance when trusted authorities gain people's consent and cooperation.

Measuring Trust

In the California study, we used a five-item scale to measure people's trust in the motives of the particular authority involved in their personal experience. The scale assesses views about the character of that legal authority and the benevolence of his or her motives. People were asked to agree or disagree that the authority: "considered my views" (67 percent agreed); "tried hard to do the right thing by me" (69 percent agreed); "tried to take my needs into account"(62 percent agreed); "cared about my concerns" (62 percent agreed); and "is someone that I 'trust'" (69 percent agreed). The results suggest that people generally express trust in those authorities with whom they come into personal contact. We combined these items to form an index of motive-based trust (alpha = 0.93).

Is Motive-Based Trust Social in Nature?

We argue that motive-based trust is social in nature; it is different from the type of instrumental, rational trust that is linked to expectations about the future behavior of others. As with procedural justice, we want to show that there is more to motive-based trust than instrumental or outcome-based evaluations.[5] To examine this issue empirically, we considered and compared the influence of four potential antecedents of motive-based trust, two of which are social in nature and two of which are instrumental.

The first potential instrumental antecedent of trust is a person's judgment about the predictability of his or her experience. A core element in rational models of trust is being able to count on other people to do what we expect them to do. For example, those who make promises will keep their promises. This idea of trust is linked to the belief that others will meet our expectations for their future behavior, and that we can reliably and accurately calibrate or calculate our behavior toward them. In this study we measured the degree to which other people's actions were predictable and expected in two distinct ways. People responded to two questions: "He/she did things I did not expect him/her to do," and, "I was surprised by the way he/she treated me." (The latter item was reversed when the scale was created.) These two items were combined into an index of predictability (alpha = 0.75).

A second potential antecedent of trust is an individual's judgment about whether an experience met his or her prior expectations, that is, whether authorities did in fact act as the individual expected them to. We have already outlined this approach to measuring expectedness. People were asked to compare the outcome they received during their experience to the outcome they had expected prior to the experience. This expected outcome judgment is one of the elements of the composite outcome favorability discussed in chapter 3. Here we use the expectation item as a separate index to assess the degree to which prior expectations were "violated" by the behavior that occurred. This index reflects the degree to which people indicated that they received the outcome from the police or the courts that they expected prior to their experience.[6] People were asked to generally indicate the degree to which their experience conformed to their prior expectations.

If the rational model of trust—people trust others when they can predict their future behavior—is correct, then being surprised by how an authority acts or feeling that his or her behavior has violated prior expectations during a personal encounter will shape a person's views about the trustworthiness of the authority's motives. If trust, as we measure it, reflects the ability to anticipate the future behavior of others, then it is linked to assessments of violated expectations and predictability, and is rational or instrumental in character. Two other potential influences on people's evaluations of trustworthiness are social in nature. We test the social character of trust by examining the relationship between the social bonds between the person and the authority, and the person's feeling that he or she can understand the motivations underlying the authority's actions.

We first examined whether people felt that there was a social bond between themselves and the authority, using a three-item scale to measure the degree to which people felt such a bond: "He/she and I had a lot in common as people"; "He/she and I shared some of the same values and concerns"; and, "We shared a similar background." These three items were combined to form an index of perceived social bonds (alpha = 0.75).

A second potential social antecedent of trust is the perception that the behavior of the authority can be understood, in the sense that people think they know the reason for that behavior. According to an attributional perspective on trust, which is focused on using behavior to understand motives, people trust someone not because they can predict that person's behavior, but because they feel that they understand *why* the person is acting as he or she is. In other words, they feel that they understand the other person's character or motives and can therefore comprehend that person's reasons for acting in certain ways.[7]

Of course, an understanding of the motives of an authority ought to be linked to a person's perceived ability to predict the future behavior of that authority, but we are focusing on the separate impact of understanding why the authority acted as he or she did. If trust is social in nature, we would expect that understanding will have a more important role in shaping perceptions of authorities' trustworthiness than will the ability to anticipate or predict their behavior.

In this case, the other person the respondent was seeking to understand was a police officer or judge. Respondents were asked to agree or disagree with these statements: "I understood why he/she made the decisions he/she made," and, "I understood why he/she treated me the way he/she did." These items were combined into an index of understandability (alpha = 0.86).

To test the importance of the four instrumental and social antecedents of trust outlined here, we examined the influence of each of the factors on respondents' evaluations of the trustworthiness of particular legal authorities. The analysis is a regression equation in which both instrumental and social factors were used to explain judgments of motive-based trust. The analysis is shown in table 5.1.

The results strongly support the argument that motive-based trust, as measured in this study, is largely social in character and not the same thing as instrumental trust. Social judgments about the degree to which respondents felt a social bond with the authorities and the degree to which respondents thought that they could understand why the authority acted as he or she did were the only factors that uniquely explained variance in the judgments about the trustworthiness of authorities. This

Table 5.1   Instrumental and Social Factors Shaping Motive-Based Trust

Beta weights	
Social factors	
"Do you share social bonds with the authority?" (High = yes)	0.33***
"Do you understand/his or her actions?" (High = yes)	0.53***
Instrumental factors	
"Their actions are as expected." (High = yes)	.01
"Their actions are predictable." (High = yes)	0.03
Total adjusted R-squared	55%

Source: California study data.
Note: High scores indicate high levels of personal trust.
***$p < .001$.

includes a significant influence for understanding why authorities acted as they did (beta weight = 0.53, $p < .001$) and a significant influence of feeling shared social bonds with those authorities (beta weight = 0.33, $p < .001$).

The findings regarding the role played by the understandability of the actions of the authority are especially striking given that the independent effect of whether the respondent felt that the actions of the authority were understandable is found in an analysis that controlled for the influence of whether those actions were expected or predictable. Thus, this effect reflects the separate influence of whether respondents felt that they could understand the motives or reasons for the actions of the authorities, not whether they anticipated what would happen or found it "surprising" or "unexpected." A person who acts in unexpected ways is not viewed as untrustworthy if people feel that they can understand why he or she acted that way. Instrumental judgments about whether the actions of authorities were expected or predictable did not have a unique influence on respondents' views about the trustworthiness of authorities' motives. There was no significant effect based either on the influence of violations of prior outcome expectations (beta weight = −0.01, not significant) or on whether the authority's behavior of the person was viewed as having been predictable (beta weight = 0.03, not significant).

Another piece of evidence of the social character of the trust that those interviewed expressed about particular legal authorities is the low correlation between motive-based trust in the authorities and expressions of fear about them ($r = -0.28$, $p < .001$). In contrast, trusting particular legal authorities is strongly linked to having respect for them ($r = 0.65$, $p < .001$). Again, the social dimension of trust is central. Trust was linked to social judgments of respect for the authority, just as it was previously linked to understanding the actions of the authority, rather than to the predictability of those actions.

This chapter outlines our conceptualization of trust as a motive inference and explains how we measure motive-based trust. It also presents evidence that trust as experienced in personal encounters with authorities is social, or motive-based, in character, rather than instrumental. When we include predictability in our model, it is not significantly linked to trust; trust in the motives of police officers and judges was clearly based on more than the judgment that their actions could be anticipated. It was also based on more than feeling that the outcome of these authorities' actions was desirable or fair. A strong social component of trust, linked to respondents' feeling that they understood why authorities acted as they did and that a social bond existed between them, emerges from our analysis.

Personal Trust and Decision Acceptance: Does Trust Encourage Deference to Legal Authorities?

An empirical question must be addressed to establish the viability of a process-based model of regulation: Do people's judgments about the trustworthiness of the motives of particular legal authorities lead them to accept more willingly the directives and decisions of those legal authorities? People sometimes receive undesired outcomes from the police and the courts, and the police are often unable to solve people's problems and frequently must cite or arrest them. The courts often resolve problems in ways that people find dissatisfying, or they punish people for lawbreaking activity. We might expect that people would not accept negative outcomes, and that their resistance would lead to compliance problems for the police and the courts.

Does trust in the motives of the authorities cause people to accept their decisions more willingly even when those decisions are negative and present them with undesired results? To address this question, we used regression analysis to compare the influence of outcome favorability judgments to the influence of judgments about the trustworthiness of the authority's motives on decision acceptance. In keeping with the discussion of instrumental trust in this chapter, we also considered the possible influence of predictability and violations of expectations.

The results of the regression analysis are shown in table 5.2. They indicate the proportion of variance in acceptance and satisfaction that was uniquely explained by the favorability of the outcome that the person received, by whether expectations were met, by predictability, and by trust in the motives of the authority.

Table 5.2   Influence of Outcome Favorability and Trust on Acceptance of and Satisfaction with the Decisions of Legal Authorities

	Procedural Justice	Willingness to Accept Decision	Satisfaction with Decision Maker
Beta weights for regression analysis:			
Motive-based trust	.73***	.72***	.76***
Outcome favorability	.14***	.13***	.16***
Predictability	.14***	.10***	.09***
Expectations violated?	.00	−.02	−.03
Adjusted R-squared for regression analysis Unique influence of:			
Outcome, favorability, predictability, and expectations	1%	1%	2%
Motive-based trust	42	39	45
Total adjusted R-squared	71	65	75

Source: California study data.
***p < .001.

To estimate the amount of unique variance explained by a particular idea, we used the overall adjusted R-squared, which reflected the total amount of variance explained by a group of variables and indicated the degree to which each construct explained variance beyond what could be explained by all the other factors being considered. In addition, we used simultaneous regression analysis to indicate the relative weight of the independent influence of each factor, distinct from the influence of other factors in the equation. The magnitude of these influences is reflected in the size of the beta weight.

The results of the regression analysis suggest that the favorability of the outcomes that respondents received shaped their responses to their personal experiences with the police or the courts. They were less willing to accept negative outcomes and outcomes that were not predictable or expected, and they felt less satisfaction with the legal authorities who provided them with such negative outcomes. On average, these effects accounted for about 2 percent of the variance in the acceptance of decisions and in satisfaction with the decision maker.

The findings shown in table 5.2 also suggest that people's willingness to accept decisions was distinctly influenced by their trust in the motives of the legal authorities. If people trusted the motives of particular authorities, they were more willing to accept their decisions. They also expressed greater satisfaction with those authorities. The average amount of unique variance explained by trust is about 43 percent.

A direct comparison of the magnitude of the influence of judgments about outcome favorability, expectedness, and predictability and of assessments of the trustworthiness of the authorities' motives on the willingness to accept their decisions suggests that people are most strongly influenced by their judgments of trustworthiness. If people trust the motives of the authorities, they are more willing to accept their decisions. Further, this influence occurs even when we control for the favorability of decisions, their expectedness, and the predictability of the behavior of the authorities. The influence of motive-based trust is larger in magnitude than is the influence of the favorability of decisions, their expectedness, or their predictability. These results lend support to the empirical foundations of a process-based model of regulation.

To test the range of the effect of motive-based trust, we conducted the same analysis among subgroups of respondents with different types of personal experiences with legal authorities. To conduct the analysis we once again divided the sample into four groups using two dimensions: the authority involved (police, courts), and whether the contact with legal authorities was voluntary or involuntary. The results of these analyses suggest that motive-based trust dominated people's reactions to their experiences irrespective of which authority they dealt with or whether their experience was voluntary.[8]

When we examine the influence of trust at varying levels of outcome favorability, we find that motive-based trust became more, not less, important as outcomes became more negative. If people trusted the motives of the authorities, their level of acceptance remained high, both as outcomes became more negative and as they became less expected or predictable. If people lacked trust in authorities' motives, their acceptance declined more sharply as outcomes became more negative and less expected or predictable. The results suggest that when people receive negative or unexpected outcomes, they focus more strongly on whether they trust the authority involved.

Summary

A key question in considering the process-based model of regulation as an alternative to sanction-based approaches is whether there are factors other than an instrumental cost-benefit analysis underlying people's willingness to accept decisions and cooperate with authorities. Our analysis of the California study data suggests that motive-based trust, rooted in people's perception that they understand and have a social connection with legal authorities, is one such factor.

The analytical results presented in this chapter strongly support the value of a motive-based trust perspective on regulation. They demonstrate that judgments about the motives of the particular police officers and judges with whom people have personal experiences have more influence on whether people accept the decisions of these legal authorities than do evaluations of the favorability of their outcomes. These findings can be combined with those on procedural justice, outlined in the previous chapter, to support the importance of social motives in shaping people's behavior toward law enforcement and other legal authorities.

These findings are especially important because they focus on the voluntary acceptance of decisions. As has been noted, when people's actions develop out of a trust in the motives of the authorities with whom they are dealing, they consent and cooperate with those authorities' directives. This cooperation facilitates the efficient and effective exercise of regulatory authority.

Chapter 6

The Overall Influence of Social Motives on Decision Acceptance

TWO SOCIAL motives, procedural justice and motive-based trust, have been considered separately, and each has been shown to influence decision acceptance and satisfaction with the decision maker. Both procedural justice and motive-based trust reflect the influence of factors that are not directly linked to the favorability, fairness, predictability, or expectedness of the outcomes of people's interactions with legal authorities.

We now turn our attention to the relationship between procedural justice and motive-based trust. When we consider these two social motives jointly, our concern is with determining whether each social motive makes a unique contribution to explaining decision acceptance. If each does not make an independent contribution, we need not separately consider issues of justice and trust and can concentrate instead on just one of the two.

The results of a regression equation, shown in table 6.1, suggest that both of the social motives we have considered make independent contributions to our understanding of why people accept the decisions made by legal authorities. The beta weight for procedural justice was 0.38 (p < .001) and for motive-based trust 0.47 (p < .001).[1] These significant effects indicate that each social motive explains variance beyond that which can be explained by the other variables in the equation.

The results of the regression analysis also confirm that people's judgments about outcome fairness, outcome favorability, and the expectedness and predictability of the outcomes within an experience explained very little of the variance in decision acceptance beyond what could be explained by procedural justice and motive-based trust. In contrast, 44 percent of the variance beyond that which could be explained by

Table 6.1   Procedural Justice, Motive-Based Trust, Acceptance
of the Decisions of Legal Authorities, and Satisfaction
with the Decision Maker

Beta weights	
Social motives	
Motive-based trust	.47***
Procedural justice	.38***
Instrumental motives	
Distributive justice	.08***
Outcome favorability	.08***
Expected?	−.02
Predictability	.04**
Adjusted R-squared	
Unique influence of social motives	44%
Unique influence of instrumental motives	1
Total	81

Source: California study data.
Note: The dependent variable combines decision acceptance and satisfaction with the decision maker.
**p < .01.
***p < .001.

instrumental motives was explained by procedural justice and motive-based trust. This reinforces the suggestion that the two social motives—procedural justice and motive-based trust—dominate the decisions that people make about whether to accept the decisions of legal authorities. In fact, the instrumental factors are not statistically significant once social motives are taken into account.[2]

The Potential Influence of Prior Values: Path Analysis

The prior analysis suggests that people's inferences about the fairness of the procedures they experience and their inferences about the trustworthiness of the motives of authorities shape their willingness to defer voluntarily to those authorities by accepting their decisions. However, this relationship is inferred from a correlation in a cross-sectional study in which all of the various views are measured at one point in time. We also need to demonstrate that people's judgments are related to their actual experiences and do not flow from their prior attitudes and values. We can test whether the relationship we observe between procedural justice, motive-based trust, and the willingness to accept authorities' decisions is caused by some prior factor, such as the views about the law and legal authorities that people bring into their interactions.

Because the design of the California study did not include a panel analysis (in which respondents are interviewed at several points in time), we rely here on data from a previous study to examine further the effect of prior values on decision acceptance. In this test we used the panel data collected in a study of 804 randomly selected Chicago residents who were interviewed twice, approximately one year apart. (For a discussion of these data, see Tyler 1990.) During that one-year period 329 of the respondents (41 percent) had a personal experience with the police or the courts. We examined the influence of that personal experience on subsequent feelings and actions among this subset of respondents, controlling on prior levels of their feelings about the legitimacy of authorities, which we established during the first interviews. In particular, we examined whether the procedural justice and trust that people reported in their interactions with a particular legal authority had an influence on their subsequent views of legitimacy that was distinct from the views they had held prior to their personal experience.

We can analyze the data from this panel study to examine the influence of people's experience-based judgments about the favorability of their outcomes and about the fairness and trustworthiness of the authorities in predicting their post-experience legitimacy judgments, controlling on their pre-experience levels of legitimacy. If judgments about the fairness and trustworthiness of particular authorities develop out of the actual nature of the personal experience, then we would expect those judgments to be distinct from prior views about the general legitimacy of authorities. We would further expect these distinct experience-based judgments to have an independent influence on people's post-experience legitimacy judgments.

In this analysis one aspect of the dependent variable—legitimacy—involved feelings of obligation to obey rules. The index was based on four items in the first phase of the study and on six items, including the original four, in the second phase, conducted one year later. All of the items used an agree-disagree format to index feelings of obligation to obey social rules. The six items were: "People should obey the law even if it goes against what they think is right"; "I always try to follow the law even if I think that it is wrong"; "Disobeying the law is seldom justified"; "It is difficult to break the law and keep one's self-respect"; "A person who refuses to obey the law is a menace to society"; and, "Obedience and respect for authority are the most important virtues children should learn."

The second aspect of legitimacy involves institutional trust. We assessed institutional trust using nineteen items that indexed three aspects of institutional trust: confidence in institutions, judgments that the authorities do or do not discriminate, and future expectations about the behavior of institutional actors. We measured institutional trust using these items in both interviews of the panel study.

Confidence in the institution is assessed through general evaluative items: "I have a great deal of respect for the police"; "On the whole, police officers are honest"; "I feel proud of the police"; "I feel I should support the police"; "The courts generally guarantee everyone a fair trial"; "The basic rights of citizens are protected by the courts"; "On the whole, judges are honest"; and, "Court decisions are almost always fair." These items reflected what earlier theorists referred to as "support" for authorities (Easton 1965).

We assessed nondiscrimination by the institution by asking respondents whether the police and the courts "treat everyone equally" or whether they "favor some people over others." The goal of this assessment was to determine whether people felt that all citizens receive the same quality of treatment from legal authorities. Prior studies of authorities of all types have made it clear that the issue of equality of treatment is distinct from the issue of the quality of treatment, and it may independently influence evaluations (Tyler et al. 1997).

We assessed expectations regarding the future behavior of institutional actors by asking people whether, if they call the police in the future, are stopped by the police in the future, or go to court in the future, three things would or would not be true: their encounter would be handled in a satisfactory way, they would receive a fair outcome, and they would receive fair treatment. Together, these variations led to nine "future expectations" questions.

We combined these nineteen items into an overall scale indexing institutional trust. During the first round of interviews, we assessed views about institutional trust prior to the personal experience. These views were also assessed during the second round of interviews, after people's personal experiences with authorities had taken place. We combined these institutional trust items into one subscale of legitimacy, while obligation to obey was the other.[3]

As noted, a subsample of those initially interviewed had had a personal experience with the police or the courts during the period between the two interviews. We examined three aspects of that experience: the favorability of the outcome, assessments of procedural justice, and judgments about the trustworthiness of the authorities involved. To determine the favorability of the outcome, we asked respondents to compare their outcome to three points of reference: their prior expectations, what they thought generally happens to people in similar situations, and the outcome they had received in the past in similar situations. We combined these three evaluations into an index of overall outcome favorability (alpha = 0.75).

We also asked respondents eight questions about procedural justice: "How fair were the procedures used?"; "How fairly were you treated?"; "Were the authorities polite to you?"; "Did they show concern for your rights?"; "Did they get the information they needed to make good decisions about the situation?"; "Did they try to bring things into the open so they could be handled?"; "Were the authorities honest in what they said?"; and, "Did the authorities do anything that you thought was dishonest or improper?" (alpha = 0.74). In addition, we asked respondents two questions about the trust they felt in the motives of the legal authority: "Did the authority try to be fair to you?" and, "Did the authority consider your input in making decisions?" We combined these two trust judgments into an overall index of personal trust (alpha = 0.73).

Our purpose was to use this panel data to test the possibility that the influence of the social motives of procedural justice and motive-based trust would disappear if we controlled on prior general attitudes about the legitimacy of the law and of legal authorities. To conduct this analysis we used the indices of obligation to obey and institutional trust established at the first (time 1) and second (time 2) interviews as two indicators of latent variables reflecting orientation toward authority prior to and following actual experiences with legal authorities. Using the 329 people who had had a personal experience with legal authorities between the two interviews, we looked at the influence of experience on time 2 legitimacy, controlling for time 1 legitimacy. In addition, we allowed time 1 legitimacy to influence the judgments that people made about their personal experiences. This analysis maximizes the possibility that the independent effects of personal experience would not be found to have significance. Two experience-based indices were considered. One indexed outcome favorability. The other was a latent variable reflecting the influence of procedural justice and motive-based trust.

The results of the causal analysis are shown in figure 6.1. They indicate, first, that people's time 2 legitimacy was strongly influenced by legitimacy at time 1 (beta = 0.83, $p < .001$). In addition, judgments about procedural justice and motive-based trust had a distinct and significant influence on time 2 legitimacy (beta = 0.22, $p < .01$). Finally, outcome favorability had no distinct influence on time 2 legitimacy (beta = 0.04, n.s.).

Further, in contrast with the California data, we were able to see an effect of prior views on people's judgments about the procedural justice of their experience and on their judgments about the trustworthiness of the authorities' motives (beta = 0.44, $p < .05$). This could have been true either because people's evaluations of their experiences were shaped by their prior views or because their prior views shaped how they acted during their subsequent personal experience, changing the nature of

Figure 6.1   Panel Analysis of the Impact of Experience

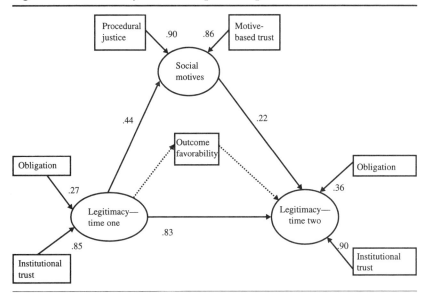

Source: Based on Chicago Study data.

that experience. Either way, these influences existed, but they did not eliminate the separate influence that judgments about a personal experience with a legal authority had on general post-experience legitimacy.

It is interesting to compare these findings to those already outlined for the California study. The results of that study suggest that controlling for general societal orientations does not disrupt the connection between procedural justice, motive-based trust, and decision acceptance. Here the same conclusion emerges. When we look at the panel data, however, it is also clear that people's prior views do have some influence on their judgments of procedural justice and motive-based trust.

These findings support the conclusion that the influence of experience-based judgments about procedural justice and motive-based trust that we found in the California study is a real effect, not just an effect resulting from the prior views about legal authorities and institutions that people bring into their personal experiences. Indeed, data from the study conducted in Chicago show that experience-based judgments about the justice of the actions of particular authorities and the trustworthiness of the motives of particular authorities are likely to influence people in ways that are distinct from any impact of their prior views about the general legitimacy of legal authorities.

Table 6.2   Influences on Acceptance and Compliance

	Voluntary Acceptance of Decisions	Compliance with Decisions
Beta weights		
Experience-based judgments		
Trustworthiness	.46***	.12*
Procedural justice	.32***	.06
Outcome fairness	.09**	.07*
Outcome favorability	.08**	.00
Expectedness	−.01	−.01
Predictability	.05**	.03
Total adjusted R-squared	69%	4%

Source: California study data.
*p < .05.
**p < .01.
***p < .001.

Acceptance Versus Compliance

As previously discussed, the voluntary acceptance of the decisions of police officers and judges should be distinguished from compliance with the decisions of those authorities. Compliance can be induced by the fear of force or punishment, while acceptance flows from consent and cooperation. In our measurement of people's responses to the police and the courts, we have focused on acceptance. Acceptance is distinct from compliance in that it involves voluntary or willing behavior. Compliance occurs when people follow rules or do as directed for whatever reason. Hence, authorities with power are more likely to obtain compliance than acceptance. We have already shown that, as we would expect, people are more willing to say that they complied with a decision than to say that they accepted it. We also expect that acceptance is more strongly related to social motives than compliance.

This distinction is reinforced by the analysis shown in table 6.2. In that analysis we returned to the California data to compare the influence of procedural justice and motive-based trust on compliance and acceptance. We measured compliance by asking people whether they did as directed by the legal authorities.

As we would expect, procedural justice and motive-based trust had little influence on compliance, but as we have already shown, they did have a large influence on acceptance. This finding supports our argument that the psychology of voluntary acceptance should be distinguished from the psychology of involuntary compliance.

Table 6.3   Elements of Fair Procedure

	Agree	Mean (Standard Deviation)
Quality of decision making processes[a]	—	1.76 (0.88)
"He/she treated me the same as he/she would treat anyone else in the same situation."	76%	—
"He/she was basically honest."	84	—
"He/she made decisions based on the facts."	82	—
Quality of treatment[b]	—	1.78 (0.99)
"He/she treated me politely."	82	—
"He/she showed concern for my rights."	74	—
"He/she treated me with dignity and respect."	79	—

Source: California study data.
Note: Low means indicate high quality.
[a]alpha = 0.82.
[b]alpha = 0.92.

Antecedents of Procedural Justice

We also want to consider those aspects of the behavior of legal authorities that may shape people's perceptions of procedural justice and motive-based trust during their personal experiences. Using the California data, we argue that procedural justice judgments are linked to two aspects of the actions of decision makers: judgments about the quality of their decision making processes, and judgments about the quality of their treatment of the people with whom they interact (Tyler and Blader 2000; Tyler and Lind 1992).[4] The items indexing each of these two constructs are shown in table 6.3. Based on the results shown in this table, it is clear that respondents generally thought that they were the beneficiaries of both high-quality decision making and high-quality treatment from legal authorities.

What causes people to feel that they are experiencing procedural justice when they deal with a particular legal authority? Why do they trust the motives of the person with whom they are dealing during their encounter? To address this issue, we conducted regression analyses in which the dependent variables were procedural justice and motive-based trust and the predictors were the two aspects of the authorities' behavior that have

Table 6.4   Antecedents of Procedural Justice and Motive-Based Trust

	Procedural Justice	Trust
Beta weights		
Quality of decision making	.32***	.30***
Quality of treatment	.51***	.55***
Outcome favorability	.12***	.08***
Outcome fairness	.04***	.05***
Adjusted R-squared		
Unique influence of the quality of decision making and quality of treatment	47%	49%
Unique influence of outcome favorability and outcome fairness	2	1
Total adjusted R-squared	75	75

Source: California study data.
***p < .001.

been outlined: the quality of their decision making process, and the quality of the treatment that people received during their encounter. As controls, we also included assessments of the favorability of the respondents' outcomes and of the fairness of their outcomes.

The results of the regression analysis are shown in table 6.4. They suggest, as we might expect, that people are more likely to think that the procedures they experienced were fair, and to trust the authorities with whom they interacted, when they received favorable outcomes (beta = 0.12 for procedural justice; 0.08 for trust).

In line with our expectations, the findings also support the argument that the quality of the decision making that people experience (beta = 0.32 for procedural justice; 0.30 for trust), as well as the quality of their treatment by the authority (beta = 0.51 for procedural justice; 0.55 for trust), have independent influences on their judgments about procedural justice and trust.

We can estimate the relative importance of these different factors by comparing the ability of each judgment to explain unique variance. Judgments about the quality of decision making and the quality of treatment uniquely explained 47 percent of the variance in procedural justice and 49 percent of the variance in trust. In contrast, the outcome of the experience uniquely explained 2 percent of the variance in procedural justice and 1 percent of the variance in trust. As these numbers suggest, both procedural justice and trust were dominated by these two influences.[5]

Table 6.5   Process Control and Decision Control

	Agree	Mean (Standard Deviation)
Process control "I had an opportunity to describe my situation before he/she made a decision about how to handle it."	69%	2.04 (1.18)
Decision control "I felt I had some influence over the decisions he/she made about my situation."	48	2.65 (1.13)

Source: California study data.
Note: Low means indicate high control.

Control

Early theories of procedural justice emphasized issues of control: people feel that procedures are fairer, the argument went, when they have more control within the context of those procedures. Control researchers now make a further distinction between process and decision control. Process control is control over evidence presentation, and decision control is control over the form of the final decisions made about the distribution of outcomes. Control theorists argue that both types of control matter (Thibaut and Walker 1975).

The indices of process and decision control are presented in table 6.5. The percentages shown in this table indicate that people are more likely to feel that they have process control than that they have decision control. Only 48 percent agreed that they had been able to influence the decision, while 69 percent indicated that they had had an opportunity to make their arguments. As we would expect, these two judgments are not completely independent of each other. Those who thought they had more opportunity to present their arguments were more likely to indicate that they had an influence on the decision ($r = 0.38$, $p < .001$).

Tyler and Blader (2000) found that control issues have no independent influence beyond that of other procedural elements—the quality of decision making and the quality of treatment. This is consistent with the finding of Lind, Tyler, and Huo (1997). If it is also true in this dataset, then we can focus our attention on the elements of procedure that we have identified—the quality of the decision making process and the quality of the treatment received—and need not directly address issues of control.

Table 6.6   Influence of Control Judgments

	Acceptance	Satisfaction
Beta weights		
Process control	−.01	−.02
Decision control	.02	.02
Motive-based trust	.42***	.35***
Procedural justice	.31***	.34***
Quality of decision making processes	.11***	.14***
Quality of treatment	−.03	.06*
Outcome fairness	.08***	.06***
Outcome favorability	.07***	.09***
Total adjusted R-squared	69%	81%

Source: California study data.
*p < .05.
***p < .001.

We tested the argument that control judgments have no independent influence using regression analysis that included indices of both control and noncontrol elements of procedures in the same equation. The analysis is shown in table 6.6. It supports the suggestion that control judgments have no independent influence on decision acceptance beyond the influence of decision making and treatment quality.

Although control judgments have no direct influence on decision acceptance, they have an indirect influence in that they affect judgments of trust and procedural justice, the quality of decision making procedures, the quality of the treatment received, and outcome favorability and fairness. The results of the regression analyses shown in table 6.7 demonstrate that control is linked to all of these judgments.

In each case, process control effects dominated over decision control effects. Even with outcome judgments, respondents' evaluations of the fairness and the favorability of their outcomes were primarily shaped by their assessments of their opportunities to participate in the process by presenting evidence, not by their control over the actual outcome.

Of course, we do not want to exaggerate this argument, since there are independent decision control influences on each of the four judgments we consider. Nonetheless, the dominant finding here, as in prior research, is that people focus more directly on whether they have an opportunity to present their arguments than they do on whether they think they are influencing the decisions made.

Table 6.7 Control Influences

	Trust in Motives	Procedural Justice	Quality of Decision Making	Quality of Treatment	Outcome Fairness	Outcome Favorability
Process control	.44***	.39***	.40***	.40***	.29***	.30***
Decision control	.26***	.18***	.15***	.16***	.22***	.24***
Adjusted R-squared	34%	24%	23%	23%	18%	20%

Source: California study data.
*** p < .001.

Although we do not focus on control issues, we want to emphasize that control is nonetheless important to the psychology of personal experience, especially indirectly through its impact on other important evaluations. In this case, people were more likely to think that authorities were using high-quality decision making procedures and to feel that they received high-quality treatment if the authorities gave them more control during their encounter. The primary form of control that people wanted was process control—the opportunity to present evidence—not decision control.

Respondents were also more likely to evaluate their outcome as favorable and fair when they thought they had more control. But did they evaluate their outcomes this way because their outcomes were actually more favorable when they had more control over them? We can address this question by looking at the coded objective favorability of respondents' outcomes. This is not a completely objective measure, since it relies on respondents' self-reports of what happened. However, it is the most objective indicator available in this study.

When we look at the influence of control on objective favorability, we find that people indicated having more control in situations in which outcomes were more objectively favorable. Both judgments of greater process control ($r = 0.22$, $p < .001$) and judgments of greater outcome control ($r = 0.28$, $p < .001$) were linked to objectively more favorable outcomes. This suggests that thinking one has control is associated with receiving objectively better outcomes. Perhaps having more control (for example, more opportunity to present evidence) enables one to achieve a more desirable outcome.

Of course, it is also possible that when people received objectively better outcomes, they then adjusted their judgments to believe that they had controlled the attainment of those outcomes. Social psychologists have widely documented such post-experience cognitive adjustments to bring judgments about pre-experience decisions into line with outcomes—for example, to claim credit for success.

As we would expect, subjective judgments of control have more influence on subjective evaluations of outcome satisfaction than the previously noted influence on objective outcome favorability. This supports the argument that people are motivated to claim credit for perceived success, even more than would be warranted by the actual level of success attained. We find influences of both process control ($r = 0.40$, $p < .001$) and decision control ($r = 0.36$, $p < .001$) on subjective outcome favorability.

Overall Model

To assess the overall model we contrasted two images of the basis upon which people are motivated to comply with police officers and

Figure 6.2   Conceptual Model for the Overall Influence of Social Motives

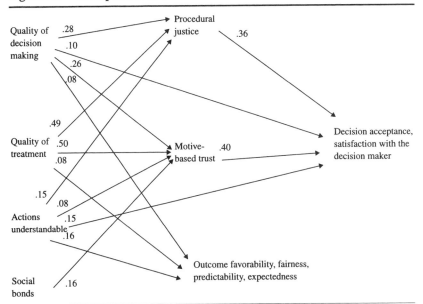

Source: California study data.

judges. The first image links compliance to the favorability, fairness, and predictability of the decisions from direct contacts with the police and the courts. The second image links compliance to gaining voluntary acceptance by using fair procedures and creating a climate of motive-based trust.

We used causal modeling to test this approach. In the model we treated decision acceptance and satisfaction with the decision maker as two indicators of a single latent dependent variable. We also treated the instrumental concerns—outcome favorability, outcome fairness, predictability, and expectedness—as indicators of a single instrumental variable. The resulting model is shown in figure 6.2.

The results shown in figure 6.2 support the argument that process-based social concerns, rather than instrumental ones, dominate people's judgments about their personal experiences with legal authorities. These results show that procedural justice and motive-based trust have distinct influences on acceptance and satisfaction. Further, these two factors are influenced, in turn, by judgments about the quality of decision making and the quality of treatment. Procedural justice is shaped by judgments about the quality of decision making, the quality of treatment, and whether actions are understandable. Motive-based trust is shaped by judgments about the quality of decision making, the quality of treatment, the understandability of actions, and the existence of social bonds.

Taken together, these findings strongly support the argument that the police and the courts can encourage consent and cooperation from the members of the public with whom they interact through process-based strategies. Those strategies rely on enacting fair and appropriate decision making procedures and creating motive-based trust by providing people with high quality treatment.

Implications

We began our discussion of the relationship between community members and legal authorities by asking whether it is possible for police officers and judges to deliver undesirable, negative outcomes without damaging their relationship with those whom they regulate. The results of our analysis so far strongly support the argument that it is indeed possible. Although the willingness to accept authorities' decisions and satisfaction with decision makers are both shaped by the favorability of people's outcomes, outcome favorability is not the only, or even the major, factor shaping acceptance and satisfaction. Both trust in the motives of the authorities and judgments about the fairness of the procedures they use have stronger influences on acceptance and satisfaction than does outcome favorability, outcome fairness, or the predictability of outcomes.

The strong influence of social judgments on decision acceptance and satisfaction with decision makers supports our argument that there are ways in which police officers and judges can create and sustain trust in their motives and, through such trust, can encourage the willingness to accept their decisions, even when they cannot deliver favorable outcomes. What would legal authorities gain by approaching their personal experiences with the public from a process-based perspective? One important gain is the greater likelihood of gaining deference within the immediate situation. Because deference is motivated, to at least some degree, by feelings of cooperation and consent, people are not focused on the coercive aspects of the interaction but directed by their own willingness to cooperate.

The process-based cooperative model lessens the likelihood that there will be an escalation of force into a negative, confrontational situation. Further, levels of hostility will be lower. (For a discussion of the possibility of such negative, hostile reactions, see Sherman's [1993] "defiance" theory.)

A further advantage to a process-based approach is illustrated by another study of police interactions with drivers—the Prince George's

County Take Away Guns (TAG) project. That project uses traffic enforcement to take away guns from drivers. Police officers are trained to explain their goals and persuade drivers to consent to searches for guns in their cars (a "procedural justice" approach). After stopping drivers for some infraction (for example, a broken tail light), the police appeal to the driver's "good citizen" identity and ask to search the car. They emphasize the voluntary nature of the program and provide motorists with a letter from the district police commander inviting any complaints or comments that people want to make. The study found that increased traffic stops (up 400 percent) led to a 49 percent decline in gun crimes. The procedurally just policing approach led to a decline not only in crime but in complaints about police misconduct, which dropped by 30 percent (Sherman 1999).

The TAG project is especially valuable because it illustrates a core point—that the police can engage in regulatory activities without alienating the public if they act in ways that treat members of the public with respect. In the TAG project, the police are careful to acknowledge citizen rights, to explain their activities, and to make avenues of complaint clear. As a consequence, they received much higher levels of voluntary cooperation than would be typical.

A Process-Based Approach and High-Risk Subgroups

Will this approach work with everyone? As we outline in part IV, the argument that a high-risk group of young minority males is "defiant" and does not respond to treatment with respect and fairness is not consistent with the data collected in the California study. The results of that analysis indicate that, in fact, the members of this high-risk group are primarily concerned about issues of respect and acknowledgment of their rights. This finding is supported by recent studies of adolescents that also emphasize the centrality of "treatment with respect" to teenagers' reactions in dealings with societal authorities (Bourgois 1996; Emler and Reicher 1995).

In commenting on juvenile delinquency, Emler and Reicher (1995, 224, 226) make an argument similar to our own:

One other false proposal that needs to be commented on is the idea that strict, punitive regimes, "short sharp shocks" or other "aversion therapies," are the solution to delinquency in general. . . . On the one hand, an experience of formal authority as cold, impersonal and punitive is hardly likely to improve one's attitude towards it. On the other, to celebrate physical "hardness," to force one into the company of others who offend and to cut one off from all other social contacts is the ideal way of ensuring that individuals will act upon this hostility. Indeed the basic premise of such regimes—punishment—is a profound misreading of delinquent psychology. . . . If delinquency is the expression of a negative orientation to formal authority . . . how is it possible to improve this orientation?

These authors propose structural solutions whose goal is to ensure that all adolescents feel that they are "equally valued" as people. Like the restorative justice model (Braithwaite 1999), this approach emphasizes the importance of communicating to all children that society, social institutions, and societal authorities value them as people, even though society may disapprove of and sanction their behavior. As we have noted, one of the most effective ways to communicate such value is through fair and respectful treatment.

Similar arguments have recently been made about acts of violence among adolescents. Kennedy and Forde (1999, 36) have argued that acts of violence are not premeditated, calculating, instrumental actions. Instead, they develop in the context of social interactions from "conversation, argument, debate, anger, and confrontation." In their study of "street youth"—young, unemployed males—they found that violence is often triggered when others "show disrespect" or commit "violations of honor" (118). These interpersonal slights legitimize the use of violence to defend one's sense of "self" and thus lead to violence on the part of the offended parties. Similarly, Anderson (1994, 82) emphasized that interpersonal violence among urban youth is linked to demonstrations of a lack of respect, that is, to not "being granted the deference one deserves."

Although these findings provide strong support for the argument that judgments of procedural justice and motive-based trust are core concepts shaping people's reactions to their personal experiences with police officers and judges, we acknowledge that there may be some people for whom these concepts are of less importance, or perhaps none at all. This does not diminish the potential value of the process-based approach.

The police may begin an interaction using a process-based approach and then, for that subgroup for whom this approach is not effective, move to a more sanction-oriented approach. This is exactly the model proposed by Ayres and Braithwaite (1992), who proposed that regulatory authorities move through a series of increasingly instrumental regulation strategies, ending up with surveillance and sanctioning of the small subset of the population who can be managed only in these ways. As these authors suggested, the identification of this small subset through an escalating model of the type outlined allows society to deploy its coercive resources in the most effective ways, that is, by focusing their application on the small subset of the larger population who are unable to exercise self-regulatory control.

This strategy of regulation is similar to the general strategy of cooperation proposed by Axelrod (1984). That strategy involves an initially cooperative approach to others. If others reciprocate by engaging in cooperation, a long-term cooperative strategy is established. If others reciprocate by engaging in competition, a long-term strategy for managing competition is established.

There are several important aspects of this overall cooperative strategy. First, it is a contingent strategy shaped by the behavior of others. As a result, it differentiates between cooperators and competitors. Similarly, the strategy advocated here allows legal authorities to distinguish between cooperators and competitors. For most interactions issues of force need never arise.

In addition, cooperators are able to reap the benefits of their mutually cooperative interactions. They can minimize the resources that they allocate to competing with others. Cooperators do better than competitors not by defeating them in direct competition but by gaining more from their other mutually cooperative interactions. Every interaction for a competitor, by contrast, is a competition.

Third, even when competing with others, the Axelrod strategy emphasizes constantly seeking to "reform" competitors by encouraging them to become cooperative. Like the restorative justice approach, this approach is motivated by the desire to activate the internal motivations of people who have engaged in instrumental behaviors—in this case, encouraging cooperation between former competitors.

The police and the courts can act in this manner by approaching citizens respectfully and cooperatively. If necessary, they can then become more force-oriented. However, even in such competitive situations, the police and the courts should keep in mind that their long-term goal is to build positive and favorable connections with the members of the community.

Long-Term Implications of a Process-Based Approach

Beyond the immediate situation, the potential for adding value through a process-based approach lies in creating a more positive, trusting orientation toward the police and the courts. Such a generalized societal orientation encourages a more favorable attitude toward the law and legal authorities. This argument has two aspects. The first of these is the suggestion that the police and the courts can encourage a more favorable orientation toward the law by exercising procedural fairness. In this way process-based approaches could have positive long-term consequences.

The second implication is that the sanction-based model may have negative long-term consequences. Legal authorities employing it may "increase rather than decrease future criminal behavior" (LaFree 1998, 180). As LaFree suggests: "A growing body of evidence from diverse sources underscores the conclusion that formal criminal justice punishment may have little effect—or even a counterproductive effect—when coupled with low levels of institutional legitimacy" (170). LaFree suggests that these negative consequences are especially likely to be found among African Americans.

The first argument about the potentially favorable effects of fair treatment flows directly from the procedural justice literature, which focuses on generating support for and a greater willingness to accept third-party decisions (Lind and Tyler 1988; Tyler 1990; Tyler et al. 1997; Tyler and Smith 1997). Procedural justice theories predict that both immediate and long-term decision acceptance will result from the use of fair decision making procedures. Procedural justice is predicted to enhance support for authorities and institutions, leading both to a greater commitment to society and its institutions and to stronger feelings of obligation to obey social rules. These are all gains associated with a focus on treatment with dignity and respect as part of a process-oriented policing strategy.

Another similarly conceived model of legal procedures is the restorative justice model proposed by Braithwaite (1999). That model seeks to use conferences between juvenile offenders, their victims, legal authorities, and members of the public to find ways to reintegrate the offenders into the community. The goal of the conferences is twofold: to find suitable punishments for wrongdoing that are willingly accepted by the perpetrator, the victim, and members of the community; and to find ways to increase an offender's commitment to law and to the community. The goal is to encourage individuals to accept responsibility for their actions, in the short term by paying compensation, engaging in restitution, and otherwise seeking to make amends for their actions, and in the long run by taking greater personal responsibility for following rules and obeying the directives and decisions of legal authorities. One way to encourage these attitudes, as our findings make clear, is for people to feel fairly treated by and to trust the authorities they encounter in their personal lives.

Several studies of long-term effects support the argument that fair treatment and decision making can have positive future consequences. In Paternoster, Bachman, Brame, and Sherman's (1997) study, offenders who dealt with the Milwaukee police because of a domestic violence complaint were interviewed after being arrested and charged by the police. The study examined whether the fairness of the police, in the eyes of those arrested, predicted their future criminal behavior, controlling on prior criminal history. The answer was yes: those offenders who thought that the police treated them fairly had 40 percent fewer repeat offenses during the six months after the interview.

Another long-term study is the longitudinal test of Braithwaite's restorative justice model in the context of court proceedings (Sherman 1999). A study of restorative justice conferences found that defendants experienced those conferences as fairer procedures for handling their case than more traditional court procedures. The study tested whether people who experienced fairer procedures during their experience with the courts were more likely to adhere to the law in the future. Two situations were studied: youthful offenders and drunk drivers. Results suggested that the use of the "fairer" restorative justice conferences both encouraged respect for the law and reduced later lawbreaking behavior (Sherman 1999).

Pruitt also examined long-term compliance. He focused on adherence to mediated agreements over time and found that the procedural justice of the mediation session influenced adherence to that agreement four to eight months later. Pruitt and his colleagues (1993) reported that there is no relationship between agreement quality and long-term adherence. However, "the perceived quality of the procedure . . . is related to both short-run and long-run success [adherence]" (Pruitt et al. 1990, 42). Interestingly, they found that those who came to the hearing in response to a complaint from others were not likely to feel satisfied with the agreement four to eight months later, but that if they thought the hearing had been fair, they were nonetheless still complying with the agreement. In other words, fair procedures had encouraged them to comply with an agreement that they did not necessarily like.

Summary

Thus far, we have examined two key assumptions underlying the process-based model of regulation. The first assumption is that people in the community will accept the decisions of the authorities they are dealing with, even when those decisions are unfavorable, if they experience the authorities as using fair procedures and if they trust the motives of those authorities. If so, then the police and the courts have a strategy for attaining deference besides sanction-based approaches that involve the threat or use of coercion. Our findings from the California study strongly support the suggestion that process-based approaches are a viable alternative strategy for policing and for managing the people who appear in the courts.

Second, we have looked at whether it is possible for legal authorities to influence procedural justice judgments and to create motive-based trust through their actions. Given that legal authorities are not always able to solve people's problems and must sometimes regulate them by delivering sanctions, it is not possible for them to demonstrate justice and build trust by delivering desired outcomes. Therefore, one might assume that it would be difficult for legal authorities to build up good-will and trust among those with whom they have personal experiences.

However, our findings suggest that the favorability of the outcomes that legal authorities deliver is not central to the justice that people experience or the trust that they feel in the motives of the authorities. Instead, people's assessments of procedural justice and motive-based trust flow primarily from their evaluations of the quality of decision making and the quality of treatment that is part of the process that the police and the courts use when dealing with the public. This supports the second important element of a process-based strategy.

Taken together, these findings suggest that a process-based approach to the exercise of legal authority can in fact be the basis for an effective model of regulation. These findings are optimistic, suggesting that it is less necessary for the police or the courts to exercise their role through sanctioning.

A process-based strategy has an important long-term advantage: it encourages people to engage in self-regulation. As we have noted, deterrence strategies are clearly effective to some degree, but they are costly and inefficient. Their inefficiencies stem from the need to engage in surveillance that can detect and punish wrongdoing. In contrast, the process-based approach to regulation encourages people to feel that they ought to accept the decisions and directives of authorities. This leads them to do so even when the potential for sanctioning is weak.

A process-based strategy can also lessen resistance to the acceptance of decisions. Because people feel fairly treated and trust the motives and intentions of the authorities, their hostility and resistance is lower than would be the case under other conditions.

The process-based strategy of regulation also increases the likelihood of adherence to agreements over time. As we have already noted, the procedural justice literature suggests that when people experience procedural justice in their dealings with legal authorities, their compliance with the law is maintained in the long term. These findings suggest that people continue to adhere to the law because they develop internal values that support intrinsically motivated, self-regulatory behavior. Feeling fairly treated and trusting the motives of those authorities with whom one interacts encourages a voluntary acceptance of decisions that continues over time.[6]

PART III

SOCIETAL ORIENTATIONS AND PERSONAL EXPERIENCES

INTERVIEWS in the California study focused on people's personal experiences with legal authorities. In our discussions up to this point we have been concerned with understanding the factors that shape people's willingness to accept decisions within the context of their own personal encounters with police officers and judges. We recognize, however, that such personal experiences occur within a broader framework.

That framework encompasses two types of societal orientations: people's general views about the legitimacy of legal authorities and institutions, and people's connections to others in their communities and to American society. In our study these connections reflect the degree to which the respondents identified with their neighbors, with residents of their city, and, more generally, with other Americans.

We are interested in determining whether societal orientations influence people's willingness to defer to the decisions of police officers and judges during their personal encounters with these authorities. It is possible that both positive and negative societal orientations have an influence. We expect those who have a more favorable societal orientation to be more willing to defer to legal authorities. We expect this to be true both for views about the general legitimacy of legal authorities and for the degree to which people identify with society. Further, we expect people with more favorable societal orientations to rely more strongly on their judgments about procedural justice and motive-based trust when deciding whether to defer to authorities. We expect those who do not have favorable societal orientations to rely more strongly on their judgments about the fairness or favorability of their outcomes. Societal orientations, we predict, shape the basis on which people decide whether to defer to legal authorities.

In examining these two kinds of influence, we are concerned with going from the general to the particular. That is, how do general social orientations influence decisions about what to do in a particular situation?

Conversely, we are also concerned with determining how personal experience influences general societal orientations. If people have a good or bad encounter with a police officer or a judge, to what extent does that shape their views about the general legitimacy of the law and the legal system, and does it influence their identification with their neighbors, with their city, or with the United States?

Finally, to the degree that personal experience does influence more general orientations, what factors in personal experience are at work? Are people influenced by social motives such as procedural justice and motive-based trust, or are they influenced by the favorability or fairness of their outcomes?

The issue of generalization from personal experience is important because it addresses the long-term impact of a personal experience, as well as its generalization beyond one type of experience to others. For example, if a person is rudely treated by a police officer during a traffic stop, does that experience influence whether he defers to another police officer in the future, and does it shape his deference to the decisions made by judges? The first part of this question involves a similar experience, with a similar type of authority, that occurs in the future. The second part involves a future experience with a legal authority different from the one previously encountered.[1]

The question of the degree to which people generalize from their particular personal experiences to their general societal views has previously been addressed by Tyler (1990). The results of that study suggested that general views about the legitimacy of the law and legal institutions are shaped by people's personal experiences with individual legal authorities. It also suggests that the key experiential element shaping their views is the procedural justice they experience during their personal encounter with the police or the courts.

Our evaluation here expands on that analysis in several ways. It considers the potential influence of both procedural justice and motive-based trust, and it examines generalization from personal experience to both views about the legitimacy of legal authorities and identification with society—in this case, one's neighborhood, city, and country. Based on the prior work of Tyler (1990), we expect that what happens during a personal experience generalizes to these broader views, but the degree of that generalization is unknown.

Our analysis of the California data here focuses on two aspects of people's general societal orientations—their views about the legitimacy of the law and legal authorities and their connections with their community, their city, and the United States. Chapter 7 examines these societal orientations and discusses how they are measured in this study. Chapter 8 explores their impact on how people react to their personal experiences and considers the influence of general views on reactions during particular experiences. Chapter 9 looks at generalization from the experience to these views, considering the influence of particular personal experiences on general views about society and its institutions.

Chapter 7

Societal Orientations:
Legitimacy and Connections
with Society

O UR FIRST concern is with people's general orientation toward the law and legal authorities. Legitimacy reflects people's views about the degree to which they feel a responsibility to support legal authorities and defer to their decisions. The argument for the importance of legitimacy is linked to the belief that people's feelings of personal responsibility and obligation shape their law-related behavior.

Tyler (1990) has directly addressed this issue and shown that legitimacy shapes everyday compliance with the law. He found that those who view legal authorities as more legitimate, as indexed by the level of general institutional trust in those authorities and by feelings of obligation to obey the law, are more likely to obey the law in their everyday lives. His study, however, did not look at the influence of general views about the legitimacy of the law and legal institutions on decision acceptance behavior within particular situations.

Legitimacy as Perceived Obligation

Tyler (1990) used perceived obligation to obey as one key indicator of legitimacy. This view of legitimacy as the perceived obligation to obey the law and the directives of legal authorities is rooted in the classic work on legitimacy of Max Weber, who was interested in people's motivations for deferring to authorities. One such motivation is the belief that one is personally responsible for obeying authorities. From this perspective, legitimacy is the property that a rule or an authority has when others feel obligated to defer voluntarily to that rule or authority (Beetham 1991; Engstrom and Giles 1972; Suchman 1995; Tyler 1999a, 2001b). In other words, legitimate authorities are those regarded by people as entitled to having their decisions and rules accepted and followed by others (French and Raven 1959). The roots of the modern discussion of legitimacy are usually traced to the previously noted writings of Weber on authority and the social dynamics of authority (Weber 1968).

Weber argued that the ability to issue commands that will be obeyed does not rest solely on the possession of power and the capacity to use it. In addition, there are rules that people voluntarily obey and authorities whose directives are voluntarily followed. Legitimacy, therefore, is a quality possessed by an authority, a law, or an institution that leads others to feel obligated to obey its decisions and directives voluntarily. It is "a quality attributed to a regime by a population" (Merelman 1966, 548).

A similar view of responsibility and obligation to others (including both issues of legitimacy and of morality) is articulated by other social scientists. As Hoffman (1977, 85) notes:

> The legacy of both Sigmund Freud and Emile Durkheim is the agreement among social scientists that most people do not go through life viewing society's moral norms as external, coercively imposed pressures to which they must submit. Though the norms are initially external to the individual and often in conflict with [the individual's] desires, the norms eventually become part of [his or her] internal motive system and guide [his or her] behavior even in the absence of external authority. Control by others is thus replaced by self control [through internalization].

As with Weber, the key issue addressed by Durkheim and Freud is self-regulation: personally taking on obligations and responsibilities and feeling responsible for deferring to society, social rules, and authorities. We follow Weber, however, in focusing on the internalization of the obligation to obey authorities, as opposed to the internalization of the responsibility to follow principles of personal morality. This feeling of obligation reflects a willingness to suspend personal considerations of self-interest and to ignore personal moral values because an authority or a rule is entitled to determine appropriate behavior within a given situation.

Kelman and Hamilton (1989) refer to legitimacy as "authorization": a person authorizes an authority to determine appropriate behavior within some situation and then feels obligated to follow the directives or rules that authority establishes. As these authors indicate, the authorization of actions by authorities

> seem[s] to carry automatic justification for them. Behaviorally, authorization obviates the necessity of making judgments or choices. Not only do normal moral principles become inoperative, but—particularly when the

actions are explicitly ordered—a different type of morality, linked to the duty to obey superior orders, tends to take over. (Kelman and Hamilton 1989, 16)

Legitimacy can be a general feeling of obligation or responsibility to obey authorities that encourages deference in any situation. However, it is also something that is created by individual police officers within the context of their encounters with members of the public—a type of "situational legitimacy" (Reiss 1971). Recognizing this, police officers focus not only on displays of force when shaping their actions but on establishing their "legitimate right to intervene" in a particular situation (Reiss 1971, 46). Police interventions into people's lives are viewed by the people affected as more legitimate when there is some additional reason for the intervention beyond the officer's personal judgment, such as a complaint from another citizen.

When legitimacy is low, the police are more likely to have to use physical force, introducing "the risk of injury to both the arrested person and the officer" (Reiss 1971, 60). Interestingly, Reiss finds that 73 percent of injuries to officers occur when the officers are interfered with, and interference most typically comes from people other than the parties involved in the immediate situation, that is, from bystanders or family members. "When such persons question the legitimacy of police intervention and a police officer reacts to control their behavior, more serious conflict may ensue as each party attempts to gain control of the situation. This results more often in injury to the officer" (60).

In addition to being created within a particular type of situation, legitimacy is also something created by individual police officers. When a police officer responds to a call or stops someone on the street, he or she taps into people's general feelings that authorities are legitimate and entitled to be obeyed. To the degree that community residents view the authority of police officers as legitimate, the task of individual officers is made easier. We find here that the people who view legal authorities as legitimate are generally more willing to defer to the directives of particular police officers.

However, each officer can also enhance (or undermine) the ability of this general institutional legitimacy to make his or her own decisions more legitimate when dealing with particular members of the public. One of the virtues of community policing, in which community residents develop a long-term relationship with particular police officers, is that it gives those officers an opportunity to build up support for their role. When police officers are strangers arriving in a patrol car, they have no personal relationship with the people in the community, and their legitimacy is derived primarily from the general feelings that people have about the legitimacy of the police as a group. In communities where the police generally are seen as low in institutional legitimacy, developing a long-term relationship with the people in the community affords particular officers the opportunity to create personal legitimacy for their actions.

Legitimacy as Institutional Trust

A second aspect of legitimacy—trust and confidence in the law and government institutions—has been widely studied by political scientists. The focus of their concerns is on people's general evaluations of the trustworthiness of political and legal actors, often labeled "confidence" or "trust" in government and in government institutions and authorities. Such trust in government has frequently been measured using a scale that assesses evaluative orientations toward the national government (Stokes 1962). This scale has been used to measure "trust in government," "confidence," "political cynicism," "disaffection," and "alienation" (Citrin and Muste 1999).

Political scientists have linked trust and confidence to a wide variety of political and social behaviors. Political scientists argue that institutional trust in political leaders and in the political process is important because it encourages conventional political participation and lowers engagement in system-challenging behavior, such as participation in political protests (Levi and Stoker 2000). Those who trust the political process are more likely to contribute time and money to campaigns, to work for candidates, and to vote, and they are less likely to support efforts to undermine the democratic political process. This argument connects to that being made here, since institutional trust is one component of legitimacy.

Cynicism About the Law

The approach to legitimacy used in our analysis also reflects the conceptual framework created by Ewick and Silbey (1998). These authors examined the motives that people infer as underlying the operation of the law. For example, they asked people whether they believed that the operation of the law is motivated by the desire of the powerful to control the poor. These authors used narrative analysis to examine people's orientations toward the law. They did not construct scales of the type used in this book, nor did they perform the type of quantitative analysis presented here. As a consequence, we developed scales to reflect their ideas and used them to analyze our data.

The key element we explore with this scale is the degree to which people do or do not feel "against" the law, in the sense that they view the law as an extension of the power of other groups or the state over them, rather than as rules created or enacted to advance their own interests. In the most extreme cases, people's orientation toward the law is negative and resistive, and they seek ways to get around the law to preserve their own dignity and honor and to advance their own interests. Certainly, people with this orientation feel little responsibility or obligation to obey the law voluntarily. Instead, they engage in "small subterfuges, deceits, and other violations of conventional legal norms" (Ewick and Silbey 1998, 49).

Affect

Legitimacy can also be measured by assessing people's affective orientation toward the law and legal authorities. This approach is based on the view that people's feelings about authorities play an important role in shaping their behavior toward those authorities. In his writing about legitimacy, Easton talked about legitimacy as an affective or feeling-based orientation toward the law and legal authorities (see Easton and Dennis 1969). He suggested that this orientation develops during childhood and is precognitive. In other words, children develop feelings about law and government before they have reasons for those feelings. Easton viewed these early feelings as an important motivating force in adult behavior.

Is Legitimacy Important?

We can test the argument that legitimacy is important in shaping everyday law-related behavior through a new analysis of the previously collected data that explored the antecedents of obedience to the law in people's everyday lives (Tyler 1990). In the earlier study, 804 randomly chosen residents of Chicago were interviewed about their law-related attitudes and behaviors at two points in time. The panel data from that study can be used to examine the influence of legitimacy on two behaviors: obeying the law, and seeking help in response to legally relevant problems.

In his original analysis, Tyler (1990) measured legitimacy using a two-part approach: people were asked about their feelings of obligation to obey the law, and then they were asked for their general evaluations of the institutional trustworthiness of legal authorities. Legitimacy was measured using a combined index of obligation to obey the law and institutional trust.

Because that was what was measured by Tyler (1990) in the original study, our concern here will be with the impact of legitimacy on an individual's everyday compliance with the law and on his or her willingness

Table 7.1   Influence of Legitimacy on Law-Related Behavior

	Time 2 Compliance	Time 2 Help-Seeking Behavior
Beta weights		
Time 2		
Legitimacy	.11***	.11**
Sanctioning risk	.07*	.14***
Time 1		
Compliance	.60***	—
Help-seeking	—	.47***
Demographics		
Age	.07*	.00
Sex	.09**	.01
Income	.06	.02
Education	.03	.05
Race	.01	.08*
Total adjusted R-squared	52%	30%

Source: Chicago study data.
Note: n = 804.
*p < .05.
**p < .01.
***p < .001.

to seek help from legal authorities. We can examine this issue using data from the earlier panel study, in which these two types of behavior were assessed during both the first and second rounds of interviews. In this analysis we control for time 1 levels of these law-related behaviors using responses given during the first round of interviews. Potential factors shaping second-round reports about behavior include time 2 judgments of the legitimacy of legal authorities, time 2 estimates of the likelihood of being caught and punished for rule-breaking, and the demographic characteristics of the respondents (age, gender, education, income, and race).

The results of the analysis are shown in table 7.1. They indicate that judgments about the legitimacy of the authorities at the time of the second round of interviews shaped both compliance with the law and requests for help from legal authorities. If people generally viewed legal authorities as legitimate, they were more likely to indicate that they followed the law in their everyday lives. They were also more likely to indicate that they sought help from legal authorities in a variety of situations in which they had legally relevant concerns or problems.

The results of the analysis indicate that legitimacy shapes both compliance with the law and help-seeking behavior. As we would expect, the primary antecedent of law-related behavior in the second round of interviews was law-related behavior in the first round (beta = 0.60, p < .001). However, even when we controlled for the prior level of compliance behavior, a distinct effect of time 2 levels of legitimacy emerged in the analysis (beta = 0.11, p < .001). This suggests that legitimacy has an important, independent role in shaping people's everyday compliance with the law and that it also influences their decisions about whether to seek help from the police and the courts.[1] In addition, people's behavior is shaped by their estimates of the likelihood of being caught and punished for wrongdoing (beta = 0.07, p < .05).

The act of initiating contact with legal authorities illustrates the potential importance of legitimacy. When people call the police, for example, they contact the police department in general, but a specific police officer shows up. People's expectations about that person are presumably drawn from their general trust in police officers as a group.

We can further use the panel data collected in the Chicago study to test the argument that legitimacy (measured at the time of the first round of interviews) predicts the subsequent willingness to initiate contact with the police and courts (at time 2). Of course, we would not expect a strong relationship, since many people who might contact the police or the courts if they had a law-related problem will not have such a problem, and therefore they have no reason to act on their willingness to initiate contact. Nonetheless, we might expect to find at least some relationship between legitimacy and the subsequent willingness to initiate contact with the police and courts.

In the Chicago panel study respondents were asked whether they had either called the police or voluntarily gone to court during the one-year period after they indicated their level of institutional trust in the first interview. These indices were combined to form an overall index of voluntary contact. Those respondents who indicated higher feelings of legitimacy during the first interviews were also more likely to say, during those same interviews, that they would seek legal help if they had a problem in the future (r = 0.26, p < .001 for minorities; r = 0.22, p < .001 for whites). An examination of the relationship between legitimacy and actual subsequent voluntary contact suggests that legitimacy is linked to help-seeking behavior (beta = 0.11, p < .05), but only among minority respondents.[2]

In the case of limiting one's law-related behavior in response to legal rules—in other words, following the law—both groups were affected by their views about the legitimacy of legal authorities. As we have already noted, those whose views of legitimacy were measured at higher levels were more willing to follow legal rules.[3]

These findings suggest that legitimacy has important behavioral consequences for people's subsequent law-related behavior. If people generally view the police and the courts as legitimate authorities on an institutional level, they are both more likely to follow the law in their everyday lives and more likely to seek the help of legal authorities when they have problems.

In contrast to the earlier study of Chicago residents, our study of Oakland and Los Angeles residents did not directly measure everyday behavioral compliance with the law or general help-seeking tendencies. Instead, the California study built on the findings of prior research, replicated in the Chicago panel analysis, and was based on the assumption that the legitimacy of the law and of legal institutions has important behavioral consequences. The California study did not, however, directly measure compliance with the law, nor did it look at the antecedents of compliance.

The Measurement of Legitimacy in the California Study

In this analysis we measure legitimacy using four types of indicators: obligation to obey, cynicism, affect or feeling, and institutional trust. Obligation refers to people's judgments about their personal responsibility to follow the law. Cynicism reflects their views about whether the law serves their interests. Affect indicates a person's positive or negative feeling about legal authorities, and institutional trust reflects general trust in the institutions and authorities of the law. To measure institutional trust, we measured general views about legal authorities. For example, we asked whether the police or courts were "generally honest" or "treat all citizens equally."[4] The items used to assess these four constructs are shown in table 7.2.

Obligation to Obey the Law   We assessed obligation to obey by asking respondents their views about three issues: "I feel that I should accept the decisions made by legal authorities"; "People should obey the law even if it goes against what they think is right"; and, "It is difficult to break the law and keep one's self-respect." The alpha for this scale was low (alpha = 0.47).[5]

Cynicism About the Law   Respondents are asked to express their views about three issues related to their trust in the basic intention of laws. In this sample, cynicism about the law—expressed as the view that it operates to protect the advantaged—is fairly high. Sixty-seven percent of those interviewed felt that the law is used by people in power to try to control people like "themselves"; 66 percent felt that the law represents the values of people in power rather than their own values; and 39 percent indicated that the law does not protect their interests (alpha = 0.70).

Table 7.2   Indices of Legitimacy of Legal Authorities

Indicators	Agree	Mean (Standard Deviation)
Obligation to obey the law[a]		
"I feel that I should accept the decisions made by legal authorities."	72%	—
"People should obey the law even if it goes against what they think is right."	77	—
"It is difficult to break the law and keep one's self-respect."	77	—
Cynicism about the law[b]		
"The law represents the values of the people in power rather than the values of people like me."	66	—
"People in power use the law to try to control people like me."	67	—
"The law does not protect my interests."	39	—
Institutional trust[c]		
"Most [police/judges] in [city] do their job well."	79	—
"Most [police/judges] in [city] treat people with respect."	75	—
"The basic rights of citizens in [city] are well protected by the police."	65	—
"The [police/courts] in [city] have too much power."[c]	51	—
"Most [police/judges] in [city] are dishonest."[c]	28	—
"Most [police/judges] in [city] treat some people better than others."[c]	75	—
Feelings about legal authorities[d]		
"Consider the [police/courts] in [city]. On a scale of 0 to 10, how would you rate the [police/courts]? The higher the number, the warmer or more favorable you feel. The lower the number, the colder or less favorable you feel. If you feel neither warm nor cold toward them, rate them a 5."		

(Table continues on p. 110.)

Table 7.2   Continued

Indicators	Agree	Mean (Standard Deviation)
Overall mean rating	—	6.13
		(2.29)
Police	—	6.20
		(2.25)
Courts	—	5.70
		(2.09)

Source: California study data.
[a] alpha = 0.47. Every respondent rated the law.
[b] alpha = 0.70. Every respondent rated the law.
[c] alpha = 0.82. Each respondent rated only the authority with whom he or she had a personal experience.
[d] Every respondent rated both the police and the courts.
[e] Indicates reverse coding.

Institutional Trust in Legal Authorities   We assessed institutional trust in legal authorities using a six-item scale that reflects a generalized view about the motives of legal authorities. In responding to these questions, people were asked to make judgments about the degree to which they felt that legal authorities as a group can be trusted to exercise their power well by: treating people with respect, providing equal treatment, being honest, showing concern for people's rights, doing their jobs well, and exercising an appropriate amount of power. This aspect of institutional trust was the most similar to that found in the data from Tyler (1990).

Most respondents indicated that the legal authority they dealt with (the police or the courts) did a good job (79 percent agreed) and treated people with respect (75 percent agreed). Slightly fewer respondents agreed that people's rights were "well protected" by the legal authorities with whom they had contact (65 percent agreed). Very few people felt that the legal authorities with whom they dealt were mostly dishonest (28 percent agreed). On the other hand, 75 percent agreed that the police and the courts treated some people better than others, and 51 percent felt that legal authorities have too much power (alpha = 0.78).

Feelings About Legal Authorities   This scale, which is an index of strength of feeling about legal authorities, is framed by reference to a thermometer. We asked respondents to think about how "warm" or "cold" their feelings were about a particular type of authority. The scale ranges from 0 to 10; low scores indicate colder feelings (as in a thermometer), and the midpoint is 5. People expressed slightly warm feelings toward both the police and the courts (overall mean rating = 6.13).

These four aspects of legitimacy are related (average r = 0.40), and so we combined them into a single index of legitimacy by averaging the standardized versions of the four subscales (overall alpha = 0.73; mean = 0.15; standard deviation = 0.76).

Connections to the Community

A second type of societal orientation reflects people's connection not to the law and legal authorities but to their community and the people in that community. We considered two aspects of people's connections to their community. The first parallels the previous discussion of legitimacy, when indexed as institutional trust, but considers trust in other people in the community rather than in the law and legal authorities. Here our concern is with the degree to which people feel that they can trust the motives of those who live and work around them.

Second, we examined the strength of people's connection with their community, rather than to the people around them. People's identification with their community refers to the degree to which they feel a psychological attachment to their community. That identification is reflected in how much people's sense of self is connected to their community (identification), to their pride in their community (pride), and to their feeling that others in the community respect them (respect) (Tyler 1999a, 1999b; Tyler and Blader 2000). Our concern is with the degree to which these elements of a person's connection to his or her community are shaped by personal experiences with legal authorities. Thus, we are again concerned with the impact of personal experiences on general societal orientations. Unlike the prior issue of the legitimacy of the law and legal institutions, the connection of personal experiences with the police and the courts to community-related issues is less straightforward. It seems reasonable that people would use the information that they gain from their personal experiences with a police officer or a judge to make evaluations of the law and of legal authorities. On the other hand, it is not clear that a person would use personal experiences with legal authorities to evaluate other people in the community or to shape his or her own degree of identification with society.

Since legal authorities represent the community as well as its values, norms, rules, and institutions, such a generalization can be viewed as reasonable. However, members of the public may also define the police and the courts as distinct from the community, or even as opposed to community norms and values, and they may not make connections between the behavior of legal authorities and their views about their community.

Why Is Trusting Others Important?

Trust in others in one's community is often viewed as important because it shapes behavioral engagement within communities. We would expect that people who trust others around them get more involved in activities in their neighborhood, including both social activities and discussion of community issues. Further, we would expect people who are trusting to be more active in civic affairs, including voting and otherwise participating in the political process. Recent work by political scientists makes it clear that societies depend heavily on the "civic engagement" of citizens in democratic communities (Putnam 1993, 1995a, 1995b).

Community activity is potentially important for many reasons. One that is central to our argument is that community activity aids in successful efforts to combat crime and social disorder in urban communities. The community helps the police and the courts to maintain social order. Members of the community report crimes and bring disputes to the attention of the police and the courts, engage in informal social control through block watches and other neighborhood activities, and willingly follow the law, freeing the police and the courts to direct their resources toward more serious dangers to the community. In conjunction with the formal activities of legal authorities, the nature of informal community responses to crime also shapes the crime rate (Bursik and Grasmick 1993; Sampson, Raudenbush, and Earls 1997; Skogan and Maxfield 1981).

Such community activity can be encouraged by the behavior of the police and the courts (Moore 1997; Moore and Stephens 1991; Skogan 1990a, 1990b; Wilson and Kelling 1982). Legal authorities can engage in policing strategies, such as community policing, that empower communities and encourage residents to feel that they can effectively combat crime and maintain social control by reporting crimes, identifying criminals, and engaging in informal crime control activities like block watches. Central to this argument is the concept that police activity can deter crime and criminal behavior and through such deterrence communicate to people that crime can be controlled (Sherman 1992, 1993; Wilson and Boland 1978). Police strategies can also influence communities in ways that go beyond lowering the crime rate; these strategies can shape people's perceptions of legal authorities, fear of crime, and feelings of effectiveness in dealing with crime in their community (Moore 1997; Moore and Stephens 1991; Skogan 1990a, 1990b). These views, in turn, shape people's behavior in their neighborhoods. Sobol, Lynch, and Planty (1999), for example, demonstrate that police arrest policies shape the willingness of residents to engage in informal social control activities in their neighborhoods.

Our argument is an extension of this perspective. We suggest that police treatment of particular community residents shapes the views of people in the community about the police, the courts, and the community itself. Our focus here is on the feelings that members of the community have about each other. We argue that if people trust others in their community, they are more likely to engage in activities within that community.

Putnam has argued that active participation in the community also aids the effective working of community governance (Putnam 1993, 1995a, 1995b). Brehm and Rahn (1997) used longitudinal data to explore the relationship between trust in others in one's community and engagement in one's community. Their data support the argument that general trust in others in one's community leads to behavioral engagement in the community, as we would predict. In addition, engagement in communities encourages greater trust in others. This supports our position that general trust in others in the community shapes people's behavioral engagement. This connection underlies our interest in exploring the impact of encounters with particular legal authorities on generalized trust in others in the community.

Our first concern is to test the validity of the argument that generalized trust in others in one's community is in fact linked to involvement in one's community and to civic engagement in the political process. If trust in others lacks behavioral impact, then it is of less interest to us. We conducted such a test using the California data. In the analysis we distinguished between two types of behavioral engagement that might be shaped by trust in others in the community. The first was voluntary engagement in community activities. The analysis did not specifically focus on anticrime activities but instead explored people's general level of association with others in their neighborhood. The second type of behavioral engagement was voluntary political or "civic" engagement.

Table 7.3 shows the items we used to measure both types of community engagement. We assessed people's voluntary engagement in the community by asking respondents whether they had recently participated in several types of community activities. They were asked whether they had gone to a public meeting, talked to their neighbors about community issues, or interacted with their neighbors on a social basis. People were most likely to indicate that they had socialized with their neighbors (62 percent responding "often" or "sometimes") or had talked to them about community issues (56 percent responding "often" or "sometimes"). Many fewer said that they had attended public meetings (25 percent responding "often" or "sometimes"). These three items were combined to form an overall index of community engagement (alpha = 0.60).

Most respondents indicated that they were registered to vote (74 percent), and a slight majority of those interviewed indicated that they

Table 7.3   Indices of Behavioral Engagement in the Community

	Often or Sometimes	Yes
Community engagement[a]		
"During the past twelve months, how often have you . . .		
Gone to a public meeting about an issue that affects [city]?	25%	—
Talked with your neighbors about issues that affect [city]?	56	—
Gotten together with your neighbors, just for fun?"	62	—
Political engagement		
"Are you currently registered to vote?"	—	74%
"Did you vote in the last presidential election?"	—	63

Source: California study data.
[a] alpha = 0.60.

voted during the last election (63 percent). These two items were combined to form an overall index of political activity. We could not compute a reliability index for that scale, since only those registered to vote can vote, making the two items interrelated. In constructing the scale, we added the two items; a high score indicates both being registered and having voted.

Measuring Trust in Others in the Community

We assessed respondents' trust in the motives and character of others in the community using a five-item scale: "Most people in [city] are basically good and kind" (75 percent agreed); "Most people in [city] are willing to put aside their personal interests to achieve a common goal" (52 percent agreed); "Most people in [city] care about what happens to their neighbors" (68 percent agreed); "Most people in [city] will return a favor if they have the chance" (75 percent agreed); and "Most people in [city] tolerate each other's differences" (67 percent agreed). These items were combined to create an overall community trust scale (alpha = 0.77).

Trust in Others in the Community and Community Engagement

Does trust in other people in one's community lead to greater levels of behavioral engagement in the community? Regression analysis indicates that trust in others in the community explained 7 percent of the variance in voluntary community engagement ($p < .001$) and 2 percent of the variance in political participation ($p < .001$). Trust in others in the community did shape the behavior of respondents in this study. Trust in others is more strongly connected to behavioral engagement in the community than political participation. This seems reasonable, since political participation is not usually focused on one's neighborhood community but rather on the larger polity.

Although these findings support our basic argument, it is important to note that we did not explore all possible types of community involvement. We did not, for example, ask more specifically about involvement in crime-related activities, such as neighborhood watch or community groups that support the police. Further, we did not distinguish between social activities and activities designed to solve community problems or discuss community issues. As a consequence, our findings are consistent with the findings of others that trust in others in one's community has behavioral implications. However, these findings do not provide a clear portrait of the implications. Our goal is simply to show, consistent with the findings of other studies, that our respondents' views about others in their community shaped their behavior in that community. It also seems likely that a more complete analysis of possible behaviors would show a stronger effect than the effect we report here using our restricted set of questions about community involvement.

Identification with the Community

Social psychologists argue that people vary in the degree to which they identify with and feel connected to the communities to which they "belong." Identification with one's community has important implications for intergroup relations, since people who identify more strongly with their community or group view it in more positive ways and evaluate the members of other communities or groups more negatively (Gaertner et al. 1994). As a consequence, identification with one's community is often linked to within-group solidarity and between-group conflict. Studies support this argument by showing that those who identify with their community or group are more likely to help others in their group (Mael and Ashforth 1992), to remain in their group (Abrams, Ando, and Hinkle 1998), and to feel an obligation to defer to group rules and authorities (Tyler and Blader 2000).

The argument that identification matters develops from the social identity model of human motivation (Tajfel and Turner 1979), as well as from other theories rooted in people's desire to belong to groups (Baumeister and Leary 1995). From this perspective, people follow community rules and defer to community authorities because the community performs an important role in shaping their sense of self and in creating feelings of self-esteem and self-worth. This argument suggests that relationships between people and their community are negotiations about identity, with those who identify with the community engaging in more cooperative behavior (Tajfel and Turner 1979, 1986). As a result, community residents' identification is valuable to communities.

As an identity-based judgment, identification with the community is not the same concept as trust in other people in the community. An element of trust in others in one's community, as with trust in institutions and authorities, is a concern about the motivations of others. People who trust others in their community have made inferences about the benevolence and trustworthiness of those others, but on a general level.

Identification, in contrast, is the use of one's community as a source of self-definition. People's identification with their community reflects not only the degree to which they define themselves in terms of membership in the community (identification) but status evaluations as well. Status evaluations include judgments about group status (pride) and about one's status in the group (respect). In this discussion, we treat all of these indices as aspects of respondents' identification with their city and with American society in general. Of course, as with generalized trust in others in the community, our concern is with the degree to which people's identification with the community is influenced by the fairness and trustworthiness of the behavior of particular legal authorities.

Identification with One's City and with the United States

To test the importance of identity issues directly we measured identification with the community. This measurement had to be linked to a model that included the elements of status that should be important in shaping people's attitudes, values, and cooperative behaviors. We argue that three aspects of group-oriented status may be important in shaping cooperation with groups: identification, pride, and respect (Smith and Tyler 1997; Tyler, Degoey, and Smith 1996; Tyler and Smith 1999).

When social identity theorists discuss *identification*, they are usually referring to the merger of the self and society in which people take on the group's norms, values, and goals as their own. Hence, the measurement of identification is linked to the degree to which people define and evaluate themselves through their membership in groups, such as their community or the larger society.

A core argument of social identity theory is that people create their sense of self and evaluate their self-worth by combining two types of status information: personal identity and social identity. Personal identity refers to the idiosyncratic aspects of the self, and social identity refers to the groups to which an individual belongs. Social identity therefore involves "the individual's knowledge that he [or she] belongs to certain groups together with some emotional and value significance to him [or her] of the group membership" (Tajfel 1972, 31). Social identity is that part of people's sense of "who they are" that is associated with self-definition in terms of group membership (Haslam 2001).

A second way to think about and measure identification is to assess people's evaluations of the status of their community (*pride* in group membership). This aspect of identification is linked to the desirability of the group. People are influenced by the favorability of the status of the groups to which they belong, and being a member of a high-status group is important because it leads to a more favorable social identity and to higher feelings of self-esteem and self-worth. It also leads to greater cooperative behavior, since people want to cooperate with communities that support their high self-esteem.

Third, in addition to being influenced by their assessments of the status of their groups, people are also influenced by their assessment of their own status within their group (the *respect* they feel from others, also called "social reputation"; Emler and Hopkins 1990). We argue that people are influenced not only by their feelings about the status of their community but by their judgments about how others in their community feel about them.

Recent studies of young, minority males emphasize the central role that respect from one's group and from society generally plays in shaping emotions and behavior (Anderson 1994, 1999; Bourgois 1996; Emler and Hopkins 1990). Being disrespected by others is often the central issue underlying the conflict and violence in interpersonal interactions among the young in gang situations (Kennedy and Forde 1999).

Several field studies have suggested that status judgments play an important role in shaping behavioral reactions toward communities. Tyler and Degoey (1995) examined the effect of status judgments on cooperative behaviors within a political community, using public evaluations of local government authorities. They tested the influence of people's assessments of the status of their community and of their own status within their community on their willingness to cooperate with community authorities by following rules governing the use of community resources.

The situation they studied was a water shortage in the city of San Francisco. Owing to water shortages, people were asked to cooperate with the Public Utilities Commission, the agency that creates rules to regulate the use of water. The results of this study suggested that actions to help the community by voluntarily following behavioral guidelines were independently influenced by status judgments about pride and respect, as well as by gain-loss evaluations (in other words, the rules help me or they hurt me).

Identification was also shown to be linked to the willingness to defer to authorities in another study of a random sample of northern California residents, this one involving 502 residents of the San Francisco metropolitan area. (For a detailed description of this sample, see Tyler and Mitchell 1994.) Respondents were asked about their willingness to defer to federal laws. Regression analysis indicated that those who felt more identified with the United States were more likely to feel an obligation to obey laws (R-squared = 4 percent, $p < .001$). This identification influence occurs through an influence of pride in the United States (beta = 0.20, $p < .001$), but not respect (beta = 0.00, n.s.).

Another community survey (Boeckmann and Tyler 1997) similarly found that people's willingness to join neighborhood organizations voluntarily and their rule-following behavior were influenced by their judgments about their status in the community (pride and respect). Resource effects on cooperation were not examined.

The results of these studies show that judgments about group status (pride) and about status within the group (respect) shape people's behavior toward groups and group authorities. The studies do not distinguish between identification, as we define it here, and pride, but instead combine them into a single index. Thus, the findings suggest that all three of these concepts—identification, pride and respect—may be linked to cooperation.

Similar results have been obtained in other studies, including studies of cooperative behavior among college students (Smith and Tyler 1997), in work organizations (Huo et al. 1996; Tyler 1999b; Tyler and Blader 2000), and in university cooperatives (Daubenmier, Smith, and Tyler 1997). In each of these studies, cooperative behavior is affected by people's identification with their community or group. The studies all suggest that people generally act more favorably toward groups when they identify with them.

In examining social identification influences in the California study data, our goal is to address whether identification is linked to important behaviors toward the law by looking at the relationship between identification and the acceptance of decisions. Prior studies suggest that people who identify with their communities are more willing to defer to the law.

Assessing Social Connection

In the California study those interviewed were asked about their identification with two of their communities: the city they lived in and the United States. In each case they were asked how important membership in that community was to their sense of themselves, that is, the degree to which they merged their own identity with membership in that community. They were also asked to make two status judgments: their degree of pride in membership in those two communities, and their feelings of being respected by others in the two communities.

Because of our focus on local legal authorities, people's identification with their city may be the most relevant aspect of identification. On the other hand, we have found in previous research that identification with being an American is important to people's self-definition (Smith and Tyler 1996). We therefore used both frames of reference.

Table 7.4 shows the items used to assess identification, pride, and respect, on both the local and national levels. The results indicate that most respondents felt proud of both their city and their country, and that they identified with both of these communities. The lowest level of agreement was found with city identification. Only 62 percent of those interviewed said that the city they lived in was important to how they thought of themselves as a person, while 89 percent said that being an American was important to their identity. Most respondents also indicated that they felt that others in their city, as well as other Americans, respected them.

We factor-analyzed these items and revealed the three factors shown in table 7.5. First, pride in being an American and identification with the United States were found to load on one factor. Second, pride in one's city and identification with that city were found to load on a second factor. Finally, feeling that one was respected by others in one's city and/or by other Americans was found to be linked together in a single factor. On the basis of this analysis, three scales were created: pride in one's city (which includes identification with that city), pride in being an American (including identification with being an American), and respect from others (in one's city and throughout the United States). As noted, each pride index combines indices of pride and identification.

Taken together, we have three indices of identification. The results suggest that the three aspects of identification are distinct, though related to one another. The average correlation is r = 0.33.[6]

Does Identification Encourage Desirable Social Behavior?

We have already noted that in other studies of the influence of identification, it is found to be associated with favorable attitudes and behaviors toward groups, organizations, and societies. Is this also true in the California study? Before directly examining the relationship between identification and decision acceptance, we look at the relationship between identification and other social orientations.

Table 7.4   Indices of Social Connection

	Agree
Pride in city	
"I am proud to be a resident of [city]."	83%
"What [city] stands for is important to me."	80
"When someone praises the accomplishments of others in [city], it feels like a personal compliment to me."	69
Identification with city	
"Being a resident of [city] is important to the way that I think of myself as a person."	62
Pride in the United States	
"I am proud to be an American."	93
"What America stands for is important to me."	91
"When someone praises the accomplishments of other Americans, it feels like a personal compliment to me."	73
Identification with the United States	
"Being an American is important to the way that I think of myself as a person."	89
Respect from Americans	
"If they knew me well, most Americans would respect what I have accomplished in life."	90
"If they knew me, most Americans would approve of how I live my life."	86
"If they knew me, most Americans would value my opinions and ideas."	88
Respect from others in the city	
"If they knew me well, most of the people in [city] would respect what I have accomplished in life."	91
"If they knew me, most people in [city] would respect how I live my life."	89
"If they knew me, most people in [city] would value my opinions and ideas."	89

Source: California study data.

We used regression analysis to examine the influence of identification on the legitimacy of authorities and on engagement in the community. The results, shown in table 7.6, indicate that identification is linked to both legitimacy and engagement. It explains 14 percent of the variance in views about the legitimacy of authorities, as well as approximately the same range of variance in engagement that is explained by trust in

Table 7.5   Factor Analysis of Indices of Social Connection

	Pride-City	Pride-America	Respected by Others
"I am proud to be a resident of [city]."	.70	—	—
"What [city] stands for is important to me."	.76	—	—
"When someone praises the accomplishments of others in [city], it feels like a personal compliment to me."	.51	—	—
"Being a resident of [city] is important to the way that I think of myself as a person."	.40	—	—
"I am proud to be an American."	—	.68	—
"What America stands for is important to me."	—	.73	—
"When someone praises the accomplishments of other Americans, it feels like a personal compliment to me."	—	.60	—
"Being an American is important to the way that I think of myself as a person."	—	.64	—
"If they knew me well, most Americans would respect what I have accomplished in life."	—	—	.70
"If they knew me, most Americans would approve of how I live my life."	—	—	.75
"If they knew me, most Americans would value my opinions and ideas."	—	—	.72
"If they knew me well, most of the people in [city] would respect what I have accomplished in life."	—	—	.55
"If they knew me, most people in [city] would respect how I live my life."	—	—	.55
"If they knew me, most people in [city] would value my opinions and ideas."	—	—	.55

Source: California study data.
Note: The factor analysis used maximum likelihood extraction and varimax rotation. All loadings over 0.50 are shown.

others in the community (7 percent). In other words, as we expected, identification with one's community has general behavioral implications. Of course, these implications should not be overstated.

Summary

Previous research suggests that societal orientations have important implications for people's everyday behavior. Legitimacy shapes rule-following behavior, trust in others shapes engagement in one's community, and

Table 7.6   Identification, Generalized Trust, and Engagement in the Community

	Legitimacy	Trust in Others in the Community	Participation in the Community
Beta weights			
Pride in the United States	.31***	.01	−.09**
Pride in city	.12***	.18***	.11***
Respect from others	.00	.14***	−.05
Total adjusted R-squared	14%	7%	2%

Source: California study data.
Note: Positive influences indicate that high levels of identification encourage greater feelings of legitimacy, more engagement in the community, and greater political participation.
**$p < .01$.
***$p < .001$.

identification shapes both legitimacy and engagement in one's community. Overall, these findings point to the societal benefits derived when community residents have favorable orientations toward the law, toward others in their community, and toward society. Such general, favorable orientations encourage desirable behaviors in community residents by increasing their engagement in the community and in community activities. Further, they encourage people to cut back on their rule-breaking activities and to otherwise limit their engagement in undesirable behavior (Tyler and Blader 2000). The strongest influence is on legitimacy, and the weakest is on participation in the community.

These findings provide a useful background for our thinking about the key issue of concern in this study—the willingness of members of the public to accept the decisions made by legal authorities. They suggest that having a favorable societal orientation creates a generally positive climate of connection between the person and the group, and that this climate leads to greater levels of several socially desirable behaviors. However, these prior findings leave unanswered the question of whether general orientations shape decision acceptance behavior in particular experiences. It is to this question that we now turn.

Chapter 8

Societal Orientations and Reactions to Personal Experiences with Legal Authorities

W̶E HAVE already examined the psychology underlying people's reactions during their personal experiences with legal authorities. We found that the behavior of legal authorities— their fairness and their motives—influences people's willingness to defer voluntarily to their decisions and directives. In particular, people are more willing to accept decisions that are arrived at through processes they understand to be fair and that are made by authorities whom they trust.

We now want to examine the additional influence, if any, of general societal orientations on what happens during people's personal experiences with legal authorities. We expect that not everyone approaches a personal experience with the same prior orientation toward the law, toward their community, and toward society. For example, some people see legal authorities as more or less legitimate than do others, some people feel more or less strongly connected to the other people in their community, and some people feel more or less identified with society. Here we focus directly on the question of whether prior societal orientations have an impact on the nature of personal experiences.

How might general societal orientations shape personal experiences? In this chapter, we test two arguments. The first argument is that favorable societal orientations encourage voluntary decision acceptance. The second is that general societal orientations shape the importance that people attach to whether they experience procedural justice during their experience and whether they feel motive-based trust toward the authorities with whom they are dealing.

Do Favorable Societal Orientations Encourage Deference Toward the Police and Toward Judges?

Tyler (1990) demonstrated that those with a greater sense of obligation to obey the law are more likely to do so. We expect that people who are more likely to view the law and legal authorities as legitimate, who feel closer ties to others in their community, and who feel more identified with American society are also more willing to defer to legal authorities.

Further, we expect that there is a direct, or main, effect of societal orientations on both deference and satisfaction with authorities. People with more positive orientations are more willing to defer than those with less positive orientations, controlling for the favorability of the outcome.

We also expect that those who are more likely to view authorities as legitimate or who identify more strongly with the United States base their judgments more strongly on the degree to which they receive procedural justice and feel motive-based trust when dealing with legal authorities. Conversely, we expect them to rely less strongly on the favorability or fairness of their outcomes.

This prediction involves an interaction between societal orientations, process-based and outcome-based judgments about experience, and deference to decisions. It suggests that societal orientations determine how much weight people put on process and outcome issues when deciding whether to defer to particular police officers and judges.

We again contrast the two basic images of how people might decide whether to defer to the decisions of legal authorities. One image links the willingness to accept those decisions to their favorability and fairness. To represent that image, we use a summary index of the favorability and fairness of the outcome. The second image links the willingness to accept decisions to evaluations of elements in the process through which the decisions are made. We consider a summary measure of procedural justice, the trustworthiness of the motives of the authorities involved, and assessments of the quality of their decision making and of the quality of their treatment of the person involved. These four aspects of procedure are collectively referred to as process-based judgments.

Here we examine conditions that facilitate or hinder process-based reactions to individual police officers or judges. To what degree do general social orientations moderate the basis on which people decide whether to accept the decisions of these legal authorities during personal experiences with them? We test the argument that generalized societal orientations matter because they change the psychology underlying people's reactions to particular legal authorities. We expect that people who have a more positive societal orientation focus more strongly on issues of trustworthiness and fair treatment when deciding whether to accept the decisions made by these authorities.

Do those with stronger social bonds with a group or group authorities more willingly accept the decisions of those authorities and follow group rules? We predict that people whose feelings of legitimacy and trust in others in their community are stronger do in fact act differently, owing to their social connections with their community and community institutions. We expect that people who feel that authorities are more legitimate or who have a stronger connection with others in their community are more focused on process issues when deciding whether to defer to legal authorities during a personal encounter.

The results of several prior studies suggest that general social orientations shape the basis on which people decide whether to defer to societal authorities, such as political and legal authorities. Tyler and Degoey (1995) examined how people decide whether to defer to rules made by a governmental organization by looking at the willingness of residents of San Francisco to accept restrictions on water use enacted by the Public Utilities Commission, a government board given the power to limit water use during a period of drought. We would expect that people accept water restrictions because those restrictions would favor them, or because they think that the Public Utilities Commission enacts regulations following fair decision making procedures.

First, the study showed, as we would have predicted, that people's willingness to defer to government regulations is heavily influenced by their views about the fairness of government decision making procedures. If people feel that the Public Utilities Commission makes its decisions fairly, they are more willing to defer to those decisions.

The study also examined the strength of people's identification with their community. It showed that those people who identified more strongly with their community relied more heavily on judgments about the fairness of decision making procedures when deciding whether to defer to the decisions of legal authorities.

Smith and Tyler (1996) looked at superordinate and subgroup identification, and at the influence of each type of identification on policy support. They found that those whites who felt more strongly identified with the United States were more willing to judge redistributive public policies on procedural grounds and to support those policies if they were made fairly. Whites who identified more strongly with other whites judged such policies by their implications for their group (outcome favorability).

Huo, Smith, Tyler, and Lind (1996) looked at the same issue we are examining here—the influence of identification on the willingness to accept particular decisions. They found that high levels of superordinate identification with an overall group (in this case, a work organization) led people to accept decisions by a specific authority from that group (their supervisor) when those decisions were fairly made. In contrast, low levels of identification led people to accept decisions based on their favorability.

These arguments suggest that legal authorities also have something to gain from encouraging a supportive social climate. Such a climate should facilitate the exercise of legal authority in specific situations by encouraging people to defer to authorities based on judgments of their fairness and trustworthiness rather than the desirability or fairness of their decisions.

Since legal authorities often deliver unfavorable outcomes, they would have greater difficulty managing interactions with people who based their acceptance of the decisions of legal authorities on the favorability or fairness of those decisions. Hence, a justice- or trust-based reaction to the decisions made by legal authorities facilitates their effectiveness. Consequently, the police and the courts gain in their ability to do their jobs when those whose behavior they are seeking to regulate have more supportive attitudes and values.

Societal Orientations in the California Study

Data from the California study can be used to explore whether people's views about the legitimacy of the law and legal authorities, their general trust in others in the community, and their identification with that community shape their behavior during a personal experience with an authority. We first examined whether general societal orientations have a direct influence on the willingness to accept decisions. Do more favorable orientations lead to more willing deference to particular authorities?

To test this idea we conducted a regression analysis. The results, shown in table 8.1, reveal that all four societal orientations—legitimacy, trust in others in the community, pride in the community, and feeling respected by others in the community—shaped the willingness to accept decisions during particular experiences with legal authorities. People with more favorable orientations of any of these four types were more accepting of decisions. The strongest influence was found with judgments about the legitimacy of legal authorities. People's prior views about the legitimacy of legal authorities have as much influence on their willingness to accept decisions as do their assessments of the favorability of their particular outcome.

The second issue we examined is whether people with more favorable societal views put more weight on process issues, such as trust-

Table 8.1   Influence of Societal Orientation on Decision Acceptance and Satisfaction with the Decisionmaker, Controlling for the Favorability of the Outcome

Beta weights				
Societal orientation				
Legitimacy	.44***	—	—	—
Trust others	—	.21***	—	—
Respect	—	—	.04*	—
Pride	—	—	—	.16***
Favorability of the outcome	.41***	.49***	.50***	.49***
Total adjusted R-squared	43%	29%	25%	27%

Source: California study data.
*p < .05.
***p < .001.

worthiness, or less weight on the favorability or fairness of their outcomes when they are deciding whether to defer to legal authorities. To conduct this analysis we used the overall indices of process-based judgments (procedural justice, quality of decision making, quality of treatment) and outcomes (outcome favorability, outcome fairness) in regression analyses. We used the two experience-based assessments—process-based judgments and outcomes—to predict the willingness to accept decisions and satisfaction with the decision makers.

The results are shown in table 8.2. They support the argument that generalized societal attitudes have a role in shaping the basis on which people deal with legal authorities during personal encounters.

The findings reported in table 8.2 indicate that there is an interaction between societal views and the degree to which people decide whether to accept decisions based on issues of procedural justice and motive-based trust rather than on outcome issues. These interactions indicate that people rely more heavily on process issues when: they view legal authorities to be more legitimate; they have more trust in other people in their communities; and they identify with their community more strongly. The interactions are significant for a combined dependent variable (decision acceptance and satisfaction with the decision maker). In each case, having a more favorable societal orientation leads to putting greater weight on process issues when deciding whether to defer to legal authorities during personal experiences with them. These results support the argument that people's societal orientations have important implications for the manner in which they react to their personal experiences with legal authorities.

Table 8.2   Do Social Motives Shape the Basis of Decision Acceptance and Satisfaction with the Decisionmaker?

	Legitimacy	Trust in Others	Respect	Pride
Beta weights				
Process issues	.77***	.86***	.84***	.87***
Outcome issues	.12***	.12***	.09***	.07***
Moderator				
Legitimacy	.03*	—	—	—
Trust in others	—	.03*	—	—
Identification-respect	—	—	.01	—
Identification-pride	—	—	—	.01
Process issues × moderator	.07***	.05*	−.01	.04*
Outcome issues × moderator	−.01	.02	.03	−.06**
Total adjusted R-squared	80%	80%	79%	80%

Source: California study data.
*p < .05.
**p < .01.
***p < .001.

In the case of identification with society, stronger identification is found to change the basis on which people react to authorities in two ways. If people have stronger ties to others in their community or greater identification with society (pride), they evaluate legal authorities more strongly in terms of process issues and less strongly in terms of outcome issues. Pride is the only element of societal orientation found to have this effect.

The degree to which people feel respected by others (respect) has no impact on how they make judgments concerning decision acceptance or on how satisfied they are with the decision maker. Respect was also the variable that showed the lowest direct influence on decision acceptance. This suggests that feeling respected by others in society is not strongly related to one's relationship to legal authorities.

Summary

These findings strongly support the argument that police officers and judges benefit when those with whom they are dealing have favorable societal orientations. Each of the elements of societal orientation that we examined—legitimacy, trust in others in one's community, and identification—facilitates the acceptance of decisions. Further, they are all elements that encourage people to accept decisions based more strongly on processes than on outcomes. Of course, we do not want to understate the importance of outcomes, because they clearly matter. However, the interaction effects we found were interactions with the importance of processes. For example, when people thought legal authority was more legitimate, they put more weight on process issues when deciding whether to accept the decisions of particular police officers.

These findings suggest that general attitudes feed back into the specific situations in which legal authorities are seeking to secure cooperation from citizens. When people have supportive attitudes and values, they are more likely to rely on justice and trust when dealing with legal authorities, who are thus better able in turn to gain their consent and cooperation.

Chapter 9

Generalizing from Personal Experiences to Societal Orientations

Our final concern is with the implications of personal experience for general societal orientations. People have to make decisions about what to do in the immediate situation when they have a personal experience with legal authorities, and that decision may have an impact on their general views about the law, the legal authorities, and society. It is to this generalization process that we now turn our attention.

Legitimacy

The findings already outlined show that people's willingness to defer to police officers and judges in personal encounters is influenced by the behavior of those authorities. To the degree that people perceive the authorities as acting fairly, they accept their decisions more willingly. The preceding analysis made it clear that two process issues—procedural justice and motive-based trust—dominate people's perceptions of an authority's behavior and shape their deference in the immediate situation.

However, we are also interested in the degree to which authorities' behavior during personal experiences may influence people's broader views about authorities, institutions, and society. In their encounters with the public, the police and the courts are not simply dealing with the particular problem or issue that has brought certain people before them. They are also engaging in political socialization, that is, they are educating those in their community about the legal system. The behavior of individual police officers and judges communicates information to members of the public that they use to make judgments about the nature of legal authority within their society.

Personal experiences with legal authorities are especially important because most people have, at best, infrequent contact with them. Unlike their managers at work or their families, people do not have ongoing, everyday contacts with particular police officers and judges. Indeed, most people have little contact with *any* legal authority. Therefore, each personal experience is likely to be memorable and to play an important role in shaping a person's views about the law and legal authority.

We argue that the experience of justice encourages the development of favorable societal orientations, enhancing deference to legal authorities. Each positive experience creates stronger and more favorable societal orientations, and such orientations lead people to engage in evaluations of the police and the courts that are more process-based. In the ideal case, this leads to a spiral in which the authorities become better able to manage and regulate the public because they treat people with greater fairness in a community that is becoming more and more process-oriented.

Conversely, a negative experience of injustice during a personal encounter undermines people's connections to society; their future experiences with legal authorities become more conflicted, and they are less likely to defer to those authorities and voluntarily accept their decisions. In the worst case, we think of the unfair actions of legal authorities as creating a spiral of increasing conflict and decreasing legitimacy. If the police act unfairly and lower general trust, then in their future personal interactions they must rely more heavily on force to gain compliance. This further undermines their legitimacy. Eventually police interactions become heavily dominated by the use of force.

Central to the development of either a spiral of conflict or a more process-oriented community is the behavior of police officers and judges during their personal encounters with the public. By their behavior in such situations, legal authorities act as agents of socialization, either encouraging hostile attitudes of distrust and resistance or helping to develop a trusting attitude that leads to lowered levels of conflict and heightened deference. In either case, the actions of legal authorities have consequences that stretch beyond the specific situation.

Does Personal Experience Influence Societal Orientations?

Beyond influencing people's acceptance behavior within the immediate situation, the procedures that people experience and the trust or distrust they feel for particular legal authorities during their personal experiences constitute one of the ways in which they acquire a civic education about the law and about legal authorities. If people do in fact generalize from their personal experience with particular legal authorities to form a view about all such authorities, then police officers and judges, through their actions when dealing with community residents, are contributing to either building or undermining general confidence in the police and the courts. Of course, we would not expect most single encounters with authorities to make a dramatic change in a person's views. That is, a person is unlikely to view all legal authority as illegitimate because of one rude judge, or to view all legal authority as legitimate because of one respectful police officer. But legitimacy or illegitimacy accumulate or decline over time, and each experience has a small positive or negative impact on people's "reservoir of goodwill" toward the police and the courts.

Our concern here is with examining the degree to which people generalize from the procedural justice or inferences of trust they experience during an individual encounter with particular authorities to their views about the legitimacy of impersonal authorities and institutions. This includes people and institutions with which the person will probably never have personal contact. Generalization may also occur with regard to trust in others in one's community and identification with the community. In addition, we are interested in identifying the aspects of personal experience that shape that generalization.

Do People Generalize from Their Personal Experiences?

Our first question is whether procedural justice and motive-based trust, as experienced in a specific interaction with legal authorities, shape people's overall societal orientations. If so, then personal experiences have a broader long-term impact on people's relationship to legal authorities and institutions. To test the possibility of generalization we examined the influence of people's experiences on their views about the law and society, using data from the California study.

To conduct this analysis we used two summary scales. The first is the process-based judgment scale, which combines judgments of trustworthiness, procedural justice, quality of decision making, and quality of treatment. The second is the outcome scale, which combines judgments of outcome fairness and outcome favorability.

The results of the analysis, shown in table 9.1, indicate that judgments made during personal experiences were in fact generalized and did influence societal orientations. The results make it clear that process issues—procedural justice and trust in the motives of the authorities whom respondents encountered—had an impact on their general views about the legitimacy of legal authorities, on their trust in others in their community, and on their identification with society. Of course, these results

Table 9.1   Influence of Personal Experiences on General Views About the
Law, Legal Authority, and Society

Evaluations of Personal Experiences	Legitimacy	Trust Others	Identification (Identification, Pride, Respect)
Beta weights			
Process judgments	.50***	.23***	.15***
Outcome judgments	.10***	.02	.08**
Total adjusted R-squared	30%***	6%***	4%***

Source: California study data.
**p < .01
***p < .001.

are limited in how compellingly they demonstrate the relationship, since in the California study we interviewed people only at one point in time. Nonetheless, to the degree that cross-sectional data can be used for this purpose, these data strongly support the argument.

People's broader views about the police, the courts, the law, and their communities are all influenced by their personal experiences. However, as we noted earlier, we would not expect a single experience to have a dramatic impact on a person's general views. But single experiences do influence those views, and that influence seems striking, especially with legitimacy: 30 percent of the variance in the overall index of legitimacy is linked to judgments about one's recent personal experience.

Is the magnitude of the influences found in this study a reasonable approximation of the typical magnitude of the impact of recent personal experiences on people's general views about the law and legal authorities? No doubt the strength of the influence of a particular personal experience depends on many factors about both the person involved and the nature of the encounter, and it would certainly vary across experiences. It is interesting, however, to compare the 30 percent influence of recent personal experiences on views about the law with the findings of the Tyler (1990) study about the impact of personal experience with legal authorities. That study focused on the impact of personal experience on general views about the *legitimacy* of the law. It found that the nature of people's most recent experience with a police officer or judge explained around 5 percent of the variance in their views about the legitimacy of the law. Of course, the legitimacy scales are somewhat different. If we create a scale modeled on Tyler's (1990), which includes only perceived obligation to obey and institutional trust, personal experience explains 24 percent of the variance in that measure of legitimacy. Hence, the magnitude of the influence found is greater for this study than that found in Tyler (1990).

Table 9.2   Role of Quality of Decisionmaking and Quality of Treatment in Shaping Institutional Trust

	Procedural Justice	Motive-Based Trust	Legitimacy	Trust in Others	Pride
Beta weights Quality of decision making	.32***	.30***	.31***	.09*	.11*
Quality of treatment	.51***	.55***	.22***	.14***	.07
Outcome fairness	.04**	.05**	.15***	.07*	.12***
Outcome favorability	.12***	.08***	−.06*	.06*	.02
Total adjusted R-squared	75%	75%	30%	5%	5%

Source: California study data.
Note: We do not consider respect, since only 1 percent of the variance in respect is influenced by these judgments.
*p < .05.
**p < .01.
***p < .001.

It is also interesting to explore which elements of personal experience shape the impact on legitimacy. The results shown in table 9.1 indicate that process issues dominate generalization from experience. On average, the beta weight for process issues is 0.29, and that for outcome issues 0.07. This suggests that the primary factor shaping people's broader views is their assessment of the process they experience when dealing with legal authorities.

We can better understand what it is that shapes generalization by looking at the influence of the two key antecedents of procedural justice: quality of decision making and quality of treatment. A regression analysis using these two factors is shown in table 9.2. The results suggest that the impact of personal experience on people's views about the legitimacy of the law and legal authorities, on trust in others, and on identification is strongly shaped by their evaluations of both the quality of the decision making and the quality of the treatment. This influence is greater than the impact of judgments about the outcome of a personal experience, although these factors also play a role.

These findings support the argument that process judgments shape legitimacy. Are those the same process elements that shape the impact of experience on procedural justice and motive-based trust? A comparison is shown in table 9.2. The results support the argument that quality of treatment dominates the impact on procedural justice and motive-based trust, but not generalizations to legitimacy. In the case of legitimacy and connections to society, the quality of decision making is as important or more important than the quality of treatment.

This finding is consistent with the results of other studies that similarly find that quality of decision making (neutrality) is central to the legitimacy of legal institutions such as the Supreme Court and Congress (Tyler and Mitchell 1994). These findings suggest that the interpersonal aspects of procedure—how people are treated by authorities—are especially important when people have a personal encounter with a specific authority. When people are evaluating more remote institutions and authorities, they shift their focus to how those authorities exercise authority—the quality of their decision making. Therefore, different procedural elements define personal feelings of trust and institutional trust.

These results suggest that personal experiences generalize to shape broader views about the law and legal institutions, trust in others in the community, and identification with society. How reliable are these findings? The primary problem is that they developed out of a cross-sectional study in which personal experience and institutional trust were measured at the same time. As a consequence, it is possible that prior societal orientations shaped both judgments about particular legal authorities and post-experience legitimacy.

Several pieces of evidence argue against this explanation for the findings of the California study. The first is the Chicago panel data analysis reported here. When we controlled on prior views about legitimacy, we still found that judgments about procedural justice and the trustworthiness of the motives of the particular legal authority shaped general views about legitimacy.

Second, the results of a similar panel analysis reported by Tyler, Casper, and Fisher (1989) also support this conclusion. That study explored the personal experiences of people accused of felonies whose cases were processed through the formal legal system. The analysis looked at the influence of this personal experience on their views about legal authorities, using a panel study approach in which people were interviewed prior to and following the disposition of their cases.

Tyler, Casper, and Fisher (1989) found that, when they controlled for prior views, judgments about personal experience continued to shape post-experience legitimacy. Although the study did not measure trustworthiness and focused on broader evaluations of the legal system and legal authorities, it found that procedural justice judgments were the key experience-based judgment that shaped post-experience legitimacy.

Summary

In this chapter, we examined the degree to which people generalize from their personal experiences with police officers and judges to form their broader views about the law and about their community. The results support the argument that people do generalize from their personal experiences. People's perception of their treatment during an experience can have three types of broader impact: it shapes their trust in legal institutions and authorities; it shapes their trust in others in their community; and it shapes their identification with their community.

By acting fairly, legal authorities are not only encouraging the immediate acceptance of their decisions but socializing community residents. Particular actions in specific contexts have an impact on people's overall confidence in their community and its legal authorities.

Those behaviors of police officers and judges that offend and alienate the public are unlikely to be effective in controlling crime in the long term. Unfair treatment by particular police officers or judges creates a climate of disrespect for the law. That climate has an impact both on the particular people experiencing unfairness and on their community. People become less willing to obey the law, and the task of the legal authorities becomes more difficult.

These findings provide a broader context for our understanding of the implications of the actions of legal authorities. To be effective in controlling crime, legal authorities need the cooperation of the communities they police. They need the voluntary help of people in those communities in reporting crimes, being willing to testify in court, and joining neighborhood groups that work to combat crime.

There are differences of opinion about the degree to which the police and the courts, through their policing and sentencing activities, shape the nature and degree of lawbreaking behavior. We noted this issue in our discussion in chapter 5 of the policing and court practices that have recently been the focus of attention in New York City. Some argue that the police and the courts influenced the city's crime rate by aggressively combating minor crimes. Others suggest that New York's crime rate has been shaped by other factors besides police and court policies. It is beyond the scope of this discussion to evaluate the influence on the crime rate of the policies followed by legal authorities (see Gottfredson and Hirschi 1990; Felson 1994). For example, studies do not find a strong connection between reactive arrest rates and crime, although support for the value of proactive, targeted policing is stronger (see Sherman et al. 1997).

Our point is that the police and the courts are aided in the fight against crime by the active cooperation of the public. The police are better able to deal with crime when community residents engage in behaviors that facilitate effective crime control. As a consequence, not only do personal experiences with legal authorities have an impact on individuals' generalized attitudes and behaviors but, because of that generalization, they also have a broader impact on communities and on the fight against crime and social disorder. Such a model underlies efforts at community policing (Kelling 1988).

On the other hand, policing practices can backfire if they are carried out disrespectfully, and they can undermine the support of the communities involved. Sometimes managing high-crime communities by using aggressive policing tactics can alienate the community and contribute to higher long-term crime rates by lowering community cooperation with legal authorities and community respect for the law.

If the public experiences legal authorities as unfair, efforts to control crime through policing falter (Eck and Rosenbaum 1994). On the other hand, when the police act in ways perceived by the public to be fair, they can regulate public behavior without alienating the public. This assessment of police fairness is primarily linked to people's evaluations of the quality of their treatment during personal experiences with police officers and judges.[1]

In previous research, the senior author (Tyler 1990) suggested that people's personal experiences with legal authorities generalize to influence their broader views about the legitimacy of the law and legal authorities. Such broader views then shape their everyday obedience to the law. These findings suggest a similar conclusion regarding the broader impact of procedural justice and trust in the motives of the authorities with whom people interact during their personal experiences. Personalized judgments are generalized to influence views about the legitimacy of the law and of legal authorities. That legitimacy is important because it is related both to people's everyday compliance with the law and to their help-seeking behavior when laws have been broken.

This finding is consistent with the suggestion of others that process-based judgments about procedural justice and trustworthiness have broader implications for people's law-abidingness. For example, in a prison setting, Sparks, Bottoms, and Hay (1996) found that a more "social" crime prevention approach (that is, one viewed by inmates as fairer) led to a reduced level of rule-breaking. Pommerehne and Weck-Hannemann (1996) also demonstrated that fairness in government decision making decreases tax evasion.

In the context of work organizations, Kim and Mauborgne (1993) and Tyler and Blader (2000) have demonstrated that employee views about the justice of organizational procedures and their trust in the motives of organizational authorities are strongly related to their compliance with organizational rules. Although organizational rules are not the civil laws enforced by the police and courts, they do define appropriate behavior within organizations. Many prohibited activities, such as stealing, are of course also violations of the formal law.

All of these findings suggest the importance of the type of generalized legitimacy that develops, in part, from experiencing fair and trustworthy conduct on the part of legal authorities. The findings support the argument that police officers and judges are agents of value socialization whose conduct can either enhance or diminish public confidence in the institutions they represent.

PART IV

ETHNIC GROUP DIFFERENCES
IN EXPERIENCES WITH THE LAW

IN DESIGNING the sample for the California survey, we focused on the race or ethnicity of the people we interviewed. The study was stratified to draw approximately equal numbers of members of three important groups, African Americans, Hispanics, and whites. We did so because past studies of the American public provide clear evidence that there have long been major ethnic group differences in people's experiences with and attitudes toward the law and legal authorities. In fact, race-ethnicity has always been considered one of the central dimensions defining the relationship between the residents of various communities and legal authorities.

When legal authorities are engaged in regulation, expressions of discontent are most widespread, and can be particularly troubling and problematic among members of minority groups. In fact, "concern about police behavior toward racial minorities is an enduring feature of twentieth century American politics and public policy. Hardly a week goes by without a newspaper or television account of an incident where police officers are alleged to have treated a person who is a member of a minority group badly, with a subtext that the person's race accounted for the mistreatment" (Mastrofski et al. 1998, 1).

In chapter 10, we discuss the background of community relations with legal authorities and give particular attention to the interactions between minority community residents and legal authorities. Using data from the California study, we explore the nature of the outcomes that minority and white residents receive from the police and the courts and their willingness to accept those outcomes.

In chapter 11, we examine the manner in which minority group members evaluate their experiences—whether they feel that the procedures they experience are fair and whether they trust the motives of the authorities they encounter. Our goal is to examine whether there are differences in the psychology of personal experience that can be linked to issues of race-ethnicity.

Finally, chapter 12 explores the impact of connections to one's ethnic-racial group. We first examine whether the match or mismatch of ethnicity-race between a person and a legal authority makes a difference during a personal encounter. Psychologically, this match or mismatch may change a within-group encounter to an encounter that crosses group boundaries. We then examine the role that ethnic group identification plays in shaping the psychology of experience. Here our concern is not with ethnic group membership per se, but with the degree of psychological connection to one's ethnic group.[1]

Chapter 10

Ethnicity and Experiences with Legal Authorities

B OTH ANECDOTAL and observation-based studies suggest that the police and the courts often subject the members of minority groups to biased treatment (Cole 1999). As a recent review concluded: "The evidence is indisputable that, compared to general population distributions, persons of color are disproportionately represented among those subjected to police use of force, where the discharge of a firearm is involved" (Locke 1995, 139). In an analysis of police encounters with members of the public in several American cities, Worden (1995) found that African Americans are more likely to be subjected to "improper force," even after controls are made for their physical resistance and demeanor during the encounter.

Beyond widespread evidence of actual bias and discrimination when minority group members deal with the police, there is evidence that minority group members feel that they are treated with bias and injustice. This is especially true for African Americans (Garofalo 1977; Hagan and Albonetti 1982; Hindelang 1974; Huang and Vaughn 1996; Jacob 1971; Peek, Lowe, and Alston 1981; Schuman et al. 1997; Waddington and Braddock 1991; Wortley, Hagan, and MacMillan 1997). Studies also suggest that African Americans are more likely to file claims of police abuse of authority (Pate and Fridell 1993). We find more negative feelings about the police among Hispanics as well, although to a lesser degree than is true with African Americans (Lasley 1994). Lasley suggests that Hispanics take a middle ground between whites and African Americans. For example, in a study of New York residents conducted in 1988, 69 percent of African Americans, 53 percent of Hispanics, and 37 percent of whites said that the police favor one group over another.

Similar concerns have also been articulated about the courts, although the potential for violence and highly visible abuse has made the police the natural focus of concerns about equal treatment. Nevertheless, minority group members are also generally found to have more negative attitudes toward the courts (Hagan and Albonetti 1982; Myers 1996; Yankelovich, Skelly, and White, Inc. 1978). In the 1995 National Opinion Survey on crime and justice (Myers 1996), minority respondents said more frequently that the courts are unfair and unequal in their treatment of the members of different social groups, and that the disregard of defendants' rights is a problem. In this study Hispanics were found to be especially dissatisfied with the courts and to view their performance as poor. In particular, Hispanics expressed the view that the courts are unable to protect society.

These actual and psychological realities are central to any strategy that seeks to gain consent and cooperation from the members of minority groups, since negative judgments, however accurate or inaccurate, undermine cooperation with legal authorities. As we have already noted, those people who enter into interactions with generally favorable views about legal authorities tend to be more law-abiding.

It is often suggested that troubled public relations are an unavoidable byproduct of the efforts of the police and the courts to control crime. One way to view the struggle to control crime is as a trade-off between the gains associated with the aggressive policing of communities (lowered crime rates) and the losses associated with the alienation of the community and its residents when people feel that the police are intruding into their lives with practices such as stopping them on the street or searching them for weapons. This trade-off perspective assumes that aggressive, crime-controlling strategies are inevitably alienating to the public.

Ironically, to the degree that this trade-off exists, it is especially difficult in poor and minority communities because it is the poor and minorities who are the primary victims of crime: 80 percent of violent crimes are same-race crimes (Kennedy 1997). Further, it is the poor who have the fewest resources to cope with their losses. Hence, the members of poor and minority communities have the most to gain from law enforcement. They can also be viewed as having suffered from neglect and indifference in the past (Kennedy 1997). On the other hand, it is also the poor and minorities who are most likely to be the targets of police harassment and overuse of force when the police do focus on suppressing violent crimes, drug use, and gang activity (Kennedy 1997).

The Relationship Between Minority Group Members and Legal Authorities

These issues are especially central to the relationship between minority group members and legal authorities. Because of structural inequalities in income and opportunity and the many damaging effects of racism and poverty, minority neighborhoods are often high-crime areas, and minority group members are proportionally more likely than whites to be engaged in criminal behavior. Hence, crime control efforts are especially likely to be directed at minority group members.

Minority group members, in fact, have a very ambivalent relationship with crime control efforts. On the one hand, they are the target of those efforts and are the most likely to be stopped, detained, and so on. This treatment should lead them to be especially distrustful of and resistant to the police and the courts. On the other hand, minority communities are typically high-crime areas, and many crime victims are minority group members. As a result, they also have a reason to welcome the crime control efforts of the police.

Similarly, minority group members often have problems for which they might reasonably seek help from the police and the courts. Thus they have a great deal to gain from legal authorities who respond to their concerns and are motivated to protect those people who call or come before them.

Consider the comments of William Bratton (2000), the former New York City police commissioner, in the wake of the acquittal of the police officers involved in the shooting of Amadou Diallo (see chapter 5). Commissioner Bratton described the relationship between minority group members and the police as "a love affair" that was "waiting to happen" because of the role of the police in lowering crime and disorder in minority communities. He observed that "minority communities are those most affected by crime, and, historically, they have not been well policed." Bratton suggested that minority communities want policing that is effective in reducing crime but that is also "sensitive, compassionate, and respectful of constitutional guidelines."

These comments highlight the important point that low-income and minority communities have the most to gain from the police and the courts (Kennedy 1997). The question is whether legal authority can be exercised in ways that enhance minority respect for and deference to the law (Tyler 1994).

Minority Outcomes from Experiences with Legal Authorities

One important question is whether minorities receive more negative outcomes from their personal experiences with legal authorities than do whites. Using the overall outcome index constructed in this study, it is possible to address the question of whether minorities experience more negative outcomes. The results of a regression analysis examining possible ethnicity influences on outcome favorability indicate that minorities are not more likely to receive negative outcomes, whether measured objectively or subjectively. The relative means of the overall standardized index of outcome favorability within the different ethnic groups shows the relative favorability of the outcomes experienced by the members of these groups. This analysis is presented in table 10.1. In considering these findings, it is

Table 10.1 Ethnicity and Outcome Favorability

	Objective Outcome Favorability (H = unfavorable)	Overall Index of Outcome Favorability (H = unfavorable)	Distributive Justice (H = unfair)	Consistent with Expectations (H = inconsistent)	Predictable (H = not predictable)
Beta weights					
Ethnicity					
Hispanic (H = yes)	.04	.07	.03	.03	.14***
African American (H = yes)	.03	.05	.10***	-.03	.15***
Experience					
Voluntary (H = yes)	-.32***	-.03	.10***	-.02	.11***
Authority (H = police)	.18***	.10***	-.02	.08**	.01
City (H = Los Angeles)	.03	-.03	.03	-.01	-.02
Demographics					
Gender (H = female)	-.02	-.03	.06*	-.05*	.03
Age (H = old)	.01	-.04	.07**	-.03	.04
Education (H = high)	.03	.03	.03	.01	.08**
Income (H = high)	.01	.01	.02	.01	.06
Party (H = Democratic)	-.03	-.03	-.01	.03	.02
Ideology (H = conservative)	.02	-.04	.00	-.01	.03
Total adjusted R-squared	11%	1%	3%	1%	7%

Source: California study data.

*p < .05.
**p < .01.
***p < .001.

important to remember that all of the information about outcome favorability comes from self-reported outcomes. We asked people to evaluate the outcomes and to indicate what those outcomes were (for example, "I was arrested"). However, there were no neutral observers to provide independent information on what happened during the encounter.

The overall mean for the standardized scale of outcome favorability was 0.00 (standard deviation = 0.55). The mean for whites was 0.00 (standard deviation = 0.50), for African Americans 0.00 (standard deviation = 0.59), and for Hispanics –.13 (standard deviation = 0.57). An overall test for the equivalence of the means suggests no significant difference ($F(2,1653) = 2.87$, n.s.), while a comparison of the means for whites and minorities indicates that minority group scores are slightly, but significantly, lower than are the scores of whites ($t(1653) = 2.17$, $p = .03$). Both tests suggest the same conclusion. Among the people interviewed in this study, ethnic differences in outcome favorability were quite small, if they existed at all.

The results shown in table 10.1 also suggest that more subjective judgments about experience show stronger minority group effects. For example, minority respondents are much more likely to indicate that they experienced the behavior of legal authorities as unpredictable and as distributively unfair. Hence, more subjective evaluations of experience were more likely to reveal ethnic group differences.

A more detailed comparison of white and minority experiences reveals a complex pattern of outcomes. Two conclusions seem warranted by the analysis. First, people in all three ethnic groups experienced their outcomes in encounters with the legal system as less than satisfactory in 25 to 30 percent of the cases. Their problems were sometimes not solved, and many experienced negative outcomes such as citations and fines. This finding supports the basic argument that, if police officers and judges had to rely on their ability to provide people with favorable outcomes, it would be difficult for them to perform their functions. Legal authorities are often presented with problems that they cannot solve to the satisfaction of the people involved, and sometimes they cannot solve them at all. Further, legal authorities must enforce rules that limit people's ability to act as they wish. These basic features of personal experiences with legal authorities are true for both whites and minority group members.

Second, whatever ethnicity differences in outcomes are found in people's personal experiences with legal authorities, they are minor in scope and reflect a complex pattern of outcome differences in which minorities receive better outcomes in some situations and worse outcomes in others. Nonetheless, an overall index of objective and subjective outcome favorability suggests that outcomes are experienced by minority respondents as slightly more negative than they are by whites. From an overall perspective, these differences, if statistically significant, do not seem very

Table 10.2   Determinants of Acceptance of the Decisions of Legal Authorities

	No Control		With a Control on Outcome Favorability	
	Acceptance	Satisfaction	Acceptance	Satisfaction
Beta weights				
Ethnicity				
Hispanic (H = yes)	−.09*	−.07*	−.06*	−.04
African American				
(H = yes)	−.12**	−.12***	−.10***	−.10***
Experience				
Voluntary (H = yes)	.12***	.19***	.11***	.18***
Authority dealt with				
(police-courts)				
(H = police)	.00	.01	.04	.04
City (H = Los Angeles)	.02	.01	.01	.00
Demographics				
Gender (H = female)	.02	.01	.01	−.01
Age (H = old)	.08**	.08**	.07*	.06*
Education (H = high)	.00	.01	.01	.01
Income (H = high)	.06*	.04	.06*	.05*
Party (H = Democratic)	−.01	−.02	−.02	−.03
Liberalism				
(H = conservative)	.01	.03	.03	.05*
Outcome favorability				
(H = favorable)	—	—	.45***	.50***
Total adjusted R-squared	5%	6%	24%	31%

Source: California study data.
Note: High scores indicate willingness to accept decisions and satisfaction with the decision maker.
*p < .05.
**p < .01.
***p < .001.

important and are unlikely to account for the substantial differences in minority and white attitudes toward the police and the courts that we outline later.

Ethnicity and Decision Acceptance

Tables 10.2 and 10.3 outline the effect of demographic factors on voluntary acceptance of the decisions of legal authorities and on satisfaction with the decision maker. These analyses indicate several things. First, minority respondents are less likely than white respondents to accept the decisions of police officers and judges willingly. Minority respondents are also less positive in their evaluations of legal authorities. The effects

Table 10.3   **Willingness to Accept Decisions and Satisfaction
with Decision Maker, by Ethnicity**

	White	African American	Hispanic
Compliance			
"I did what I was asked to do."			
Agree or agree strongly	99%	97%	97%
Agree strongly only	88	88	82
Acceptance[a]			
"I willingly accepted the decision." (agree)	88	80	89
"In a similar situation in the future, I would like to see the situation handled in the same way." (agree)	65	53	59
"I considered going to someone else to try to change the decision."[c] (agree)	16	23	30
"The situation could have been handled better."[c] (agree)	36	50	61
Satisfaction[b]			
"The person generally did a good job dealing with my situation." (agree)	79	66	70
"I was generally satisfied with the way he/she handled the situation." (agree)	73	61	69

Source: California study data.
[a] alpha = 0.80.
[b] alpha = 0.92.
[c] Indicates reversal in scoring.

are stronger for African Americans compared to whites, but there are also differences between Hispanics and whites. These effects remain if we control for differences in the favorability of people's outcomes using the overall index of outcome favorability.

Second, age and income influence the willingness to accept the decisions of legal authorities, with older and higher-income people expressing more willingness to accept them voluntarily. Older respondents also expressed more positive feelings about the legal authorities they encountered.

Within the group studied here, we found no strong differences in the favorability of the outcomes that people received from legal authorities. However, minority group members were found to be more likely to resist the police officers and judges with whom they interacted. Further,

Table 10.4   Ethnicity, Justice, and Motive-Based Trust

	Procedural Justice	Distributive Justice	Motive-Based Trust
Beta weights			
Ethnicity			
Hispanic (H = yes)	−.09***	−.06*	−.09***
African American (H = yes)	−.12****	−.18****	−.16****
Experience			
Voluntary? (H = yes)	.23****	.08***	.30****
Type of authority (H = police)	−.03	.02	.00
City (H = Los Angeles)	−.01	.03	.00
Demographics			
Sex (H = female)	.01	.03	.03
Age (H = old)	.07*	.04	.09****
Education (H = well educated)	.02	−.01	−.05
Income (H = high income)	.05	.04	.01
Adjusted R-squared	8%****	4%****	13%****

Source: California study data.
Note: High scores indicate that the respondent felt that he or she was fairly treated or that he or she received a fair outcome; it also indicates higher levels of trust in the motives of the authorities.
*p < .10.
**p < .05.
***p < .01.
****p < .001.

they reported more negative feelings about the individual legal authorities they encountered.

We have already outlined a general model of the psychology of personal experiences with legal authorities. That model helps us to understand why minorities might feel negatively toward the police and the courts even when they do not experience a higher number of negative outcomes. That model suggests that minorities report that they experience less procedural fairness and that they are less trusting of the motives of legal authorities.

Minorities and Procedural Justice

Are there minority differences in respondents' assessments of the fairness of the procedures used during their encounters with legal authorities? To examine this possibility we used a variety of background factors, including ethnicity, to predict judgments of distributive and procedural justice. The findings are shown in table 10.4. They indicate,

Table 10.5   **Ethnicity and Procedural and Distributive Justice**

	White	African American	Hispanic
Procedural justice[a]			
"How fair are the procedures he/ she used to make decisions about how to handle the situation?" (fair)	82%	68%	72%
"Overall, how fairly are you treated?" (very or somewhat fairly)	83	75	72
Mean (standard deviation)	1.61 (0.89)	1.95 (1.07)	1.94 (1.01)
Distributive justice[b]			
"According to the law, I received the outcome I deserved." (agree)	74%	56%	69%
"I received the outcome I feel I deserved." (agree)	67	54	65
"The outcome I received was fair." (agree)	79	63	69
Mean (standard deviation)	1.93 (0.98)	2.38 (1.14)	2.15 (1.07)

Source: California study data.
Note: Low means indicate a fair procedure and a fair outcome.
[a] alpha = 0.91
[b] alpha = 0.92

as already noted, that minority respondents were more likely to say that they received an unfair outcome. That is, minorities were more likely to say that they received an outcome that was more or less than they deserved. Further, they were more likely to say that the procedures used by the authorities during their personal encounter were unfair and to express low levels of trust in the motives of the authorities. A comparison of the justice responses of the three ethnic groups is shown in table 10.5. The percentages of trust for each group are shown in table 10.6.

The results also indicate that other factors influence motive-based trust. Respondents were less likely to say they felt that the motives of the authorities were trustworthy when their contact with them was involuntary. As we might expect, the problems of legal authorities become greater when they impose themselves on people, compared to situations in which people have gone to the authorities for help. Although, as we have shown, respondents' outcomes were often negative, irrespective of

Table 10.6   Ethnicity and Motive-Based Trust

	White	African American	Hispanic
Social trust[a]			
"During my personal experience, the . . . Authority considered my views."			
(agree)	72%	63%	65%
Authority tried hard to do the right thing by me." (agree)	76%	64%	67%
Authority tried to take my needs into account." (agree)	69%	57%	60%
Authority cared about my concerns." (agree)	70%	59%	66%
"I trust him / her."			
(trust a lot or trust some)	80%	59%	66%
Mean (standard deviation)[b]	1.93	2.29	2.21
	0.96	1.12	1.03

Source: California study data.
Note: Low scores indicate high trust.
[a] alpha = 0.93.
[b] A comparison of whites to minorities shows a significant difference in overall trust $(t(1649) = 6.11, p < .001)$.

the type of contact, involuntary contact seemed more likely to generate hostility and resistance.

Minorities and the Meaning of Fairness

As before, we can use regression analysis to examine whether minority group members were more likely to indicate that the quality of the decision making processes or the quality of the treatment they received was lower than that experienced by whites. Such a regression is shown in table 10.7. These results show that, compared to whites, minority respondents indicated that they received both a lower quality of decision making and a lower quality of treatment. Percentages are shown in table 10.8.

The regressions in tables 10.7 also suggest that the actions of the authorities with whom minority respondents dealt were less understandable to them. Further, African American respondents indicated that they felt weaker social bonds with those authorities.

Table 10.7   **Ethnicity and the Importance of the Antecedents of Justice and Motive-Based Trust**

	Quality of Decision Making	Quality of Treatment	Actions Understandable	Social Bonds
Beta weights				
Ethnicity				
Hispanic (H = yes)	−.09***	−.07*	−.10*	−.04
African American				
(H = yes)	−.19***	−.14***	−.18***	−.16***
Experience				
Voluntary				
(H = voluntary)	.24***	.26***	.16***	.21***
Authority (H = police)	−.06*	−.05	−.03	.07**
City (H = Los Angeles)	.01	−.01	−.00	.02
Demographics				
Sex (H = female)	.02	.04	−.01	−.09***
Age (H = old)	.09***	.11***	.07*	.13***
Education				
(H = well educated)	−.04	−.03	−.03	−.02
Income				
(H = high income)	.04	.02	.06*	−.01
Party (H = Democratic)	−.01	.00	−.01	−.05
Ideology				
(H = Conservative)	.04	.02	.03	.01
Total adjusted R-squared	10%	11%	6%	10%

Source: California study data.
Note: High scores indicate a fair decision making procedure; fair treatment; actions are understandable; and social bonds exist.
*p < .05.
**p < .01.
***p < .001.

Summary

The findings discussed in this chapter suggest that minority group members are less willing to defer to the decisions made by legal authorities. They are also less likely to report that their experiences with legal authorities are procedurally fair, and less likely to trust the motives of legal authorities. Thus, minorities generally report that, on a social-psychological level, their experiences are more negative than are those

Table 10.8   Ethnicity and Relational Concerns

	White	African American	Hispanic
The quality of the decision making process			
"He/she treated me the same as he/she would treat anyone else in the same situation." (agree)	81%	70%	77%
"He/she was basically honest." (agree)	93	78	80
"He/she made decisions based on the facts." (agree)	85	71	79
Mean (standard deviation)	1.55	1.94	1.79
	(0.70)	(1.10)	(0.89)
The quality of the treatment received			
"He/she treated me politely." (agree)	88%	79%	78%
"He/she showed concern for my rights." (agree)	83	74	79
Mean (standard deviation)	1.60	1.90	1.87
	(0.86)	(1.07)	(1.01)
Actions were understandable			
"I understood why he/she made decisions." (agree)	88%	69%	77%
"I understood why I was treated as I was." (agree)	84	68	77
	1.64	2.05	1.90
	(0.86)	(1.13)	(0.96)
Social bonds			
"We had a lot in common as people." (agree)	43%	38%	53%
"We shared values and concerns." (agree)	78	53	54
"We shared a common background." (agree)	29	22	30
	2.53	2.89	2.68
	(0.75)	(0.93)	(0.91)

Source: California study data.
Note: Low means indicate high quality, understandability, and shared bonds.

of whites. However, it is hard to account for these findings using outcome favorability as the explanation. In this sample the favorability of the outcomes received by the members of all three groups was roughly similar. Therefore, we need to look at the social aspects of people's experiences to understand the roots of their negative feelings.

Chapter 11

Variations in the Psychology of Experience

W HAT ROLE do procedural justice and motive-based trust play in gaining decision acceptance from individuals of different ethnicity?

To address this question, we used regression analyses in which the dependent variable was a combined index of decision acceptance and satisfaction with the decision maker. We then used procedural justice or motive-based trust to predict that dependent variable, controlling for the influence of outcome favorability and fairness. The results indicate that both procedural justice and motive-based trust shape acceptance and satisfaction, and that both have approximately the same influence. This is true among all three ethnic groups (see table 11.1). The results shown here indicate that everyone, irrespective of ethnic group, is primarily concerned with issues of procedural justice and motive-based trust when deciding whether to defer to legal authorities.

A second analysis using the procedural elements is shown in table 11.2. That analysis also suggests that acceptance by the members of all three groups is dominated by judgments about the quality of decision making and the quality of the treatment they receive from the police and the courts. Interestingly, African American respondents focus relatively more heavily on issues of decision making, while whites and Hispanics focus relatively more heavily on quality of treatment. However, these relational concerns of quality of decision making and quality of treatment dominate the reactions of all respondents.

The Role of Process Issues in Shaping Acceptance

It is possible that the role of process issues or outcome issues is different between ethnic groups in shaping individual reactions to legal authorities. One obvious argument is that minorities are both less influenced by

Table 11.1   Ethnicity and the Role of Procedural Justice and Motive-Based Trust in Shaping Acceptance-Satisfaction

	White		African American		Hispanic	
Beta weights						
Procedural justice	—	.78***	—	.78***	—	.76***
Motive-based trust	.78***	—	.83***	—	.74***	—
Favorability-fairness of the outcome	.17***	.16***	.11***	.15***	.20***	.16***
Total adjusted R-squared	75%	75%	78%	73%	71%	72%

Source: California study data.
***p < .001.

Table 11.2   Ethnicity and Procedural Elements Shaping Acceptance-Satisfaction

	White	African American	Hispanic
Beta weights			
Quality of decision making	.20***	.34***	.27***
Quality of treatment	.36***	.26***	.33***
Social bonds	.04	.11***	.05
Actions understood	.26***	.23***	.19***
Favorability-fairness of the outcome	.19***	.11***	.18***
Total adjusted R-squared	74%	77%	71%

Source: California study data.
***p < .001.

judgments about process and more influenced by evaluations of their outcomes. This argument flows from the more contentious relationship between legal authorities and the minority community.

To test this argument we examined the influence of judgments about processes and outcomes on the willingness of members of different ethnic groups to accept the decisions of legal authorities, using the previously outlined indices of process-based judgments and outcome-based judgments. This analysis is similar to analyses we have already reported. However, it adds interaction terms for the joint effect of ethnicity and processes, on the one hand, and ethnicity and outcomes, on the other. These additional interaction terms allow us to assess whether minority

Table 11.3   The Role of Processes and Outcomes, by Ethnicity

	Decision Acceptance	Satisfaction with Decision	Overall
Beta weights			
Process issues (A)	.85***	.89***	.91***
Outcome issues (B)	.16***	.12***	.15***
African American versus white (C)	.01	.02	.02
A × C	−.04	−.04*	−.04*
B × C	.06**	.00	−.03
Hispanic versus white (D)	−.02	.02	.00
A × D	−.12**	−.05**	−.09***
B × D	−.02	.00	−.01
Total adjusted R-squared	68%	80%	80%

Source: California study data.
*p < .05.
**p < .01.
***p < .001.

group members place more or less weight on each of these two factors than do whites.

The results of the analysis are shown in table 11.3. They suggest that the members of all groups are most strongly influenced by process issues. In addition, there are clear ethnic group differences. Subgroup analyses indicate that these interaction effects occur because African Americans and Hispanics are a little less concerned about process issues than are whites. In other words, not everyone evaluates experiences in exactly the same way. White respondents are especially likely to rely on their assessments of the process, in comparison to minority respondents. On the other hand, there is only weak evidence that minority group members put more weight on outcome issues. In the case of decision acceptance, for example, African Americans put more weight on outcomes relative to whites, but again, the magnitude of the difference is small.

Despite ethnic group differences, the results continue to support the optimistic argument that people's reactions to their experiences are not dominated by the favorability of their outcomes during their personal experiences with legal authorities. It is striking that, as with whites, the favorability of the outcomes received is not the most important determinant of the willingness to accept decisions in either of the two minority groups. Therefore, while there are some differences in the psychology of acceptance and of evaluation that are linked to ethnic group membership,

Table 11.4   Ethnicity and Control

	Process Control	Decision Control
Beta weights		
Ethnicity		
Hispanic	−.06	.01
African American	−.04	.05
Experience		
Voluntary	.31***	.09***
Type of authority	−.00	−.01
City	.01	−.02
Demographics		
Sex	.01	−.04
Age	.05	.04
Education	−.01	−.06
Income	−.01	−.05
Total adjusted R-squared	10%	14%

Source: California study data.
***p < .001.

these differences do not change the premise that process-based issues are important to everyone, regardless of their ethnicity or race.

Ethnicity and Control

Do ethnic differences in respondents' judgments about the amount of control they have over the decision or over the process contribute to the ethnic differences already seen in their assessments of the procedural justice of their experiences and in their judgments about the trustworthiness of the authorities they encountered? To examine this possibility we used regression analysis to explore the influence of ethnicity on control judgments. The results of this regression analysis are shown in table 11.4. They indicate that there were no significant ethnicity effects on control judgments. The only significant influence on control judgments was whether an experience was voluntary. As we would expect, people were less likely to indicate that they had control during involuntary experiences.

These findings suggest that whatever the reasons for the differences in people's judgments about their degree of control during their experiences with legal authorities, those reasons are not linked to their ethnic background. Thus, we can reasonably ignore issues of control in our analysis.

Young, Minority, and Male: High-Risk Respondents

Police officers and judges are generally concerned about their ability to gain desired behavior from the public. Achieving success "is an important test of officers' [and judges'] skills and an essential element of effective governance" (Mastrofski, Snipes, and Supina 1996, 269). From the perspective of authorities, therefore, the key question is whether they are able to shape people's behavior.

Concerns about the ability to shape behavior are often focused on a particular "high-risk" group: young, minority males. Legal authorities view this group as very power-oriented, highly volatile and confrontational, and likely to make trouble by resisting legal authority and escalating the level of tension, hostility, and violence in personal encounters with police officers and judges. As we have noted, it was not the goal of our sampling frame to include large numbers of members of this high-risk group. Instead, we sought to include diverse samples of three major ethnic groups. Hence, it is an open question whether, and to what degree, our findings speak to the motivational forces shaping the behavior of "high-risk offenders."

The population to which high-risk characteristics are attached is young (eighteen to twenty-five), male, and minority. A small group in our sample, 123 respondents, fit these demographic characteristics. We focus now on this high-risk subgroup to test possible limits of the overall findings reported.

Young, minority males provide an interesting focus for analysis for several reasons, and they may be related. First, this is the group whose members are most likely to be in gangs and most likely to be involved in violent, gun-related crimes. Members of this group also commit a high number of crimes relative to their proportion of the population. As a result, this group is the focus of police efforts to restrict and control people's behavior. Second, young, minority males are viewed by legal authorities as especially problematic and troublesome to deal with because of their hostile and provocative attitudes toward the police and willingness to escalate conflicts.

A replication of our analysis among the members of this high-risk subgroup is shown in table 11.5. The results make it clear that the basic findings we have outlined extend to this potentially problematic subgroup. Like people in general, high-risk young minority males are willing to defer to the decisions of legal authorities according to their assessments of the procedural justice they experience and the trustworthiness of the authorities' motives.

Table 11.5   The Role of Procedural Justice and Motive-Based Trust in
Shaping Acceptance and Satisfaction Among Eighteen- to
Twenty-Five-Year-Old Minority Males

	High-Risk Subgroup (N = 123)		Other Respondents (N = 1,533)	
Beta weights				
Procedural justice	—	.84***	—	.77***
Trust in the motives of the authority	.78***	—	.79***	—
Favorability-fairness of the outcome	.16**	.11*	.16**	.16**
Total adjusted R-squared	67%	74%	76%	74%

Source: California study data.
*p < .05.
**p < .01.
***p < .001.

Table 11.6   Procedural Elements Shaping Acceptance and Satisfaction
Among High-Risk Offenders

	High-Risk Offenders	Others
Beta weights		
Quality of decision making	.19***	.28***
Quality of treatment	.40***	.31***
Common background	.09	.07***
Actions understood	.30***	.22***
Favorability-fairness of the outcome	.06	.17***
Total adjusted R-squared	78%	74%

Source: California study data.
***p < .001.

A further analysis suggests that high-risk respondents were especially
concerned about issues of quality of treatment. That analysis, shown in
table 11.6, shows that this subgroup had an unusually strong concern
about the quality of the treatment they received, relative to other respondents. Most respondents focused on both the quality of decision making
and the quality of treatment. In contrast, high-risk respondents were
more concerned about quality of treatment, and less concerned about the
quality of decision making.

We find that young, minority males react to legal authorities in basically the same way as do people in general. Contrary to the expectations
that legal authorities may have about this group—for example, that issues

of dominance, power, and outcomes are the key to shaping interactions—young, minority males are not in fact more focused than everyone else on the instrumental bottom line. Their willingness to defer to the police and the courts is based on the same issues that shape the willingness of people in general to defer to legal authorities.

What are these issues? Our results suggest that the two key concerns of these high-risk respondents are the fairness of the procedures used by the police or the courts during their personal experience with those authorities and trust in their motives. These two interrelated judgments are more important than assessments of either the fairness or the favorability of the outcomes that these young men receive. For them, procedural justice and motive-based trust are linked, in turn, primarily to the quality of the treatment they received when dealing with police officers and judges, although the quality of decision making procedures also plays a secondary role. If police officers or judges want to increase the willing acceptance of their decisions and voluntary deference to their authority by young, minority males, as well as receive more favorable evaluations of their own performance, they can most effectively do so by focusing on how well they treat members of this subgroup in their interactions. As previously noted, "treatment" in the study design is evaluated by the degree to which people felt they were treated politely, with dignity, and with respect for their rights.

The suggestion that young, minority males react primarily out of a sense of procedural justice and motive-based trust may run counter to the intuitions of many police officers or judges. However, our finding that this group cares about issues of trust, justice, respect, and status is consistent with a large literature suggesting that issues of respect and dignity are critical to young, minority males, even the career criminals or gang members who are often portrayed as amoral and instrumental "superpredators" (see Anderson 1994; Bourgois 1996; Emler and Reicher 1995; Kennedy and Forde 1999).

Of course, we need to emphasize again that the California study did not target this high-risk subgroup. A telephone survey is likely to miss many high-risk respondents, and they are also more likely to refuse to be interviewed. Hence, research directed at this group is needed to test the arguments made here. However, in other research (Casper, Tyler, and Fisher 1988; Tyler, Casper, and Fisher 1989), the senior author has studied the members of this high-risk group and reached conclusions similar to those outlined here.

Our findings, together with other findings on similar respondents, suggest that the process-based model may also apply to high-risk people. What subgroup of young, minority males, we should ask, are responsive to polite and respectful treatment? Addressing this question is beyond the scope of this study, nor is this the place to examine the issue of whether "hard-core" offenders and "career" criminals can be regulated using this approach.

Overall Model of Ethnic Influences on Acceptance of and Satisfaction with Decisions of Legal Authorities

The findings of our regression analyses suggest that minority respondents were less willing to accept decisions and less satisfied with decision makers. They were also less likely to report that they had received procedural justice, and they were less trusting of the motives of legal authorities. Finally, they were more likely to say that the quality of the decision making process and the quality of their treatment were poor.

The question we now address is whether these psychological judgments explain the impact of ethnicity on decision acceptance. If psychological judgments explain or mediate the influence of ethnicity on decision acceptance, it means that minority group respondents were less willing to accept decisions because they felt less fairly treated and were less trusting.

To test this argument directly we conducted a path analysis. The dependent variable was treated as a latent variable with two indicators—decision acceptance and satisfaction with the decision maker. Outcomes were also treated as a latent variable with four indicators—outcome favorability, outcome fairness, predictability, and unexpectedness.[1] The four aspects of procedures—quality of decision making, quality of treatment, common background, and understandability—were treated as observed variables.

The possible paths are shown in figure 11.1. This model is a conceptual model of the possible influences. The results of the analysis are shown in figure 11.2. In this model, only significant paths are shown. The model fits the data well (NFI = 0.94; CFI = 0.94; 78 percent of the variance in the dependent variable is explained).

The findings support the argument that the impact of ethnic group differences on people's willingness to accept decisions and their satisfaction with decision makers is mediated by their judgments of procedural justice and motive-based trust. Once those variables have been included in the equation, there is no direct influence of ethnic group membership on decision acceptance. Thus, when minority group members received treatment that they judged to be equivalent to that accorded to whites, they were just as willing as whites were to comply.

The lack of direct influences of ethnicity on decision acceptance indicates that the psychological judgments included in the model explain

Figure 11.1   Ethnicity and Reactions to Decisions

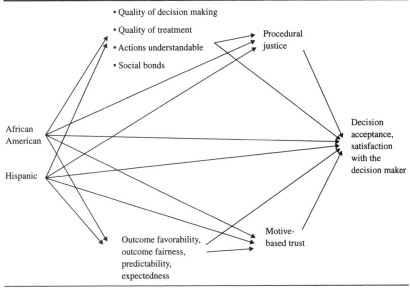

Source: Based on California study data.

Figure 11.2   Ethnicity and Reactions to Decisions

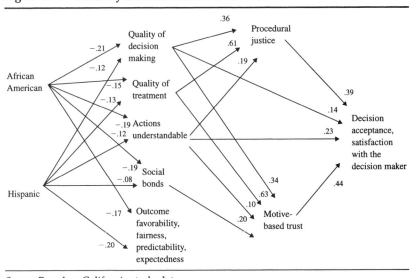

Source: Based on California study data.

why minority group members are less willing to accept decisions. Hence, the psychological model accounts for the widely reported ethnic group differences in behavior toward the police and the courts.

The results shown in figure 11.2 can also be used to make several other important points. One is that instrumental judgments do not independently influence decision acceptance once all of the influences of processes and motive-based trust are taken into account. This reinforces the prior argument that hostility toward the police and the courts is not rooted in the nature of the outcomes they deliver to the people they deal with.

Second, as shown in prior analyses, procedural justice and motive-based trust have distinct influences on decision acceptance. In other words, though the two judgments are related, each explains distinct aspects of decision acceptance and satisfaction with the decision maker.

Understanding Ethnic Group Differences

These results suggest that the key to understanding ethnic group differences in the acceptance of the decisions of legal authorities lies in understanding why people of differing ethnicities experience their personal encounters with legal authorities differently—that is, why they view the authorities with whom they deal as less procedurally just and less worthy of their trust. The findings suggest that neither the objective nor the subjective outcome of personal experience is the key to understanding ethnic group differences. Instead, we need to focus on the fact that minority respondents are more likely to report that they do not feel fairly treated and do not trust the motives of the authority with whom they interact.

These findings are optimistic in their implications for the process-based model of regulation in that they suggest that ethnic group differences are not linked to the outcomes that minorities receive from the police and the courts. However, the findings also make it clear that, relative to whites, minority group members do not view the treatment they receive as fair and do not trust the motives of authorities. This leads us to focus again on the issue of how procedural justice and trust inferences are made during personal experiences with legal authorities.

From the perspective of the process-based model, the implications of these findings are quite optimistic. They suggest that the most important issue that needs to be addressed in response to minorities' perceptions of injustice when dealing with the police or the courts is their experience of disrespect and lack of concern for their rights. In addition, other issues—honesty, factuality, lack of bias, ability to participate—that are central to assessments of the quality of the decision making process are important. These issues can all be addressed through training and changes in management practices.

If, in contrast, minority feelings were found to be linked to the favorability of the outcomes they receive, then that finding would suggest an unavoidable clash between strategies of policing that are linked to effective crime control and those that would support subjective feelings of justice. It is a statistical fact that, owing to the association of minority group status with disadvantaged economic and social status, minorities commit a disproportionate number of crimes. Therefore, crime control practices, ranging from traffic stops to street stop-and-frisks for weapons, are often directed at minorities.

These findings suggest that minorities do not object to crime control efforts per se. Rather, the objections revealed by this analysis are primarily to experiencing disrespect from legal authorities during personal encounters. In addition, people react to evidence of unfair decision making procedures, such as bias, dishonesty, or the lack of an opportunity to provide input.

Of course, we do not want to exaggerate our conclusions about these findings. It is clear that what legal authorities do in the context of personal experience has important implications for whether their decisions are accepted. However, the willingness to accept decisions is also linked to general societal orientations. Since minority group members have already been shown to have less positive societal orientations, there will always be other factors shaping their resistance to the decisions of legal authorities in a given situation.

In this analysis, we do not separate out the actions of particular legal authorities from the formal policies of legal institutions. However, Tyler and Blader (2000) have made this distinction in the context of work organizations. They found that both the respect for employees shown by the formal rules of the organization and the respect conveyed in supervisors' personal treatment of employees distinctly shaped judgments of procedural justice. Hence, there are potentially two routes that police departments and courts can take to enhance the public's perception of procedural justice on the part of the police and the courts.

The first is the training of police officers and judges. Many police officers and judges believe that their role requires them to dominate people and places, but that attitude can lead them to neglect the feelings of the people with whom they are interacting. Training can emphasize that treating people with dignity has an important impact on their willingness to defer to authorities.

The second route is the establishment of clear policies and standards that mandate treatment with dignity and respect, and the articulation of those standards by senior law enforcement officials. Such formal declarations have an impact both directly on public perception and indirectly through their impact on the behavior of particular police officers on the street and judges in their courtrooms.

Of course, in addition to quality of treatment, quality of decision-making is an important factor. Traditional training procedures already focus on the need to make objective and neutral decisions, something that needs to be reinforced. The use of empirical methods such as profiling can also be helpful if the authorities make it clear to people that the procedures are not arbitrary or capricious. One important element of the use of such decision making procedures is the need to explain to people how decisions are being made so that they understand that neutral, objective criteria have been used. After all, most people have no idea why judges make the decisions they do, or why police officers stop them in their car or on the street. These decisions need to be explained to the public.

Chapter 12

Group Boundaries and Subgroup Identification

IN THIS chapter, we examine two issues that arise in interactions between legal authorities and minority group members. The first is the consequence of dealing with an authority who is outside of one's ethnic group. The second is the role of loyalty to one's ethnic subgroup in shaping reactions to legal authorities.[1]

Group Boundaries

When people deal with particular legal authorities, one aspect of the interaction is whether they view the authority as a member of their own group. It has been suggested that minorities have different experiences when they involve minority legal authorities. This is one of many arguments underlying calls for increasing the number of minority police officers and judges.

There are two views about this issue. Social-psychological studies do suggest that cross-group interactions are more instrumental and that people care less strongly about process issues in the context of such interactions. This suggests that the police and the courts will find it easier to gain deference when the authority and the person with whom he or she is dealing share group membership. On the other hand, it is often noted that all police officers are viewed by the public as members of a single group, not as white or black but as "blue"; minority community residents might easily see all police officers as belonging to a different group regardless of their actual ethnicity.

Tyler, Lind, Ohbuchi, Sugawara, and Huo (1998) demonstrated that the presence of salient group boundaries changes the basis on which people decide whether to accept decisions in conflict situations. Their results show that people focus more strongly on process issues when dealing with people whom they view as members of their own group.

Interactions with those outside of one's group, on the other hand, are more strongly shaped by outcomes. This supports the argument that the authorities would benefit from being viewed as belonging to the same group as the people they are seeking to influence. Using the California study data, we directly examined the influence of the ethnic group match in interactions between individuals and legal authorities.

Subgroup Identification

In evaluating the influence of the ethnic group match, it may be the psychological connection to various groups that really matters—that is, the way in which people construct their subjective model of who is in their group rather than their actual group membership. In other words, the key issue may be the prominence of various group boundaries from the perspective of the respondent. Interactions with an authority who shares a person's age, gender, and ethnic background are more likely to be viewed as a within-group or intragroup experience. However, it is unclear whether differences in background characteristics lead people to think that they are dealing with insiders or with outsiders. As we have noted, people may view police officers and judges as outsiders regardless of similarities in their ethnicity or other characteristics.

We have already shown that people's psychological connection to society—their superordinate or societal-level identification—matters. Those who feel more pride in their social group are more likely both to defer to authorities and to base such deference on process issues. Here we need to consider the degree to which people feel a connection to their ethnic group and the impact that such an identification has on their reactions to legal authorities.

Research based on the relational model of authority (Tyler and Lind 1992) shows that people are concerned about the quality of their relationships with authorities and other group members. This line of research suggests that people are more likely to accept an authority's decision when they feel that they are being treated fairly, independent of the nature of the outcome (Tyler 1988, 1990; Tyler and Lind 1992). We have already shown that this is generally true among the people in the California study. People who have a stronger connection to society are more willing to accept the decisions made by legal authorities and to base such deference more strongly on procedural judgments.

The relational model deals primarily with within-group processes—that is, with the relationship between an individual and his or her reference group. It was developed to explain why individuals care about relational issues when evaluating group authorities (Lind and Tyler 1988; Tyler 1989; Tyler and Lind 1992). We discuss the relational model at this point because it helps us to understand how we might think about people's relationships to their ethnic groups.

The basic premise of the relational model is that people derive a sense of self-worth from group membership. Individuals assess their status within groups by evaluating the extent to which important group representatives, such as authorities, treat them fairly. When people feel that they are treated without bias and with benevolence and respect, their sense of self-worth is bolstered and their attachment to the group is affirmed (Smith et al. 1998). People thus value fair treatment by legal authorities because it communicates a message about their identities— that they are respected and valued members of society.

Although it is a theory of within-group rather than between-group processes, the relational model nonetheless makes a specific prediction about the condition under which procedural concerns will matter in interactions between members of different ethnic groups. The theory suggests that concern about processes will be limited to interactions between members of a shared social category. Therefore, process considerations should be less relevant in the interactions between an authority and an individual from a different ethnic background. These types of interactions may turn on more instrumental considerations and prove to be more difficult to manage (Tyler et al. 1998). If the authority figure is perceived to represent a group with which the individual feels little or no attachment, then relational issues may become less relevant (Tyler and Lind 1990).

However, the relational model does not suggest that we should necessarily expect ethnic group identification to be important unless it also undermines identification with the societal or superordinate group. The key issue should be the degree to which the person feels a connection to the group that an authority represents. It is the overall connection to American society that should determine the importance of process-based approaches to regulation, not the connection with a particular ethnic group.

Effect of Ethnic Matches in the California Study

We first consider the issue of match. The frequency of within- and between-group interactions in this study is outlined in table 12.1. Of course, it is important to recognize that in this analysis we treat all minorities as members of one group. African Americans, for example, might regard a Hispanic police officer or judge either as within their group (since they are minority group members) or as an outsider. However, for the purposes of this analysis, we make a simple distinction between white and nonwhite respondents. We combine the two ethnic

Table 12.1   The Ethnic Match with the Authority

	White (N)	African American (N)	Hispanic (N)
Authority			
White	56% (326)	59% (330)	58% (295)
Nonwhite	35 (204)	34 (193)	36 (183)
Unknown	10 (56)	7 (38)	6 (31)
N (total)	(586)	(561)	(509)

Source: California study data.

Table 12.2   The Willingness of Respondents of Differing Ethnicity to Accept Decisions and Be Satisfied with the Decisionmaker

	White	African American	Hispanic
Beta weights			
The favorability of the outcome of the experience	.48***	.50***	.52***
Match	.09*	−.02	−.05
Total adjusted R-squared	24%	24%	27%

Source: California study data.
*p < .05.
***p < .001.

groups for ease of presentation, since separate analyses distinguishing between the two groups did not suggest any differences between them.[2]

With the sample combined into two ethnic groups, the majority of white respondents had a within-group interaction, since they dealt with a white authority 56 percent of the time. Most minority respondents had a between-group interaction: African Americans dealt with a white authority 59 percent of the time, and Hispanics did so 58 percent of the time.

As in previous chapters, we can test for the possible influence of ethnic group identification by including ethnic identification with outcome favorability in a regression equation linked to decision acceptance. Our concern is with whether ethnic group identification influences people's willingness to accept decisions separately from the favorability of those decisions. This analysis is shown in table 12.2. The results indicate that only whites appear to be affected by whether the authority is in their own ethnic group.

Although we are often concerned about the relationship between minority community residents and white police officers, the results of

Table 12.3   Interaction Effects, by Ethnicity

	White	African American	Hispanic
Beta weights			
Process issues	.78***	.86***	.79***
Outcome issues	.16***	.09**	.15**
Match	.01	−.02	.00
Match × process issues	.06*	−.01	.04
Match × outcome issues	−.03	.00	−.04
Total adjusted R-squared	80%	81%	78%

Source: California study data.
*p < .05.
**p < .01.
***p < .001.

this analysis suggest that only whites are influenced by the ethnicity of the police officer with whom they are dealing. Among minority group members, ethnicity match has no impact on whether people are willing to accept decisions. However, among whites, people are influenced by the ethnicity of the authority. Subgroup analysis suggests that whites are significantly more likely to accept decisions made by white police officers (mean = 3.09 for minority officers; 3.26 for white officers; t (528) = 2.04, p < .05; high scores indicate high acceptance).

We might further ask whether the basis of decision acceptance changes for within- and between-group interactions. Results of that analysis are shown in table 12.3. These results indicate that, again, only whites are influenced by the ethnicity of the police officer with whom they are dealing, and that in those cases there is a significant change in the weight given to process issues of procedural justice and motive-based trust. Separate subgroup analyses suggest that white community residents focus more strongly on whether minority police officers and judges are following fair procedures. No effect is found among minority group members, who are always primarily focused on process issues.

We can also look at whether the ethnicity match has an indirect influence on decision acceptance by shaping people's evaluations of their experiences. To explore this possibility, we looked at the correlations between match and judgments about personal experience within each ethnic group. These correlations are shown in table 12.4. As we would expect, minority group members are more likely to say that they lack social bonds with white police officers. Interestingly, whites are equally

Table 12.4   The Relationship Between Match and Judgments About Experience

	White	African American	Hispanic
Procedural justice	−.09*	−.02	−.09*
Motive-based trust	−.10*	−.03	−.15**
Quality of decision making	−.13**	−.05	−.11*
Quality of treatment	−.12**	−.02	−.10*
Actions understandable	−.08*	−.02	−.13**
Social bonds	.01	−.25***	−.21***

Source: California study data.
Note: Entries are Pearson correlations. Negative correlations indicate that people make more negative judgments following an experience with an authority who is not from their own group. For example, minority respondents are less likely to say that they have social bonds when dealing with a white legal authority.
*p < .05.
**p < .01.
***p < .001.

likely to feel that they have social bonds with white and with nonwhite police officers and judges.

Degree of Ethnic Group Identification

The second issue of interest is not group membership per se but ethnic group identification. We have already shown that people's identification with society (their community and the United States) influences the manner in which they deal with legal authorities. Does their identification with their ethnic group also shape their relationship to the law and to legal authorities? As we noted, people can engage in many types of self-categorizations (Turner et al. 1987).

People are potentially members of many different groups, and some of these groups may be a more important source of identity than others (Brewer 1991; Tajfel and Turner 1986). For example, when a person identifies with an ethnic subgroup included within a larger category (for example, as an Hispanic, but also as an American), the extent to which the person identifies with the larger category (American) versus the ethnic subgroup within it (Hispanic) should determine when relational concerns take precedence over instrumental concerns. When the authority is empowered by a societal group, an individual's perceptions of fairness and acceptance of decisions should turn on relational considerations to the extent that he or she identifies with the larger societal group more than with the ethnic subgroup. As identification with the subgroup becomes the primary self-categorization, disputes among those who belong to different subgroups take on the qualities of intergroup conflict (Brewer and Kramer 1986; Gaertner et al. 1994; Hornsey and Hogg 2000; Kramer 1991), and instrumental concerns should become more dominant in people's reactions to the decisions made by authorities.

In our earlier work (Huo et al. 1996), we found evidence consistent with this line of reasoning. Using an acculturation framework developed by Berry (1991), we identified three groups of individuals based on their responses to questions about their identification with society as well as their ethnic subgroup: assimilationist (high societal identification and low subgroup identification), separatist (low societal identification and high subgroup identification), and biculturalist (high societal and subgroup identifications). As predicted, we found that assimilationists were more concerned about the quality of their treatment and less concerned about whether they benefited from the decision. In addition, we found that separatists were less concerned about relational issues and more concerned about the outcome of the decision. Here we test the prediction that a relational approach hinges primarily on societal identification (something we have already shown) and is not affected by subgroup identification (something that we test here).

Measuring Subgroup Identification

In analyzing the California data, we measured subgroup identification using a measurement structure designed to correspond to the manner in which we measure identification with society. We used two scales: pride-identification and respect. One index explored people's feelings about the stature of their ethnic group and the degree to which they merged their sense of self with their membership in that group. The other index examined the degree to which each respondent felt that other members of their own ethnic group respected them. The frequencies are shown in table 12.5.

To determine whether an individual's connections to his or her ethnic group mattered when he or she was deciding whether to accept decisions, we conducted two types of analyses. First, we looked at whether subgroup identification directly influenced decision acceptance. We examined whether ethnic group identification influences decision acceptance and satisfaction with decision makers independently of the previously examined influence of societal identification. The results are shown in table 12.6. They suggest that ethnic identification had little independent direct influence. The only influence found involved African American respondents' pride in their ethnic group, which shaped their decision acceptance (beta = 0.10, $p < .05$). Those who felt more pride in their ethnic group were more willing to accept decisions, however, so there is no evidence of a *negative* effect of subgroup identification.

Table 12.5   Indices of Identification with Own Ethnic Group

	White	African-American	Hispanic
Pride in ethnic group			
Proud to be in the group	66%	99%	98%
What community stands for is important	47	95	97
Praise to group is compliment to me	24	88	92
Mean (standard deviation)	2.29	1.29	1.30
	(0.83)	(0.43)	(0.45)
Respect			
Respect my accomplishments	79%	94%	93%
Respect how I live my life	77	56	88
Respect my values	79	92	91
Mean (standard deviation)	2.06	1.51	1.63
	(0.67)	(0.59)	(0.65)
Identification			
Ethnicity is important to how			
I think of myself as a person	37%	86%	93%
Mean (standard deviation)	2.82	1.53	1.41
	(0.90)	(0.93)	(0.71)

Source: California study data.
Note: High means indicate low pride, low respect, and low identification.

Table 12.6   Influence of Ethnic Identification on Decision
Acceptance and Satisfaction with Decisionmaker

	White		African American		Hispanic	
Beta weights						
Outcome favorability	.48***	.49***	.47***	.49***	.50***	.52***
Ethnic pride and identification	.04	—	.10*	—	.06	—
Ethnic respect	—	−.01	—	.02	—	.00
Pride and identification– connection with society	.18***	—	.25***	—	.19**	—
Respect from society	—	.14**	—	.03	—	.05
Total adjusted R-squared	27%	25%	29%	24%	30%	27%

Source: California study data.
Note: High scores indicate that people are willing to accept the decision or are satisfied with the decision maker. High scores indicate a favorable decision and high levels of identification.
*p < .05.
**p < .01.
***p < .001.

Table 12.7   Influence of Ethnic Identification on the Basis on Which Decisions to Defer to Legal Authorities Are Made

	Interaction with Pride and Identification	Interaction with Respect
Beta weights		
Process issues	.86***	.85***
Outcome issues	.15***	.13***
Connection to ethnic group		
Pride-identification	−.01	—
Respect	—	−.01
Ethnic group connection		
× pride and identification	−.04	−.03
Ethnic group connection		
× respect	−.04	.00
Total adjusted R-squared	80%	81%

Source: California study data.
Note: The dependent variable is a joint evaluation of willingness to accept the decision and satisfaction with the decisionmaker.
***p < .001.

We also looked for evidence of interactions between ethnic identification and the basis on which people accept decisions. The results of such an interaction analysis are shown in table 12.7. We find no support for an ethnic identification effect on the basis on which people decided whether to defer to authorities.

Taken together, these findings support the argument that ethnic group identification is not generally an important influence on people's reactions to legal authorities. We find very few differences between the reactions of whites and minorities, and the differences found are small in magnitude. It seems that the reactions of all people are similar regardless of their ethnicity.

Does Experience Shape Ethnic Identification?

In previous chapters, we found that people's personal experiences shaped their societal orientations to some degree. Here we look at the impact of personal experience on subgroup identification. As we have noted, it is the subgroup identification of minority respondents that especially interests us. The findings of a regression analysis are quite striking. They suggest that personal experience had no influence on ethnic group identification. Combined indices of process and outcomes explained 0 percent of the variance in ethnic pride-identification among African Americans and 0 percent among Hispanics.

These findings reinforce the general argument that ethnic group identification is largely unrelated to personal experiences with the police and the courts. Although critics of multiculturalism warn of the divisiveness introduced by ethnic loyalties, this finding offers a more optimistic outlook for the viability of multicultural societies. It suggests that authorities can effectively regulate behavior and elicit cooperation even in environments where people exhibit great pride in and loyalty to their ethnic subgroup, since deference to authorities is linked to societal identification rather than ethnic subgroup identification.

These generally optimistic conclusions are tempered by recognition that minority group members have less positive societal orientations. Since societal orientations have an influence on decision acceptance, minority group members have more negative relationships with legal authorities. However, these problems are not linked to identification with their minority group.

PART V

IMPLICATIONS AND CONCLUSIONS

O UR DISCUSSION has focused on people's personal experiences with legal authorities, with the goal of understanding how police officers and judges might gain cooperation and consent for their decisions within the context of those interactions. We find that people are responsive to two social aspects of their experience with legal authorities—their feelings about the procedural justice of their experience and their trust in the motives of those authorities. Further, people's perceptions of justice and trust in the context of a personal encounter are linked to two process-based issues: the quality of the decision making and how well they are treated by the authorities. These findings lead to the argument that legal authorities should focus on *process-based regulation*—that is, on gaining cooperation by treating citizens well and being fair in their decision making.

It is also possible to conduct a parallel analysis on a more general level. Regardless of whether a person has had any personal experience with the police or the courts, they can still evaluate the performance of those authorities and the institutions they represent. Such general evaluations are similar to the measures of "trust and confidence" in the government evaluations collected by political scientists.

We explore public evaluations on this general level in chapter 13. The dataset in the California study was not designed to investigate this issue directly, so we use several other datasets for our analysis. Our goal is to establish the degree to which people consider issues of procedural justice and motive-based trust when they are making system-level evaluations of authorities and institutions, such as the police and the courts. Such system-level evaluations are important because they speak to the political feasibility of adopting the process-based approach to regulation that we advocate. If the general public does not care about process-based issues, it is hard to see how a process-based strategy could win broad political support.

In chapter 14, we discuss the application of process-based strategies to policing. Although policing is not the only form of social regulation, interactions with police are the most frequent way in which people encounter legal authorities. Further, many of the problems in the relationship between community residents and legal authorities center on reactions to the approach and tactics used by the police. For these reasons, we first direct our attention to issues of policing.

Chapter 15 summarizes our arguments for the value of a process-based approach to regulation. In it, we review our findings and outline their implications. We address two issues in particular. The key issue, and the focus of this book, is the ability to gain consent and cooperation from citizens through a process-based, rather than instrumental, approach. We argue that voluntary deference is linked primarily to feelings of procedural justice and motive-based trust, which authorities can enhance through the quality of their treatment and their decision making. This suggests that a process-based approach to regulation is viable.

Finally, in chapter 16, we move beyond the specific findings of the California study to the general issue of psychological jurisprudence. Our suggestion is that process-based regulation is only one of many areas in which the law and legal authorities would benefit from a better understanding of the psychology of the person. If legal authorities have an accurate view of what motivates people's deference to legal authorities, they are better able to act in ways that encourage cooperation and consent. The work presented in this book, in other words, is but one of many possible examples of the value of taking psychology seriously when developing and implementing the law.

Chapter 13

General Views About the Law and the Legal System

J UST AS it is often assumed that the outcomes that people receive when they deal with specific police officers and judges shape their reactions to those encounters, it is often believed that instrumental issues, such as the cost of going to court, court delays, or police performance in fighting crime, dominate the overall evaluations of legal institutions that are measured in public opinion polls. If true, this has important implications for the political viability of a process-based strategy. It suggests that the police and the courts face strong public opposition to the implementation of a fairness-based model, which might be perceived as weak on crime control or unrelated to the "real" issues of cost and delay in courts. (For a more detailed presentation of the findings presented in this chapter, see Tyler 2001f.)

In the case of the courts, a variety of instrumental concerns have been put forward in critiques of their operation. When people are litigants in civil court, they are believed to be unhappy about the costs of going to court and about the delays in getting their cases resolved (Tyler 1988, 1989, 1997a, 1998). Evaluations of criminal courts, primarily on the part of victims and their families, stress the nature of the decisions and the sentences imposed. According to these evaluations, too many guilty people go free and those who are convicted often receive sentences that are too lenient.

With evaluations of the police, a key instrumental focus is the ability of the police to fight crime. Police effectiveness in combating crime is a key concern not only of suburban residents, who fear the spread of crime, but of inner-city residents, who are the primary victims of crime. Surveys have shown that both groups of citizens, for their own reasons, strongly support those police actions that lower the level of crime.

Here we argue that, in contrast to what is often believed, public confidence in the police and the courts is not strongly linked to judgments about cost, delay, and performance. On the contrary, people's primary concerns on this general level are very similar to their concerns on a personal level. The issues that people care about most deeply when considering the police and the courts are whether these authorities treat people fairly, recognize citizen rights, treat people with dignity, and care about people's concerns. In other words, evaluations of the quality of the police and the courts are a reaction to views about how legal authorities deal with community residents. These findings are true of all community members, regardless of whether they are white or minority group members, and regardless of whether they live in a low- or high-crime area.

If true, this view of the public's concerns implies that a process-based model of regulation could be effective, since it would address the concerns found in general public evaluations of the police and the courts. However, we must ask an important question: To what degree would both minority and white respondents support the police and the courts as institutions because they treat people fairly? To answer this question we examined the ability of legal authorities to create and support the confidence of the general public through the perception of fairness in the behavior of those authorities.

Survey research data allowed us to examine the basis of public confidence in, and public support for, legal authorities. Such judgments are made by all respondents and influence their political support for the police and the courts. We examined the basis of such public support using four studies of general public evaluations of the police and the courts: the Chicago study, the 1997 Oakland study, the Hearst national survey, and a study conducted by the National Center for State Courts.

The Chicago Study

First, we considered the results of the study of Chicago residents described in earlier chapters (Tyler 1990). In that study a random sample of 1,575 respondents were interviewed about their confidence in and support for the Chicago police and courts. Three aspects of public views were explored: confidence, obligation, and help-seeking. Confidence reflected people's general evaluations of the quality of police and court performance. Obligation reflected the general willingness to accept legal rules and decisions. Help-seeking reflected the degree to which people indicated that they would bring relevant problems to the attention of the authorities.

In this study confidence was assessed using a ten-item scale. People were asked to indicate how good a job the police and courts were doing ("very good" to "very poor") and to indicate whether they: respected the police; thought the police were honest; felt proud of the police; felt they should support the police; thought the courts protected citizen rights; thought judges were honest; thought court decisions were fair; and thought the courts guaranteed everyone a fair trial. These items were combined to produce an overall index of confidence, or institutional trust, of the type already outlined (alpha = 0.86).

Feelings of obligation to accept rules and decisions were established through a four-item scale—again, of a type already outlined. Respondents were asked to agree or disagree with these statements: "People should obey the law even if it goes against what they think is right"; "I always try to follow the law even if I think it is wrong"; "Disobeying the law is seldom justified"; and, "It is difficult to break the law and keep one's self-respect" (alpha = 0.59).

Help-seeking was indexed through respondents' indications of the likelihood that they would seek help from the police or the courts in several relevant situations: if their home had been burglarized; if they had a complaint against a neighbor; to resolve a neighborhood dispute; in an emergency; to report suspicious neighborhood activity; to protest an unfair ticket; to handle a small claims dispute. These items were combined into an index of help-seeking (alpha = 0.61).

Our concern is with why people have favorable or unfavorable reactions to the police or the courts. We considered two possible antecedents of such reactions: people's views about the competence of the police or the courts, and their views about the quality of the treatment they receive from these authorities. The questions we considered focus on general assessments of how legal authorities treat community residents, not on respondents' views about how they personally have been treated, or will be treated, by those authorities.

Competence was assessed using a four-item scale that indexed how often the police provided satisfactory service when called, how often the police handled stops of community residents satisfactorily, and how well the courts solved problems (two questions; alpha = 0.61). Quality of treatment was determined using a four-item scale. That scale reflected how fairly the police treated people (two questions) and how fairly the courts treated people (two questions; overall four-item scale; alpha = 0.72).

In this study the findings were that both judgments about the quality of police service and judgments about how fairly the police treat community residents have an impact on residents' overall evaluations of the quality of the legal authorities (see table 13.1). Together, the two judgments explained 59 percent of the variance in confidence in legal authorities. The primary influence was from quality of treatment (beta = 0.49), with a lesser influence of competence (beta = 0.28). Obligation to obey the law was similarly influenced by quality of treatment (beta = 0.17),

Table 13.1   Evaluations of Legal Authorities by Chicago Residents

	All Respondents	Whites	Minority Group Members
Evaluations of legal authorities (confidence–institutional trust) Beta weights			
Quality of service (competence)	.28***	.29***	.28***
Quality of treatment (fairness)	.49***	.51***	.47***
Race	–.02	—	—
Total adjusted R-squared	59%	55%	50%
Obligation to obey the law Beta weights			
Quality of service (competence)	.02	.08	–.04
Quality of treatment (fairness)	.17***	.17***	.17**
Race	.08***	—	—
Total adjusted R-squared	3%	5%	2%
Seeking legal help Beta weights			
Quality of service (competence)	.05	.07	.04
Quality of treatment (fairness)	.16***	.16***	.16***
Race	.18***	—	—
Total adjusted R-squared	6%	4%	4%

Source: Reanalysis of data from Tyler (1990).
Note: Beta weights reflect the relative influence of each factor in the equation. The adjusted R-square indicates how much of the variance in the dependent variable is explained by all of the judgments considered together.
**$p < .01$.
***$p < .001$.

but not by competence (beta = 0.02, n.s.). Finally, help-seeking was influenced by quality of treatment (beta = 0.16), but not by competence (beta = 0.05).

A separate subgroup analysis among the white and minority group members' interviews suggested that both groups placed essentially the same weight on quality of treatment when evaluating their confidence in legal authorities and their obligation to obey the law and when determining whether to seek the help of legal authorities.

These findings suggested that all Chicago residents—both white and minority—were very concerned about how the police generally treated people. They did not make their evaluations of the police primarily in terms of police effectiveness in solving particular community problems.

Instead, residents were strongly influenced by whether they believed that the police and the courts treated people with respect, dignity, and fairness and did not harass them or subject them to rude or inappropriate treatment.

The 1997 Oakland Sample

In a separate study of residents of Oakland conducted during the spring of 1997, Tyler and Canelo-Cocho (1999) focused on the residents of high-crime and predominantly minority areas of Oakland. Mail-return questionnaires were completed by a random sample of 346 people living in selected high-crime areas of Oakland comprising eight police beats. The sample was 68 percent African American, 11 percent Hispanic, 11 percent white, and 11 percent "other."

Sixteen percent of the surveys mailed to residents' homes were returned. There was no random selection of respondents within households—any adult within each household was invited to complete and return the questionnaire. As a consequence, the findings of this study do not reflect the views of a random sample of the residents of the areas studied, or of the city of Oakland. The respondents were most likely to be those who held the strongest views about the police. The responding population was older (the average age was fifty-four) than that of the census tracts studied, and more predominantly female (58 percent).

Respondents were also likely to be those who had had personal contact with the police: 57 percent indicated that they had called the police in the past year, 8 percent that the police had stopped them on the street, and 21 percent that the police had stopped them in their cars. Altogether, 65 percent of those interviewed had had personal contact with the police during the year prior to completing the questionnaire.

The questionnaires were completed during a period of very aggressive policing activities designed to suppress gangs and control gun-related crimes in Oakland. Some of the questionnaires came from areas that the police had targeted for such activities, and others did not. The survey included questions to assess police performance in terms of the impact that the public thought the police were having on the crime rate. Respondents were also asked about the quality of the treatment that the public received from the police.

To establish police performance, respondents were asked whether the level of crime had "increased, decreased, or stayed about the same" during the prior year. These judgments reflected their views about the influence of policing on the crime rate. Respondents were also asked to report how well the police were controlling four types of crime: "violent crime," "gangs," "drugs," and "gun violence." The goal of some other questions was to estimate the magnitude of four potential neighborhood problems: shootings and violence by gangs, drug dealing in the streets, gangs trying to take over the neighborhood, and people being attacked or robbed. Finally, respondents evaluated the effectiveness of the police in controlling each of the following types of crime over the past year: violent crime, gangs, drugs, and gun violence.

Five questions asked respondents about their fear of being victimized by crime: "How safe do you feel in your neighborhood?"; "How safe do you think it is to walk around your neighborhood at night?"; "How safe do you think it is for people to run businesses within your community?"; "How much do you worry about having your home burglarized?"; and, "How much do you worry about being the victim of a robbery or an assault in your neighborhood?"

Respondents were also asked how well they thought the police treated residents. These questions used an index of police character, judgments about the degree to which the police were trying to solve community problems, judgments about police intentions, and an evaluation of the degree to which the police harassed or belittled members of the public. Respondents were asked whether they agreed or disagreed with these statements: "The police respect your basic rights"; "The police are generally honest"; "The police treat all citizens in the neighborhood equally"; "Your rights are well respected by the police"; and, "The police are trying to make your neighborhood a safer place to live." Respondents were also asked how often they saw police officers in their neighborhood. Additional items with which respondents were asked to agree or disagree were: "The police listen to your views before deciding how to handle problems"; "The police usually treat citizens with respect"; and, "The police are concerned about your problems." Finally, respondents were asked to rate how significant the following problems were for their neighborhood: police stopping people on the streets without good reason; police being too tough on the people they stopped; police being rude to members of the public; and police using ethnic slurs against members of the public.

Evaluations of the Police

Tyler and Canelo-Cocho (1999) used these specific judgments about police behavior and performance to explain people's general evaluations of the police. In particular, they explored the impact of respondents' judgments on two evaluative indices: their evaluation of the quality of police services, and their willingness to pay higher taxes to support the police. They created an index of overall evaluation of the police and police services by combining a rating of job performance ("excellent" to "poor") and agreement or disagreement with the statement that "the police do their jobs well."

In the second index respondents were asked whether they would agree to pay higher taxes to support the police. Two questions were asked: "How willing would you be to pay six dollars per month to support fifteen hours per week of intensified police activity targeted at street-level drug dealing in your neighborhood?"; and, "How willing would you be to pay one dollar per month to support fifteen hours per week of intensified policy activity targeted at street-level drug dealing in those neighborhoods in Oakland where drug crime is most prevalent?"

This study was testing the argument that people distinguish between two basic aspects of policing: police performance in combating crime, and the quality of their treatment of members of the public. To test this argument the indices already outlined were factor-analyzed. The results suggested that respondents' judgments were based on two factors: performance (factor 1) and quality of treatment (factor 2).

Regression analysis was used to examine the influence of performance evaluations and judgments about the quality of treatment on people's evaluations of the police. The results are shown in table 13.2. These results indicate that quality-of-treatment assessments dominated people's performance evaluations of the police. The quality of treatment indices uniquely explained 26 percent of the variance in evaluations of the police, while performance evaluations uniquely explained 5 percent of the variance in evaluations of the police. Judgments about quality of treatment also had a greater effect on people's willingness to pay more taxes, uniquely explaining 6 percent of the variance, as opposed to the 1 percent of the variance uniquely explained by performance judgments.

When making evaluations, people focused most strongly on their inferences about the character of the police—whether they respected people's rights, were honest, and treated all people equally. When deciding whether they would provide additional funds for the police, people also focused more strongly on how the police treated members of the public. If they did not see the police as making an effort, people did not support additional police funding (beta = 0.23, p < .001). In addition, people were influenced by their evaluations linked to performance issues, including their fear of crime, their judgments about police effectiveness, and their views about the size of the crime problem in their neighborhood. However, performance judgments did not have the same impact on respondents as did quality-of-treatment judgments. In the case of paying higher taxes, quality of treatment explained 6 percent of the additional variance, and performance only 1 percent. That is, support in this study was primarily linked to judgments about how the police treated people, not to whether they were effective in controlling crime.

Table 13.2   Antecedents of Evaluation in the Oakland High-Crime Study

	Evaluations of the Police	"Would You Give More Money to Support More Police Services?"
Beta weights		
Performance		
Fear of crime	.10*	.09
Crime rate change	.07	.02
Police controlling crime?	−.03	.04
Magnitude of crime problem	−.12*	.08
Effectiveness of police efforts	−.05	.22**
Quality of treatment		
Character of police	.17***	.00
Trying?	.07	.23***
Do the police care?	.16**	.06
Do the police harass people?	.44***	.05
Total adjusted R-squared		
Unique influence of performance	5%	1%
Unique influence of the quality		
of treatment	26	6
Total	66	8

Source: Tyler and Canelo-Cocho (1999).
**p < .01.
***p < .001.

Personal Experiences in the 1997 Oakland Study

The 1997 Oakland study also included questions about personal experiences with the police. All respondents were asked whether they had called the police for help, had been stopped by the police on the street, or had been stopped by the police in their car during the year prior to the interview. Sixty-five percent (N = 224) indicated having had one contact. Of that group, 56 percent said that they received a satisfactory outcome, 72 percent said that the police used fair procedures, and 75 percent reported being fairly treated by the police.

The influence of judgments about the favorability of the outcome of a personal experience was compared to the impact of people's judgments about the fairness and quality of their treatment. This analysis showed that public evaluations of the police were shaped by both of the types of experience-based judgments we have outlined, with quality of treatment having a stronger influence than outcome favorability (beta = 0.37, p < .001, for quality of treatment; beta = 0.26, p < .001, for outcome favorability). These experience-based judgments explained 34 percent of the variance in overall police evaluations. Experience-based judgments also influenced the willingness to provide funding for additional police activities (overall R-squared = 11 percent, p < .001). In this case, quality of treatment influenced the willingness to support the police (beta = 0.36, p < .001), but outcome favorability did not (beta = −0.02, n.s.).

These findings about the influence of personal experience with the police should be treated with considerable caution, since no information was collected about the details of people's experiences. However, the findings are consistent with the results of other studies reviewed here, which also show that the key issue shaping people's reactions to personal experiences is the fairness of those experiences and the quality of the treatment they feel they received from the police. The favorability of the outcome is a secondary consideration. Further, general support for the police and additional policing activities is most strongly linked to process-based concerns—both in personal experiences and in evaluations of the broader police-community relationship.

Hearst National Survey on the Courts

During the winter of 1999 the Hearst National Survey on the Courts conducted telephone interviews with a random sample of 1,826 people.[1] The interviews focused on people's views about the American courts—in particular, their views of local and state courts. Those interviewed represented a random sample of 1,200 Americans, with an additional sample of African Americans and Hispanics.[2]

We divided the questions asked of those interviewed into three clusters: questions about group-based distributive justice, questions about the quality of people's treatment by the courts, and questions about court performance.

Group-based distributive justice questions were asked to determine how people felt about the relative experience of members of different social groups. These questions were based on the argument that the members of various groups should all receive equal treatment by the courts (distributive justice). People were asked to indicate whether they felt that, when dealing with the courts, each of a series of groups received better treatment, the same treatment, or worse treatment than others. The argument underlying this approach was that the key to discontent with institutions is fraternal deprivation—unequal treatment of groups (see Walker and Smith 2002).

The groups presented to respondents were: "people like you," "men," "women," "African Americans," "Hispanics," "non-English-speaking people," "middle-class people," "working-class people," and "wealthy people." In our analysis of this data, we folded the rating scales (so that "better" was equal to "worse"), with the result that one end of the scale represented the belief that the courts treat everyone equally and do not favor any of these groups, and the other end represented the view that some groups receive unequal treatment. We combined the folded fairness ratings for the nine groups into a single overall index of group-based distributive fairness (alpha = 0.86).

Respondents were also asked about five items that index the quality of the treatment that people receive from the courts: "The courts protect defendants' rights"; "Judges are generally honest and fair"; "Court rulings are understood by the people involved in cases"; "The courts make an effort to ensure that people have adequate attorney representation"; and, "Court personnel are helpful and courteous." We combined these items into an overall index of court treatment (alpha = 0.61).

Respondents were then asked about six items that measured the quality of court performance: "Judges do not give adequate attention to each case"; "Courts are out of touch with what is going on in their communities"; "Courts do not make sure that their orders are enforced"; "If a person sues a corporation, the courts favor the corporation"; "Judges' decisions are influenced by political considerations"; and, "Elected judges are influenced by having to raise campaign funds." We combined these items into an overall index of quality of job performance (alpha = 0.68).

Respondents were also asked about four items to index cost judgments: "How much do court fees contribute to the cost of going to court?"; "How much does the slow pace of justice contribute to the cost of going to court?"; "How much does the complexity of the law contribute to the cost of going to court?"; and, "How much does the amount of personal time required contribute to the cost of going to court?" We combined these items into one overall index of costs (alpha = 0.68).

Court Evaluations

We assessed people's evaluations of the courts in two ways. First, we used people's overall evaluations of "their level of confidence in the courts" in their local community. Overall, 23 percent of the respondents who expressed a view indicated having a great deal of confidence in their local courts; 52 percent had some confidence; 17 percent had only a little confidence; and 8 percent had no confidence at all.[3]

Performance ratings were also collected during the study. Respondents were asked to indicate whether the courts did an excellent, good, fair, or poor job handling five types of cases: civil (53 percent said performance was excellent or good); criminal (51 percent excellent or good); small claims (53 percent excellent or good); family relations (43 percent excellent or good); and juvenile delinquency (35 percent excellent or good). We combined these five ratings into an overall performance rating (alpha = 0.80).

Analysis

The results of a factor analysis support the separation of quality of treatment from performance measures. That factor analysis is shown in table 13.3. It indicates that people do not distinguish between structural problems and cost considerations, two elements that were measured separately. As a result, these two aspects of court performance were combined to form one factor. However, issues of group-based outcome fairness and quality of treatment form distinct factors.

We used regression analyses to examine the influence of the four factors outlined—group-based distributive fairness, quality of treatment, quality of performance, and cost—on evaluations and performance ratings of the courts. In addition, since the factor analysis suggests that people do not distinguish between structural performance problems and cost issues, we also conducted these analyses using a combined index of cost and performance problems. The results of the analysis are shown in table 13.4.

The results of our regression analysis indicate that, however we measure issues of performance, the primary influence on overall evaluations and overall ratings of performance is the quality of the courts' treatment of members of the public and, through judgments about the fairness of the outcomes produced by the courts—that is, the degree to which they treat all groups similarly—the quality of the treatment they provide to members of the public.

In the case of evaluations, for example, these two fairness judgments—fair outcomes and fair procedures—uniquely explained 16 percent of the variance in evaluations, while overall performance assessments uniquely explained 3 percent.

With overall performance ratings, fairness of outcomes and quality of treatment uniquely explained 15 percent of the variance in overall performance ratings, while performance assessments uniquely explained 3 percent. If we ignore the factor analysis and treat performance as reflecting two indices, we see similar results.

When we consider the relative influence of the different factors, it is clear that the primary concern shaping public evaluations of the courts

Table 13.3   Factor Analysis in the Hearst National Survey on the Courts

	Distributive Justice	Performance	Quality of Treatment
Unequal men	.59	—	—
Unequal women	.57	—	—
Unequal African Americans	.71	—	—
Unequal Hispanics	.73	—	—
Unequal non-English speakers	.62	—	—
Unequal middle-class	.58	—	—
Unequal working-class	.60	—	—
Unequal wealthy	.49	—	—
Unequal "those like you"	.60	—	—
Rights are protected	—	—	.58
Judges honest and fair	—	—	.65
Decisions understandable	—	—	.39
Adequate representation	—	—	.43
Staff helpful and courteous	—	—	.32
Inadequate attention to cases	—	.42	—
Out of touch with community	—	.45	—
Orders not enforced	—	.35	—
Corporations favored	—	.44	—
Politics influences actions	—	.59	—
Influenced by political contributions	—	.52	—
Court fees hurt	—	.42	—
Slow pace hurts	—	.55	—
Legal complexity hurts	—	.52	—
Costs of lost income going to court hurts	—	.45	—

Source: Authors' compilation.
Note: Maximum likelihood estimation and varimax rotation were used. All loadings over 0.30 are shown.

is the assessment of how well the courts treat members of the public. This factor is more important than evaluations of outcome fairness, assessments of structural problems in the courts, and evaluations of the costs of litigation.

Personal Experience

Analysis of data from the Hearst survey suggests that people with prior personal experience with the courts are less concerned about performance issues and more concerned about quality of treatment when they evaluate the courts. This finding is consistent with the view that people who have not been to court and personally experienced rude or unfair treat-

Table 13.4   Factors Shaping Views About the Courts

	Total Performance Independent Variables		Two Performance Independent Variables	
	Evaluation	Performance	Evaluation	Performance
Beta weights				
Treatment of people				
Fairness of outcomes	.12***	.12***	.12***	.11***
Quality of treatment	.35***	.33***	.35***	.33***
Performance				
Structural problems	—	—	.14***	.19***
Costs of litigation	—	—	.07*	.00
Total performance	.17***	.16***	—	—
Adjusted R-squared				
Unique effect of treatment	16%	15%	15%	14%
Unique effect of performance	3	3	3	4
Total	22	20	22	21

Source: Authors' compilation.
*p < .05.
***p < .001.

ment tend to view quality of treatment as less important than those who have been personally affected. Instead, those without personal experience focus more heavily on more abstract policy issues related to the courts.

These findings are consistent with those of a study of the Utah state courts conducted by Olson and Huth (1998). That study was based on telephone interviews with 602 Utah residents. It found that the primary factor shaping opinions about whether the courts were doing a good job was the respondent's evaluation of court fairness (partial correlation = 0.28). As in the Hearst study, evaluations of the cost and difficulty of using the courts were less strongly related to evaluations (partial correlation = −.08), as were judgments about whether proceedings and delays were unreasonably long and court trials too inefficient (partial correlation = −.15).

Further, personal experiences with the Utah state courts made a "dramatic difference" (Olson and Huth 1998, 54) in the basis on which people evaluated the courts (59 percent had had some type of court experience). The results of the Utah analysis suggest that those with court experience placed more weight on fairness when evaluating the courts (partial correlation = 0.30, as opposed to 0.19 for those without experience). The results of the Hearst analysis support this finding by suggesting that the quality of a court's treatment of people is more central to court evaluations among those who have had personal experience with the courts.

Ethnic Group Analysis

We can also divide the Hearst sample by ethnic group membership and perform separate analyses within each major ethnic group.[4] When we conduct separate subgroup analyses, we find that African American respondents were especially likely to be influenced by their judgments about whether the courts treated different groups unfairly. Hispanics and whites were especially likely to be affected by their judgments about the quality of the treatment that people received from the courts. The strongest impact of performance assessments was found among whites, who were affected by their judgments concerning the structural problems in the courts. None of the groups seemed particularly influenced by cost-related evaluations. However, all ethnic groups placed their primary emphasis on issues of quality of treatment rather than on performance assessments or outcome fairness judgments.

The National Center for State Courts Survey

We can test the generality of the Hearst findings by comparing them to the results of a more recent survey conducted for the National Center for State Courts. Conducted during the spring of 2000, this study focused on public evaluations of local courts. The study was based on telephone interviews conducted by the University of Indiana Public Opinion Laboratory. The total sample included 1,567 respondents selected from a national sample, using a stratified sampling approach that led to an oversample of minority residents. The findings we report were not based on a weighting framework that made response frequencies representative of a national sample of respondents, although such weighting would have been possible.

Respondents were asked to evaluate the local courts by responding to six items: "How would you rate how you feel in general about the courts in your community?"; "How do the courts in your community handle: . . . criminal cases involving violence?"; ". . . criminal cases involving drug abusers and drunk drivers?"; "... civil cases, such as auto accidents and medical malpractice claims?"; "... family relations cases, such as divorce, child custody, etc.?"; and, "... juvenile delinquency cases?" We combined these evaluations into an overall evaluative index (alpha = 0.86).

We next considered three factors that might shape respondents' evaluations. Our analysis assessed performance by looking at ratings of whether "cases are resolved in a timely manner"; whether "it is affordable to bring a case into court"; and whether "the courts make decisions based on facts." From these items we formed a performance index (alpha = 0.63). We measured discrimination by considering whether or not the members of four groups received equal treatment: African Americans, Hispanics, non-English speakers, and people with low incomes. We combined these items into a single discrimination index (alpha = 0.86).

Finally, we assessed the fairness of treatment by asking respondents whether "the courts are concerned with people's rights"; whether "the courts treat people with dignity and respect"; whether "the courts treat people politely"; whether "judges are honest"; whether "courts take the needs of people into account"; whether "courts listen carefully to what people have to say"; and whether "the courts are sensitive to the concerns of the average citizen." We used these items to create an overall quality of treatment index (alpha = 0.88).

We used regression analysis to test the role of performance, discrimination, and quality of treatment in shaping evaluations of the courts. The results are shown in table 13.5. They support the suggestion that the key antecedent to evaluations of the courts is the judgment about how the courts treat members of the public. That judgment has more influence than either evaluations of the degree of discrimination or performance evaluations.

We can further examine the antecedents of evaluations by dividing the sample of people into groups based on their experience: those with recent personal experience (in the last year; 594 respondents); those with past personal experience, but not recent personal experience (295 respondents); and those with no past personal experience (578 respondents). A subgroup regression among the members of each group supports our earlier argument that those with recent personal experience rely most heavily on process evaluations to make their judgments about the courts. Those who have never personally been to court place the least weight on how they think people are generally treated by the courts, relative to the weight given to treatment by those with recent personal experience. However, they still give this factor more weight than either discrimination or performance. Those with past, but not recent, personal experience fall in the middle in terms of their attention to quality-of-treatment issues.

Table 13.5   Determinants of Evaluations of the Courts

	Evaluations of the Courts	
	Without Demographic Controls	With Demographic Controls
Beta weights		
Quality of court treatment of litigants	.34***	.35***
Discrimination by the courts	.08**	.06*
Performance of the courts	.18***	.18***
Demographics		
Hispanic (yes or no)	—	-.01
African American (yes or no)	—	-.05
Gender	—	.02
Income	—	-.04
Education	—	-.02
Age	—	.05*
Total adjusted R-squared	26%	27%

Source: Authors' compilation.
*p < .05.
**p < .01.
***p < .001.

We can also divide the respondents in the study by their self-reported membership in one of three major ethnic groups: whites, African Americans, and Hispanics (ignoring a small group of respondents from other groups—for example, Asians). The sample contained 815 whites, 404 African Americans, and 304 Hispanics. A subgroup analysis using the members of each group indicates that all groups relied primarily on their judgments about the quality of the treatment that people received when making court evaluations.

Of course, we do not want to overstate the case. Performance does matter. However, among all the ethnic groups considered, performance was less important than judgments about quality of treatment. These findings, therefore, support the view that, when making general evaluations of the police and the courts, people are primarily concerned about the quality of the treatment that they think these institutions provide to the public.

As we noted, 594 of the respondents interviewed in the National Center for State Courts survey had appeared in a local court during the year prior to the interview. The study asked people to make judgments about their experience. Procedural justice was assessed by agreement with the statement: "Fair procedures were used to make decisions about how to handle the situation." Trust was assessed by agreement with these five statements: "My views were considered"; "The judge and court staff did *not* care about my concerns (reversed)"; "Differing views of people were taken into account"; "The needs of people were *not* taken into account (reversed)"; and, "My rights were taken into account." We combined these five items into a single index of trust (alpha = 0.89). We measured outcome fairness by agreement with the statement: "The outcome of those procedures was fair."

We used these judgments as predictors in an analysis focused on future-oriented judgments, which we measured by asking respondents whether, "if you appeared in a court" in the future, "the judge would treat you fairly" and "you would receive a fair outcome." We also asked them whether, if they were to have another problem similar to the one that had taken them to court in the past, they would go to court in the future.

The results of a regression analysis indicate that process judgments dominated the impact of personal experience on future expectations and on estimates of the likelihood of going to court in the future. First, whether people thought they would receive either a fair outcome or be treated fairly in the future was primarily determined by whether they said that they had been treated fairly, and whether they had trusted the authorities, during their past encounter. Second, whether people said that they would go to court in the future was primarily determined by whether they had been fairly treated and had trusted the authorities when they went to court in the past. Thus, people's reaction to their experience is shaped largely by whether they think that they have been fairly treated by trustworthy authorities.

When we combined the three indices of expected future behavior into an overall index of future orientation toward the court, we found that the best predictor of future orientation is past trust and procedural fairness. When we used trust and outcome fairness to explain future orientation, the primary factor was trust (beta = 0.63, p < .001), followed by outcome fairness (beta = 0.16, p < .001). Together they explained 52 percent of the variance in future orientation. When we used procedural justice and outcome fairness to explain future orientation, the primary factor was procedural justice (beta = 0.53, p < .001), followed by outcome fairness (beta = 0.23, p < .001). Together they explained 45 percent of the variance in future orientation. When we used all three factors at the same time, the primary influence was trust (beta = 0.48, p < .001), procedural justice was second (beta = 0.22, p < .001), and outcome fairness was least important (beta = 0.13, p < .001). The three factors explained 54 percent of the variance in future orientation.

It is striking that although trust and procedural justice were highly correlated (r = 0.74), each explained significant independent variance in future orientations. This finding supports the suggestion made earlier, using the data from interviews conducted in California, that trust and procedural justice, while related, have distinct psychologies. As in that earlier analysis, two distinct but interrelated influences were found.

When we examined the factors that shape evaluations among the members of major ethnic groups more closely, we found that the findings remained consistent across ethnic groups: the primary determinant of future behavior was the fairness experienced in the past. This was true for whites, African Americans, and Hispanics.

To determine what people mean by "fair treatment" in their personal experience, we examined responses to a series of questions that assessed four key elements of procedural fairness: trust in the authorities, neutrality, treatment with respect, and opportunity to participate.

Neutrality was measured by asking respondents to agree or disagree with these statements: "Judges were neutral in the way people were treated"; "A person's race or ethnic group made no difference in how the courts treated them"; "The court staff was neutral in the way people were treated"; "I was treated the same as everyone else"; "Decisions were made based on facts"; and, "My race or ethnic group made a difference in how I was treated (reversed)." We combined these items into an index of neutrality (alpha = 0.70).

Treatment with respect was measured by asking respondents to agree or disagree with these statements: "People were treated politely"; "Court staff showed concern for people's rights"; "People were treated with dignity and respect"; "I was treated politely"; "I was treated with dignity and respect"; and, "Judges did not show concern for people's rights (reversed)." We combined these items into an index of treatment with respect (alpha = 0.92).

We measured participation by asking for agree-disagree responses to these statements: "I was able to say what was on my mind"; "I was able to make my views known"; and, "The court did not give people an opportunity to tell their side of the story (reversed)." We combined these items into an index of participation, process control, or voice (alpha = 0.83).

Table 13.6 shows a regression analysis that examined the antecedents of procedural justice and trust judgments among those who knew, and did not know, their outcomes. The results suggest that the primary factors shaping people's evaluations of the procedural justice of their experience with the courts are process-based assessments. In particular, people place the greatest weight on whether the authorities are neutral. In addition, they are influenced by whether they are treated with respect. When the outcome is not known, treatment with respect is espe-

Table 13.6   Antecedents of Assessments of Fair Procedure and of Trust
When the Outcome Is Known and When It Is Not

Judgments About Personal Experience	Total	Outcome Is Known (N = 511)	Outcome Is Not Known (N = 147)
Influences on judgments of procedural justice			
Beta weights			
"The authorities acted neutrally."	.42***	.48***	.18
"I was treated with dignity and respect."	.32***	.31***	.38***
"I had an opportunity to speak."	.06	.03	.20
"The outcome was fair."	.07*	.06	.12
Adjusted R-squared	62%	63%	56%
Influences on judgments of trust			
Beta weights			
"The authorities acted neutrally."	.23***	.25***	.15
"I was treated with dignity and respect."	.39***	.34***	.54***
"I had an opportunity to speak."	.30***	.36***	.12
"The outcome was fair."	.06*	.04	.15*
Total adjusted R-squared	76%	79%	69%

Source: Authors' compilation.
*$p < .05$.
***$p < .001$.

cially important. When the outcome is known, neutrality is especially important.

People's judgments about their trust in the legal authority with whom they dealt were influenced by respect, voice, and neutrality. When people knew their outcome, they relied on respect, voice, and neutrality. When they did not know their outcome, they relied primarily on respect.

Interestingly, there are ethnic group differences in how people define a fair procedure. Whites and African Americans rely on trust, neutrality, and treatment with respect, while Hispanics focus heavily on evidence of neutrality. However, all of the people interviewed focused most heavily on questions of procedure and process, including the questions of trust that have been central to our discussion. The fairness of past outcomes had little to do with procedural fairness judgments among any ethnic group.

Summary

These findings suggest that a process-based approach to regulation is viable. People's evaluations of the police and the courts are not predominantly linked to performance-based judgments such as the cost or speed of litigation. Instead, people's main consideration when evaluating the police and the courts is the treatment that they feel people receive from those authorities.

In discussions of regulation it is often suggested that reforms of the type advocated here are politically unrealistic because the public evaluates legal authorities and the political authorities who manage them in terms of their success in fighting crime. In New York City, for example, the success that aggressive policing is believed to have had in causing the crime rate to decline is often cited as one of the primary justifications for such tactics.

It is beyond the scope of this book to address the relationship between aggressive policing and the crime rate. It has been argued that the crime rate is controlled by other factors and would have declined in New York City regardless of the actions of the police. On the other hand, it has also been suggested that changes in the style of policing used in the city had a dramatic impact on the crime rate. In either event, the widespread belief that aggressive policing lowered the rate of crime in New York created a political argument in favor of such policing tactics and the accompanying actions by court officials.

Our point is that, contrary to this belief, the public does not evaluate the police and the courts by focusing primarily on either the impact of such institutions on the rate of crime or other instrumental issues such as delay or cost. Instead, people base their judgments on how well the police and the courts treat the public.

Of course, outcome issues are not irrelevant to people's evaluations of legal authorities. We consistently find that they do have an influence. However, they are very far from being the only decisive factor in such evaluations, as is often suggested by the media and by political officials. Interestingly, even the members of high-crime and minority communities focus heavily on how they think legal authorities treat people.

These studies further find that those members of the public who have had personal experience with the police or the courts focus even more heavily on issues of quality of treatment. Prior dealings with legal authorities, in other words, lead people to give greater attention to the quality-of-treatment issue when evaluating those authorities. Consistent with our argument, having had a personal experience with a legal authority changes how an individual thinks about those authorities and about the institutions associated with them. When making general evaluations of legal authorities and institutions subsequent to a personal experience, people are more strongly influenced by their perceptions of treatment quality and less strongly influenced by their judgments about the outcomes they received.

Within their personal experiences, the respondents in these surveys followed the predictions of our process-based perspective and reacted to their experiences by judging the quality of their personal treatment by legal authorities. These respondents, in other words, acted as we hypothesize that members of the public will generally act—focusing primarily on how they are treated by legal authorities rather than on their outcomes.

Overall, the findings of these studies suggest support for the process-based perspective being advocated here. We found that in their general evaluation of the police and the courts, people were very sensitive to their own perceptions of the quality of treatment that community members received from these legal institutions. When they felt that legal authorities were polite and respectful, sincere and concerned for their rights, and did not harass community residents, they were more supportive of the law and legal authorities.

Chapter 14

Implications for Policing

THIS BOOK is not only about policing. Members of the public deal with both the police and the courts. However, as the findings of the studies reviewed suggest, police officers are the legal authority with whom people most frequently interact in their everyday lives. Further, many of the problems that have recently dominated discussion about the relationship between the public and legal authorities have been policing problems. Although the courts also exercise authority over the public, the police are especially likely to control people through the threat or application of force and are a natural focus of public hostility and resistance. Therefore, many of the implications of this research are especially relevant to the police and to policing practices.

Our results suggest that legal authorities have something to gain by adopting policing strategies that incorporate the process-based model.[1] More willing acceptance of a police officer's decisions in personal encounters, greater satisfaction with the police officer following the encounter, and a more favorable long-term view of the police as an institution are some of the gains we have discussed. Achieving these gains, however, would require integrating the concepts of the process-based model into policing strategies and, to some degree, reconceptualizing how police officers interact with the public.

Currently, the police often, but certainly not always, approach members of the public with a "force" or "control" orientation. They do so with two goals in mind: protecting themselves from injury or death, and controlling people in an effort to make arrests, stop illegal behavior, and otherwise suppress crime.

The police use a "command and control" strategy to achieve these objectives: they establish and maintain control over people and places through a show of force—and if necessary, the use of force. To this end, police officers carry nightsticks, mace, and guns. As has been discussed, members of the public may experience shows of force as confrontational, abusive, disrespectful, or unfair. As a consequence of how people experience this type of policing, such approaches may ultimately be damaging to the goals of the police.

The command and control strategy is one of the dominant models for how many police officers approach their jobs. However, it is important not to exaggerate the importance of command and control as a policing practice. There is considerable variation among police officers in their acceptance of command and control styles of exercising authority. In addition, ours is not the first discussion of policing that focuses on these issues. Muir (1977), for example, outlined the variety of philosophies behind the actions of the police officers he interviewed, four of which he presented in depth. Officer Justice used fear, saying, "You can't do much when they don't fear the law. . . . Coercion was essential to gaining control of individuals who were otherwise ungovernable" (20). In contrast, Officer Ingersoll "thought the policeman was obligated to help the individual, to cure him, to treat him solely as an end, never as a means" (31). Muir concluded: "The four [officers] had opposing conceptions about the means of coercion. [Two] were comfortable using coercive means to manipulate others. . . . [Two others] were uncomfortable with coercion. They knew of few, if any circumstances under which force could produce good results. They would rather deal with people than dominate them" (35).

Self-Protection

The police focus on their personal safety for obvious reasons. To minimize risk they always attempt to stay ahead on the "force curve"—that is, they use a higher level of force than the people with whom they are dealing. This approach has the benefit of allowing police officers to protect themselves. However, the hidden risks of this kind of focus on power and control also have an impact on officer safety.

By focusing on issues of power and control, the police are defining their interactions with members of the public in a certain way. Unfortunately, a power orientation in a personal encounter can lead to an increasing spiral of conflict. When conflict escalates irrationally into a test of dominance and power, people lose sight of their objective goals and become invested in "winning" the conflict (Pruitt and Carnevale 1993; Pruitt and Rubin 1986). A control approach encourages such spirals by provoking hostility and encouraging resistance and defiance. Consider, for example, how a police officer operating under a control orientation responds to disrespect from the public. Viewing such hostility and disrespect as a threat to control, he or she is provoked into a greater show of force. This reaction, in turn, encourages greater defiance and disrespect.

The core point we wish to emphasize is that such spirals of conflict also increase the risk to officers. Although spiraling conflict clearly threatens members of the public with injury, it also carries the possibility of injury to police officers.

What is the alternative to a control orientation? The approach that is most consistent with the research reviewed here is to treat members of the public fairly and respectfully, listening to them and communicating explanations for police actions. This approach dampens and deescalates conflict. Although the benefits to the public of such an approach are obvious, we want to emphasize that police officers also can gain from the use of conflict-dampening approaches.

Consider a specific example of such an approach. The Memphis Police Department uses a therapeutic model of policing when dealing with mentally ill people. Officers specially trained in nonconfrontational tactics are sent to resolve conflicts that involve the mentally ill. As we would expect, this approach has reduced the number of injuries to mentally ill persons in their encounters with the police, but it has also led to reductions in injuries to officers. Both groups have gained from an approach that minimizes the likelihood of conflict (Dupont 2000).

This example also makes it clear that the ideas presented here are not new to the field of policing. Police forces have confronted the issues outlined in this book and come up with solutions that are similar to those we advocate. Therefore, this book might be viewed as an empirical demonstration for a set of ideas that many police officers are aware of from their own personal experience. These ideas can also be derived from observation of policing, as Muir (1977) did in his classic study.

Controlling Crime

In most encounters with members of the public, police officers are focused on securing compliance with the law within the particular situation. In personal encounters, nonconfrontational approaches decrease hostility and resistance and increase the likelihood that people will voluntarily accept the officers' directives. Further, as we have already noted, the likelihood that people will abide by those directives and adhere to the law over time is increased.

It is also possible to view the relationship between the public and legal authorities from a broader perspective. The police depend heavily on people's cooperation in their efforts to control crime. Many of the crimes that come to the attention of the police are voluntarily reported by community residents, and many residents aid the police in solving crimes. In addition, most people voluntarily follow the law most of the time (Tyler 1990), freeing the police to focus their efforts on a subset of more problematic situations and people. To reap the benefits of public cooperation, the police need to maintain and build the public's trust and confidence. They can do so by focusing on the issues that matter to people when they evaluate the police. Such a focus on public concerns need not interfere with the control of crime. Community residents do not object to policing activities per se. For example, they do not object to being stopped on the street or in their cars when police officers handle those encounters sensitively. As a consequence, police officers are not giving away their ability to manage social order and control crime by engaging in policing tactics that are sensitive to issues of interpersonal treatment.

In fact, the experience of residents of cities such as Boston suggests that, if community residents are involved in a partnership with the police and the courts in which both parties jointly frame strategies for maintaining social order, the community itself may advocate and initiate police activities. In Boston it was community church leaders who targeted persistent criminals and worked with the police to curtail the criminal activity of those individuals. The community did so because the police solicited the involvement of community leaders in designing crime control strategy, treated community concerns with respect, listened to community leaders, and generally gave the community an important role in developing social control activities. As suggested by our argument, such treatment encourages the public's active and voluntary efforts to cooperate with the police and the courts.

It is also important to emphasize the generality of our findings regarding public concerns about policing activities. We find very similar concerns among white and minority community residents, among the rich and poor, the young and old. Perhaps most important, we find such concerns expressed by the young, minority males who are typically viewed by the police as the members of the public who are most potentially dangerous and difficult to manage. Of course, we should not find this surprising, since the literature on gangs emphasizes the importance that young, minority men place on being treated with respect by others in their community.

We also find that similar concerns are central to people's views about their personal experiences and to their general views about the law and about legal authorities. Therefore, public opinion about the police is shaped strongly by judgments of how the police *generally* treat people. As a consequence, a particular encounter shapes not only the views of the person involved but the broader views of those who observe it or learn about it through neighbors, friends, family, or the media.

As we have noted, one benefit of a process-oriented approach is that it lowers the level of conflict and hostility in particular situations, increasing the likelihood of gaining voluntary cooperation and acceptance. Another benefit of lowering the likelihood of escalating conflict, as we have noted, is reducing the likelihood of injury not only to police officers themselves but to members of the public. Yet another important benefit is the development of legitimacy, which facilitates subsequent police efforts to fight crime. Community residents who do not question the legitimacy of the police are more likely to cooperate with legal authorities, to defer to them voluntarily, and to obey laws. They are also more likely to report crimes and criminals, to help solve crimes by coming forward as witnesses, and to generally act in law-abiding ways.

To be agents of socialization, the police need to act in ways that people experience as respectful and fair. Efforts to gain public support for the police emphasize the need for respectful treatment of the public, as in the New York City Police Department slogan "Courtesy, Professionalism, Respect." Similarly, community policing initiatives are designed to increase personal interactions with police officers so that people can learn that the police are professional and fair (Friedmann 1992; Rosenbaum 1994; Skogan and Hartnett 1997).

One way to view the struggle to control crime is as a trade-off between the gains in terms of the lowered crime rates associated with aggressive policing and the losses associated with the alienation of the community and its residents stemming from police intrusions into their lives (stopping them on the street, searching them for weapons, and so on). Our argument is that the police and the courts do not need to view the effort to lower crime as necessarily requiring police behaviors that alienate the public. It is possible to lower the crime rate while maintaining high public confidence in the police and the courts. By emphasizing the fair and respectful treatment of all residents, the police and the courts will build public trust and confidence and draw people into the fight against crime by encouraging them to consent to and cooperate with the efforts of legal authorities.

Consider the sensitive topic of street stops to search for guns or question people about crimes. People accept being stopped and searched by the police without anger if the police act professionally, explaining their reasons for the search and treating the person with decency. It is actions that convey a lack of respect, that affront people's dignity, and that seem demeaning and biased that create resentment and mistrust. If the police account for their actions ("we are looking for guns") and apologize for inconveniencing innocent people, they can engage in intrusive crime control activities without diminishing trust and confidence in either the particular officers involved or the police more generally. In other words, effective police activities do not need to lead to public distrust of the police. Even when people have difficult and unpleasant experiences with the police, the key factor shaping their reactions is how they are treated.

Changes in police attitudes and practices that increase fair, respectful treatment can therefore increase public support for the police without diminishing police efforts to control crime. As a recent review of research on crime prevention suggests:

> One of the most striking findings is the extent to which the police themselves create a risk factor for crime simply by using bad manners. . . . The less respectful police are towards suspects and residents generally, the less people will comply with the law. Changing police "style" may thus be as important as focusing on police "substance." Making both the style and substance of police practices more "legitimate" in the eyes of the public, particularly high-risk juveniles, may be one of the most effective long-term police strategies for crime prevention. (Sherman et al. 1997, 8-1)

The process-based approach to regulation lessens these problems by encouraging people's consent and cooperation. The findings of this study suggest strongly that if legal authorities act justly, it is possible to gain such cooperation even when they are unable to solve problems and must cite, fine, or jail people who break rules.

Areas for Focus

Enacting new process-based policing strategies may require broadening the scope of police training. Rather than concentrating primarily on tactical decision making, training for police officers needs to put a stronger emphasis on interpersonal sensitivity. By approaching people in non-threatening ways, treating people with respect, explaining why they are engaging in policing actions, and allowing people to express their views, the police can gain public cooperation. All of these aspects of interpersonal sensitivity can be learned through training and integrated into policing tactics.

How effectively can these behaviors be taught? Studies in the field of organizational psychology show that training in the principles of procedural justice can be effective. For example, a short training program for union leaders was found to increase feelings among union members that the union was being managed fairly (Skarlicki and Latham 1996, 1997). This suggests that the behaviors associated with a process-based approach to policing can be learned through training and implemented in ways that lead to similarly process-based reactions to the problems encountered during policing activities.

In addition, the police need to consider expanding their goals. Their role is not just to make arrests in an effort to control crime but also to enhance their legitimacy and build the public's confidence and trust in them. By using a process-based approach in working with the public and with the community, the police can create an environment of encouragement of cooperation and consent among community residents. In the long run, eliciting these behaviors is a key facilitator of effective policing.

Chapter 15

Process-Based Regulation

WE HAVE examined various strategies that the police and the courts can use to regulate people's behaviors. Our particular interest is in those behaviors that legal authorities can engage in to enhance the willingness of the public to support and accept their decisions.

We have distinguished between two possible strategies for effective regulation. The deterrence strategy dominates current thinking about how to bring people's behavior into line with the law and the directives of legal authorities. Deterrence relies on gaining compliance through the power of legal authorities to sanction people. In implementing this approach, police officers and judges use the possibility of sanctioning to pressure people to comply with their directives. As we have noted, research suggests that deterrence does affect people's behavior, but that those effects are often weak. It is an effective but inefficient way to handle regulation.

The second strategy is to encourage the judgment that the police and the courts are using fair procedures in exercising their authority and to develop the public's trust in the motives of legal authorities. We refer to these strategies as process-based regulation because they are based on seeking to gain the cooperation and consent of members of the public through the fair, respectful behavior of legal authorities.

We have shown that process-based regulation offers several advantages. First, it lessens defiance and hostility, making it easier for societal authorities to gain acceptance for their decisions from the public. In personal encounters with legal authorities, members of the public are more likely to accept their decisions when they feel that they are fairly treated by those authorities and can trust their motives.

Second, because people are accepting the decisions of authorities more voluntarily, they are more likely to adhere to those decisions over time. When people unwillingly give way before the force of police officers or judges, who have the power to arrest, fine, or jail them, their compliance does not develop from internal motivations. Once the immediate threat of punishment is lessened, people revert to their prior behaviors. Therefore, legal authorities must often revisit problems and people over and over again to remind them of the possibility of sanctioning. To the degree that people have willingly accepted authorities' decisions, their motivation to continue abiding by those decisions in the future is greater.

Therefore, the first conclusion of this analysis is that process-based regulation enhances both the public's immediate acceptance of the directives of legal authorities and its consent and cooperation over time. In both the short term and the long term, people are more willing to accept decisions when they believe that legal authorities are following fair procedures and have trustworthy motives for their behavior.

Societal Orientations and Decision Acceptance

In addition to being influenced by their judgments about the behavior of the particular police officers and judges they encounter, people's willingness to defer voluntarily to legal authorities is shaped by their broader societal orientations. The results we have outlined clearly show that legitimacy, trust in others in one's community, and social connections with others all facilitate decision acceptance within particular situations.

The strongest influence comes from legitimacy, as we would expect, since legitimacy is directly linked to the characteristics of the law and legal authorities. However, the results also support the suggestion that the strength of people's connections to their community and to society in general influence their behavior.

The second conclusion of this analysis therefore is that general societal orientations, such as the legitimacy of legal institutions, have an influence on how people behave during their personal experiences with legal authorities. When people feel that the law and legal authorities are more legitimate, they are more willing to defer to particular police officers and judges. This is also true when people feel that they have ties to other people in the community or when they identify with society.

Interestingly, not all general societal orientations have a direct influence on people's reactions during personal experiences. In particular, people's identification with their ethnic group does not influence their decision on how to react to particular police officers and judges. Hence, ethnic group identification neither hinders nor helps police officers and judges seeking to gain the cooperation of community residents.

We identified two types of influence. First, societal orientations directly influence decision acceptance. Those with more favorable orientations are more likely to accept the decisions of legal authorities. Second, we found an indirect effect of societal orientations on how people decide whether to accept decisions. Those who feel more favorably disposed toward society and societal institutions focus more strongly on process issues when deciding whether to accept decisions.

Generalization from Personal Experience

The findings of this analysis also suggest that people generalize from their personal experiences to their broader views about the law, legal authorities, others in their community, and society. By acting fairly and encouraging trust, legal authorities are not only encouraging the immediate and long-term acceptance of their directives but also engaging in the socialization of community residents. Encouraging more positive general attitudes, in turn, facilitates the ease with which legal authorities can function in future encounters with the public. Those who view authority as more legitimate, who are more generally trusting of others, and who identify more strongly with society can be expected to defer to particular legal authorities more willingly.

These findings show that particular actions in specific situations have a broad impact on people's judgments about the legitimacy of the police and the courts, their trust in others in their communities, and their social connections to their community. These general attitudes support several types of desirable social behaviors. One is compliance with the law. Another is behavioral engagement in the community and in the political system. When residents generally trust others in their community and feel connected to their community, they are more likely to engage in such actions.

Looking at these issues another way, we can say that police and court activities that offend or alienate the public are unlikely to be effective in controlling crime in the long term. Unfair or disrespectful treatment by particular police officers or judges influences people's general evaluation of the police and the courts and their overall respect for the law. Losing respect for the law has a broad influence: both the individual and others who learn of his or her experience become less likely to obey the law in the future. As a result, the job of the legal authorities becomes more difficult. It is striking that even minor personal experiences with legal authorities—dealing with a fender-bender traffic accident, a burglary, or a street stop—have a strong general influence on people's views about the police and the courts. Although our focus in this study has been on people's recent experiences with legal authorities, many other studies of personal experiences with the police and the courts have found that some people report experiences from many months before with great emotion.

In sum, the findings of this analysis provide clear empirical support for the argument that process-based regulation can be a viable and effective approach in personal interactions between police officers and judges and members of the public. This does not mean, of course, that people do not care about the outcomes they receive. They do. However, their predominant concerns are with the nature of their treatment by authorities. Since legal authorities have more control over how they treat the public than they do over their ability to solve problems or avoid sanctioning, this finding provides a focus for the efforts of societal authorities. Regardless of the favorability or type of outcomes they are providing to the public, legal authorities can act in ways that encourage people to accept their decisions and to assess them more favorably as decision makers.

Minorities and the Law

The findings of this analysis suggest that whites and minority group members react to their personal experiences with police officers and judges in similar ways. Both groups focus on whether they experienced procedural justice and whether they could trust the motives of the authorities with whom they were dealing. Minority group members are more resistant to accepting the decisions of legal authorities, according to these results, because they are more likely to feel that they did not receive procedural justice and could not trust the motives of the authorities with whom they were dealing.

The study further suggests that minority group respondents, like white respondents, are influenced by their general societal orientations. As a result, no single personal experience determines how people respond to police officers and judges. Rather, the behavior of the authorities and the individual's general societal orientations both shape deference. This suggests that cooperation with legal authorities may develop or be undermined over the course of many personal experiences, and that over time people's societal orientations change in response to those experiences, making the job of legal authorities more or less difficult.

On the other hand, these findings suggest that people's loyalty to their ethnic subgroup is not important in shaping their reactions to legal authorities. There is no reason why we would want people to abandon their loyalty to and identification with their ethnic subgroup, especially in light of our findings that such loyalty does not interfere with people's relationships with society, law, or the political system. Our focus ought to be on people's relationship to society and to social and legal institutions.

Public Opinion of Legal Institutions

We also examined the public's general evaluations of the police and the courts as institutions and authorities. It has often been argued that instrumental concerns dominate reactions to general regulation, just as it is often suggested that instrumental concerns dominate reactions to personal experience. Our findings suggest, however, that people's system-level evaluations of the police and the courts are heavily shaped by their judgments about how the police and the courts treat people in their communities. Certainly, people care about the performance of legal authorities. However, their overall performance evaluations are strongly shaped by additional concerns about whether the police treat people with respect and dignity, show concern for their rights, and refrain from harassing them. Issues of quality of treatment and quality of decision making, in other words, enter into people's system-level evaluations of the social regulatory system.

These findings support our argument that a process-based model of regulation is viable. Such a model is promising as a way to facilitate the effective exercise of legal authority during everyday interactions between the public and legal authorities. Further, it suggests a way to build general attitudes that both support the everyday exercise of legal authority and encourage everyday compliance with the law and engagement in communities. Finally, it addresses the concerns that are found in general public evaluations of the police and the courts.

Chapter 16

Psychological Jurisprudence

T HE PROCESS-BASED strategy of regulation that we advocate is one aspect of a more general strategy of psychological jurisprudence. Psychological jurisprudence is the effort to build our system of law and regulation on an accurate model of the psychology of the person. Psychological jurisprudence has many aspects (see Tyler and Darley 2000), but our comments here focus on issues of human motivation.[1]

Psychological jurisprudence provides a distinctly empirical, rather than normative, perspective on the problems presented by the law. According to this view, our conception of the person should be based on empirical research about human motivation, such as the research outlined in this book. Like psychology in general, the application of psychology to jurisprudence is an effort to define human nature through systematic and scientific empirical study. Our long-term goal is to establish a role for empirical findings in shaping the law—that is, to create evidence-based legal policies. Like the proponents of the earlier legal realism movement, we argue that the roots of effective legal doctrine must lie in an accurate understanding of the nature of the social world and of the people within that world. Psychological jurisprudence carries this premise further by taking advantage of the methodological skills of psychology to establish that knowledge.

Deterrence: The Standard Approach to Social Control

When we consider possible motivations for people's law-related behavior, whether public or private, we can draw upon the extensive social-psychological literature that explores the factors shaping people's behavior. Historically, those concerned with producing compliance with the law have focused on the manipulation of the environment through changes in rewards and sanctions. Social psychologists suggest that this is only one of several possible ways to motivate behavior.

Those legal authorities who are concerned with producing compliant behavior among members of the public have primarily taken the approach of shaping environmental contingencies in particular ways, that is, by encouraging behaviors that manipulate the impact of anticipated gains or losses. These manipulations are based on calculations not only of the likelihood of potential gains and losses but of their expected utility (the amount to be gained or lost). This approach is the classical subjective expected utility theory. Taken together, these calculations tell people whether engaging in some action is likely to be beneficial to their self-interest.

The idea that people's behavior with respect to the law is shaped by their calculations of expected gain and loss is the core premise of the rational choice theory (Blumstein, Cohen, and Nagin 1978). Within legal circles, the model is referred to as the "deterrence" or "social control" model of behavior, and it seems to us that it is this model of the person that dominates law and public policy at this time. It is the model on which legislators and regulators seem to rely when they are contemplating statutory changes.

To regulate behavior, the rational choice model focuses on adjusting criminal sanctions to the needed level so that the expected losses associated with lawbreaking will lessen the likelihood that people will break the law. According to this model, the judgment that those engaged in regulation must make is deciding which acts should be prevented, and then specifying penalties, whether threats of physical violence, fines, or prison terms, that are severe enough to discourage the prohibited behavior. Police officers, for example, gain compliance by calibrating their displays of force—from the threat of ticketing and arrest to the possibility of injury from the use of nightsticks and mace, and ultimately to their capacity to kill a person with their guns.

What if the prohibited behavior continues to be committed with unacceptable frequency? There is an easy remedy within this model: if the observed rate of criminal behavior is thought to be too high, the remedy is to increase the sanctions threatened or delivered—that is, to increase the expected disutility of the prohibited actions so that people who would otherwise commit the behavior will be deterred. The task is to adjust the magnitude of the punishment to an appropriate level.

The social control model is the primary model of human motivation that has guided the recent efforts of the American legal system, both the police and the courts, to manage society. The application of this model of human motivation to regulation efforts has had dramatic effects on the nature of American society. Consider the case of the American prison population (Haney and Zimbardo 1998). Because of the belief that crime is deterred by the threat or experience of punishment, a large number of Americans have been convicted and sentenced to spend time in prisons. Today the United States is a world leader in the proportion of its citizens held in its prisons.

Does a social control model work? As we have noted, some research supports the suggestion that variations in the perceived certainty and severity of punishment do shape people's compliance with the law. In particular, people's behavior is often, although not always, found to be shaped by their estimate of the likelihood that, if they disobey the law, they will be caught and punished. However, research also suggests that estimates of the likelihood of being caught and punished have, at best, a minor influence on people's behavior.

One approach to the problems of deterrence is to try to fix the deterrence model. Recently such efforts have led to the idea of targeted deterrence strategies. One such strategy targets people. Ayres and Braithwaite (1992), for example, suggest that those charged with regulation should first approach people by appealing to their moral values. By taking this approach, they can then isolate the small group of people who are unable to respond to such an appeal. Those people should subsequently be the focus of surveillance and social control. This approach allows authorities to concentrate their resources on those people likely to need social control.

A second targeted deterrence strategy focuses on situations. Sherman (1998) has argued that the current deployment of police resources is more strongly shaped by political clout than it is by crime rates. As a consequence, police officers seldom patrol most heavily in the highest-crime areas. He suggests that a greater effort is needed to practice surveillance where the crime problem lies. Both of these strategies accept the basic deterrence argument and suggest that the issue is how to implement deterrence more effectively.

Despite these efforts to improve the use of the deterrence model, an increasing number of observers are raising questions about whether this model is in fact fundamentally flawed. If so, then we need to rethink the model of human motivation that we are applying to the law. To address the problems encountered by the legal system, we need to develop a broader model of motivation. We do so here by expanding the scope of our conception of possible motivating factors to be more consistent with psychological models of the person.

Intrinsic Motivation as the Basis for an Alternative Model

Our expanded model leads us to examine a second factor that social psychologists view as a central determinant of people's behavior—intrinsic or internal motivations. In previous chapters, we have examined two types of intrinsic, experience-based motivation that underlie people's willingness to defer voluntarily to the decisions made by police officers and judges. One such motivation arises out of people's perception of procedural justice and motive-based trust. This motivation develops from the behavior of police officers and judges—that is, people are motivated to accept decisions because of the inferences they make about the particular authorities they are dealing with.

The second type of intrinsic motivations are general societal orientations—the legitimacy of legal authorities, trust in other people in the community, and identification with society. Both types of internal motivation encourage cooperation with legal authorities that develops from the person and is not directly linked to issues of material reward or force.

Our argument is that the influence of these intrinsic motivations on behavior suggests an alternative model upon which an effective legal system can be created and maintained. Further, we would argue that this model is a uniquely social-psychological model. It builds on the recognition by social psychologists that people make and act on judgments that are not simple expressions of rational self-interest. These judgments are distinct from contemporaneous judgments of self-interest and clearly exercise an important independent influence on people's behavior. We refer to those judgments as social judgments concerning procedural justice and motive-based trust.

A central feature of judgments about procedural justice and motive-based trust is that their influence separates a person's behavior from the influence of environmental factors. Intrinsic motivations are a part of a person and lead him or her to exercise self-regulation. As a consequence, people do not so much comply with the law as they accept and consent to it, deferring to the law and those legal authorities whom they view as acting in a procedurally fair and trustworthy manner because, they feel, it is the right thing to do.

This model recognizes that it is not necessary to shape people's behavior by threatening them with punishment for wrongdoing. People take the responsibility themselves for accepting decisions and following rules. They do so if they feel that the actions of the authorities are reasonable and fair; under those conditions, it makes sense to them to cooperate with legal authorities—that is, to participate in society by accepting its rules. They then become willing to be governed by the law and take on the responsibility for following laws and obeying the directives of legal authorities.

Creating and Sustaining
Confidence in the Law

This perspective inverts the question that the legal system traditionally asks of psychology: "How can the legal system bring people into compliance with the law?" The correct answer, we suggest, is to create a set of law-enforcing procedures and authorities that treat people fairly. That is, our focus is on the feelings of the members of the public. Instead of taking a top-down perspective on those people whose behavior is to be controlled, our approach begins by taking the subjective experience of members of the public seriously. Rooting our model of process-based regulation in public conceptions of justice and trust, we build it on efforts to engage and address such public concerns.

Our perspective represents an important program of action for legal psychologists to articulate and advocate within the legal community. It represents an important contribution that social psychologists can make to our understanding of how societal authorities can regulate behavior, maintain social order, and promote an effective and efficient society.

Although our emphasis here is on how legal authorities can create acceptance by treating people fairly, the argument we are making is much broader. People are also generally more likely to defer to the law and to legal authorities if they think that the law accords with their social values (Tyler 1990).

Two important values are the belief that legal authorities are legitimate and ought to be obeyed and the belief that following the law is morally right. These ethically based judgments are not simple reflections of short-term calculations of gain or loss. Studies of Americans find that people's feelings of obligation to obey the police and the courts—legitimacy—are generally quite high (Tyler 1990), even in the face of widespread expressions of dissatisfaction with the law and with legal authorities (Tyler 1997a, 1998).

Our argument is that, although the threat of punishment is always in the background when dealing with legal authorities (Levi 1997), most people accept their decisions, not only, or even primarily, because they fear them but because they view their actions as reasonable and appropriate. Put another way, we need to be concerned with developing the public's confidence in the law and increasing people's willingness to defer to legal authorities. To do so we need authorities and laws capable of sustaining that confidence.

The results of the California study illustrate a core premise of the psychological jurisprudence perspective—that legal authorities benefit when they make it a priority to gain the consent and cooperation of citizens. This effort involves focusing on citizens' experiences and on their judgments about the practices and policies of legal authorities. Thus, psychological jurisprudence is a psychological perspective on the effective rule of law. The key to the successful rule of law, in this view, lies in understanding the views of the public.

We put this approach forward as a general model of regulation. At the same time we want to reiterate a few notes of caution. This analysis is not directed at hard-core criminals. We do consider the subset of respondents in the California study—young, minority males—who have the characteristics of high-risk offenders. And we find that those respondents behave in a manner similar to the behavior of our larger sample. Further, other studies of similar respondents also find that this group is concerned with issues of procedural justice and trust. However, what is really needed is a study that directly targets those people whom legal authorities feel are most likely to be antagonistic, confrontational, and defiant.

Procedural Justice

Our findings reinforce the general suggestion of recent research on social justice that people's views about the fairness of procedures have an important influence on their reactions to the law and to legal authorities (Tyler 2000; Tyler et al. 1997). It is clear that people's evaluations of the fairness of their experiences have a powerful and direct influence on their willingness to defer to legal authorities.

Further, the results of this analysis support the arguments of the relational perspective on procedural justice (Tyler and Lind 1992). That argument is that people's conception of fair procedures is linked to the quality of their interpersonal treatment by authorities (see also Tyler and Blader 2000). Are they treated politely and with dignity? Are their needs considered? Are their rights respected? People also define the fairness of procedures partially by the fairness of the decision making and consider issues such as neutrality.

Taken together, these findings support the general argument of this book—that when people choose to defer to legal authorities, social motives play an important role that is distinct from the impact of instrumental or rational motivations. As we would anticipate, one reason people defer to authorities is that they receive desirable, or at least acceptable, outcomes. In addition, however, people are motivated by their views about procedural justice and, in particular, by how well they are treated.

Trust in Others

Beyond the issue of regulation by legal authorities is the broader question of how authorities can obtain and maintain cooperation (Tyler and Blader 2000). This question includes the types of dealings with hierarchical social relations and with institutional authorities that are central to the exercise of legal authority.

Studies have suggested that the importance of trust to such authority relations extends beyond legal settings. Tyler and Degoey (1996) found that motive-based trust is also central to authority relations in political, managerial, and family settings. In all of these settings, motive-based trust shapes the voluntary acceptance of decisions.

The importance of motive-based trust also extends to horizontal relationships with other people in situations such as bargaining and negotiation, to equal-status teams and social relationships, and to other relationships that are not organized by hierarchical control mechanisms. This motive-based trust, in turn, leads to increased willingness to defer to others. Although the role of motive-based trust in such horizontal relationships is not the focus of this study, we speculate that it is important even when people are not dealing with societal authorities. This speculation is based on our argument that in dealing with others people rely on their inferences about the character of those others. It is sometimes possible—but often it is not—to observe others' behavior to verify their performance. Most typically, we can know something about the actions of others but we do not have complete information. In that event, we must make inferences about others.

The ubiquity of this motive-assessing inferential process is illustrated by the centrality of attributional thinking in social interaction (Heider 1958). Social psychologists recognize that people focus their thinking on the goal of assessing the character and motives of those with whom they are dealing. As a result, their actions are keyed to their ability and willingness to make and rely on judgments about the character of others. These judgments are more than simple predictions of expected future behavior, although they are connected to such predictions. They are assessments of character that lead people to believe that they can understand why people are acting as they do in given situations.

Of course, one reason people try to infer motives is to be able to predict the future behavior of others. In this sense, our findings are not completely distinct from the rational models of trust we reviewed in the previously discussed literature. However, our findings suggest that rational motivations do not completely account for inferences about trust. People also place considerable weight on their inferences about character and motivation. These inferences help people to understand *why* others behave as they do.

This analysis, in other words, speaks to the nature of people's social motivations in interactions with others. It suggests the important social role of trust in people's decisions about whether to defer to authorities. Our findings illustrate the importance of considering both the rational and the social elements of trust when seeking to understand people's relationships with society and regulatory authorities.

Social Motivations

The central message of our findings is that people's social motivations play an important role in shaping their reactions to legal authorities. If people believe that the authorities with whom they are dealing are exercising their authority using fair procedures and that their motives are trustworthy, then they are more willing to defer voluntarily to those authorities.

This social conception of authority relations is not meant to replace instrumental or rational models of either justice or trust. Social motivations operate against the backdrop of people's instrumental concerns about their gains and losses. But it is clear that social motivations contribute to our ability to understand people's reactions to regulatory authorities beyond what can be understood through instrumental motivations. In particular, social motivations help us to understand voluntary deference to authority.

Notes

Chapter 1

1. An alternative view is that people's feelings may become more positive when they have a good experience, and less positive when they have a bad experience. If so, then the key question is the mean level of experience— whether most experiences are good or bad. However, research shows that people are not equally influenced by all types of experience. That is, negative experiences make people's attitudes less positive, but positive experiences have little or no impact on their feelings (Katz et al. 1975). As a result, the influence of having many positive experiences on people's feelings and judgments can be overshadowed by having one negative experience, since a negative experience has greater psychological impact on the person and on observers.

2. If, for example, the police come to my door and tell me to stop the music at my party, I will not want to do so. I am enjoying my party, would like to keep on doing so, and am inclined to ignore any inconvenience or discomfort being suffered by my neighbors. However, I recognize that the police can cite me for violating the law and even arrest me and take me into the police station to await sanctioning by the courts. The risk of these applications of force outweighs any estimated gain I might have for continuing my loud party, and I comply with the police.

3. It is possible to develop an even more powerful critique of deterrence approaches: threats may undermine intrinsic motivations for going along with the decisions of authorities. The introduction of threats or negative incentives may "crowd out" and undermine the internal motivations that lead people to accept voluntarily the decisions of legal authorities (see Frey 1997).

4. Our interest in the value of procedural justice and motive-based trust as an alternative mechanism through which compliance with the law can be obtained is part of our general effort to understand the role of people's attitudes and values in shaping their behavior toward rules and authorities in organized groups (Tyler 1999a; Tyler and Blader 2000). Our ideas thus apply equally to legal, political, and managerial authorities.

Chapter 2

1. Interestingly, a replication of this study in Indianapolis and St. Petersburg did not find that the coercive balance of power influenced public compliance (see McCluskey, Mastrofski, and Parks 1998). This finding is consistent with the general finding that deterrence effects are weak: they are sometimes found, and sometimes not found; and even when they are found, they are usually weak in magnitude.

2. People were also influenced by the degree to which the police treated them respectfully—a point we discuss in more detail later.

3. It is also true that many murders occur within families or couples and are therefore relatively easy to solve.

Chapter 3

1. It is possible to use the samples collected to make population estimates by using appropriate weighting procedures. However, those weighting procedures are not used in any of the analyses presented in this book.

2. The low intercorrelation of these indices of outcome favorability highlights the problems associated with self-report when measuring outcome favorability. Clearly, the degree to which we can view individuals as regarding their outcome as favorable depends heavily on how we ask them the question.

3. A wide variety of societal authorities are in the business of responsibility management. For example, teachers encounter difficulty when they seek to shape their jobs in response to student-teacher evaluations. The customer service model therefore may not easily generalize to the encounters of those concerned with regulation.

Chapter 4

1. Those unfamiliar with the social-psychological literature on social justice are often skeptical when they first hear that people's feelings and behaviors might be shaped by judgments about justice or injustice. They are especially skeptical that such justice-based concerns might outweigh the influence of people's judgments about the desirability or favorability of outcomes. There is a pervasive intuitive notion within American culture that people are primarily, if not exclusively, concerned about what they get from others—their self-interest—and that self-interested judgments guide feelings and behaviors. This belief has been labeled "the myth of self-interest" to reflect the fact that it is a widely held view about the nature of human motivation that may or may not correspond to reality (Miller and Ratner 1996, 1998). This set of assumptions about what motivates

people is consistent with the dominance of an outcome-based perspective on individual motivation within the academic social science literature, as well as in public consciousness.

2. This analysis also shows a relationship between procedural justice and trust. That relationship is discussed in chapter 6.

3. In the case of voluntary contacts with the police, 74 percent of the variance was explained. The beta weight for procedural justice was 0.67, for distributive justice 0.13, and for outcome favorability 0.20. In the case of voluntary contacts with the courts, 74 percent of the variance was also explained. The beta weight for procedural justice was 0.78, for distributive justice 0.07, and for outcome favorability 0.10. In the case of nonvoluntary contacts with the police, 81 percent of the variance was explained. The beta weight for procedural justice was 0.71, for distributive justice 0.31, and for outcome favorability −0.14. In the case of nonvoluntary contacts with the courts, 67 percent of the variance was explained. The beta weight for procedural justice was 0.79, for distributive justice 0.08, and for outcome favorability −.04.

4. The most important theory of justice is that of Rawls (1971, 1999, 2000, 2001), who has equated "justice" with issues of outcome fairness. Others have also linked the justice of a society to its principles of distributive justice (Miller 1999). Hence, it is important to note that this analysis makes a distinction between the justice of processes—procedural justice—and the justice of outcomes—distributive justice. However, unlike these philosophers, we have assessed these ideas subjectively by interviewing people. It was the judgment of each respondent that he or she did or did not receive a fair outcome, and that it was or was not arrived at using a fair procedure, that is key to our analysis.

Further, unlike philosophical treatments of justice, this analysis does not consider issues involving the overall distribution of outcomes in society. That issue can be empirically studied (see Tyler et al. 1997), but we do not do so in this study. (The one exception is in chapter 13 on general views about the police and the courts.) Instead, we focus on people's views about whether they personally received a fair outcome.

Chapter 5

1. Hardin's key point about encapsulation is that I consider your interests only if I feel that I will benefit from an exchange relationship. Thus, I would make sure that there is something in our interactions that benefits you so that you will continue to interact with me. My reason for so doing is that I benefit from my continued interaction with you. To take a simple example, suppose that during one of our meetings you drop your wallet on the street as you walk away. My decision about whether to return the wallet to you is based on my estimate of the likelihood that you might think I took the wallet; such

a suspicion would disrupt our productive exchange relationship. If I think that you will think you lost your wallet on the street and that you will not connect that loss to me, then I will keep the wallet and further enhance my personal gains from our interaction.

2. At first glance, this articulation of the idea of motive-based trust sounds similar to that of encapsulated interests (Hardin 2002). How does this motive-based conception of trust differ from Hardin's model? Hardin argues that we can trust that another person will act out of concern for our interests when we have an ongoing, mutually beneficial exchange relationship. However, should that relationship be disrupted, the other person will suddenly become uninterested in acting in ways that meet our needs. In contrast, the concept of motive-based trust, like fiduciary responsibility, is linked to motives that are more ethical or moral in nature. Authorities are viewed as acting in trustworthy ways in situations in which the person cannot know whether the authorities have acted in his or her interests or, if he or she does know, lacks the power to act against the authorities. Therefore, how the authorities act is not simply linked to their instrumental concerns in the situation. The actions of authorities are linked to other concerns they have, such as their sense of personal morality, professional integrity, and feelings of ethical responsibility.

3. The Diallo case illustrates the role of expertise in a very compelling way. It was widely noted that the officers shot forty-one bullets at Diallo. This fact was linked in the popular press to the suggestion that the police showed bias toward this minority suspect. However, experts noted that the police were using military bullets supplied to them by the NYPD rather than typical police bullets. Typical police bullets are designed to knock a person down by flattening on impact, thus transferring their energy to the person's body. Police officers are trained to fire at a suspect until that person is knocked down. Police officers carry shotguns rather than military-style high-powered rifles for the same reason: shotguns have great power to knock down suspects. In contrast, military bullets are designed to penetrate body armor and do not flatten on impact. As a result, such bullets go through a person's body. The military bullets fired by the police at Diallo went through his body without knocking him down. The officers saw that Diallo was not falling down and believed, consistent with what they had been taught, that they had missed their target. In other words, one reason the police officers fired forty-one shots, experts determined, was that they had been supplied with an inappropriate type of ammunition, given how they had been trained to act in shooting situations. Knowing this heavily influences a person's inferences about the intentions of the officers.

In addition, the military bullets not only went through Diallo's body but bounced off the wall behind him. Experts believe that one reason the police thought they were being fired on and continued to "return fire" was because their own bullets were bouncing back at them after going through Diallo's body. Again, this is very relevant to the officers' statements that they fired because they thought they were being fired on, even though the popular press generally dismissed this claim as ridiculous and hard to believe.

This type of technical information bears considerable importance to any evaluations of the intentions of the officers, but it was generally not reported in popular press discussions of the case. This is one example of how expert knowledge that would not generally be available to the public can be very important to making objective evaluations about what happens in policing situations.

4. Judges' training in the law allows them to apply legal principles to the solution of the problems that come before them in court. The people who appear in court may like or dislike the rulings they receive in their cases, but they are seldom in a position to evaluate whether those judgments are consistent with the law. They must trust the authority involved to understand the law and apply it correctly to the case. When we are dealing with an authority, we make some inferences about the authority's motives and thus about whether the authority can be trusted. Should we trust the police when they say that they made a sincere effort to solve the burglary but are unable to recover what was stolen? We make these inferences despite limitations in our knowledge and expertise.

5. In the case of procedural justice, we contrast procedural justice influences with the influence of evaluations of the favorability and fairness of outcomes.

6. The scale provides three alternatives for evaluating the quality of the outcome of the experience: "better than expected," "as expected," and "worse than expected." Here "better than expected" and "worse than expected" are both treated as violations of expectation, while "as expected" is treated as a confirmation of expectation.

7. This effort to understand why people are acting as they do is not confined to people's interactions with authorities. When judging those charged with crimes, people's judgments are difficult to predict based simply on what happened. Rather, people seek to understand why a person acted as he or she did—that is, to understand their character and motivations. Punishment is based on inferred character, not on the surface features of a person's actions.

8. In the case of voluntary experiences with the police, 79 percent of the variance was explained. The beta weight for motive-based trust was 0.73, for outcome favorability 0.22, and for predictability 0.06. In the case of voluntary experiences with the courts, 77 percent of the variance was explained. The beta weight for motive-based trust was 0.77, for outcome favorability 0.13, and for predictability 0.14. In the case of nonvoluntary experiences with the police, 70 percent of the variance was explained. The beta weight for motive-based trust was 0.72, for outcome favorability −.01, and for predictability 0.27. In the case of nonvoluntary experiences with the courts, 64 percent of the variance was explained. The beta weight for

motive-based trust was 0.80, for outcome favorability −.01, and for predictability 0.08.

Chapter 6

1. Beta weights index the influence of a factor, controlling for the influence of other factors in the equation. If we look at the influence of procedural justice while motive-based trust is also included in the equation, then finding a significant influence of procedural justice indicates that procedural justice explains variance in the dependent variable that cannot be explained by motive-based trust.

2. To determine whether the four instrumental variables were significant, we created a structural equation model in which we treated the four instrumental variables as indicators of a latent instrumental factor, while treating motive-based trust and procedural justice as indicators of a latent factor that reflected social motives. We used these two latent factors to predict latent dependent variables shaped by decision acceptance and satisfaction with the decision maker. In that analysis the latent variable for social motives emerged as highly significant, while the instrumental latent factor was not statistically significant.

3. It is also possible to treat all of the items as indices of one scale of legitimacy. If we do, we find that the reliability of the scale is high (alpha = 0.90, time 1; alpha = 0.90, time 2).

4. As noted previously, in earlier presentations of this model motive-based trust was included as an antecedent of procedural justice. Here we treat motive-based trust and procedural justice as two judgments that flow from quality of decision making and quality of treatment to evaluations of the behavior of the authorities.

5. It is also possible to explore the impact of relational judgments on evaluations of the fairness of the procedures that people experienced among subgroups of respondents who received outcomes of varying favorability. The results of such an analysis indicated that relational issues continued to be important even when the outcomes received by the respondents were negative.

6. This study is cross-sectional and does not directly test the adherence that occurs over time. Hence, the argument that adherence over time is enhanced by procedural justice and motive-based trust rests on the other studies we have cited.

Part III

1. Of course, this question can be further broadened. We can ask how experiences with legal authorities shape views about all social institutions—the government, the press, the church, and so on.

Chapter 7

1. The analyses shown were also conducted separately for whites and minorities. In this panel study of a random sample of the residents of Chicago, there were 460 whites and 344 minorities. The primary minority group included was African Americans. On average, minorities expressed greater institutional distrust in legal authorities (mean trust for whites = 2.34; for minorities = 2.42; $F(1,802) = 4.21$, $p < .05$; with high scores indicating distrust).

    Within both groups—whites and minorities—legitimacy had a significant positive influence on people's compliance with the law. However, legitimacy was not a significant determinant of help-seeking among all respondents. Interestingly, it was minority group members whose help-seeking behavior was most strongly shaped by their views about the legitimacy of legal institutions. Legitimacy had less impact on help-seeking behavior among whites.

    We might speculate that mistrust of the law and legal institutions discourages some minorities from approaching legal authorities with their legally relevant problems. Whites do not appear to have an equally strong hesitation. This supports our prior finding from the data collected in the California study that whites are more likely than minorities to initiate contact with legal authorities by calling the police or by going to court.

2. Interestingly, this relationship differed by the race of the respondent. Among minority respondents, legitimacy was linked to subsequent voluntary contact ($r = 0.11$, $p < .05$), with those who were more trusting being more likely to indicate that they later contacted legal authorities. However, among white respondents there was no relationship between legitimacy and subsequent voluntary contact ($r = 0.03$, n.s.).

3. We might expect that people who think legal authorities are more legitimate would be more likely to follow the law and less likely to have been stopped by the police between the time 1 and time 2 interviews. If we examine the relationship between legitimacy as expressed at time 1 and reporting being stopped by the police during the period between the two interviews, however, we find no significant relationship between earlier legitimacy and being stopped at a later time ($r = -.03$, n.s.).

    This lack of a relationship between legitimacy and subsequent nonvoluntary contact with legal authorities does not support our argument. However, it is not entirely surprising, since people have very little control over whether they are stopped by the police. Although anyone can choose to call the police or go to court, people do not choose whether the police will stop them. They can exercise some influence over the likelihood that they will be stopped by the choices they make in their law-related behavior, since the police are especially likely to stop people who are breaking the law, but that linkage is very loose. Most lawbreaking behavior, such as speeding while driving your car, is unlikely to result in being stopped.

4. Such judgments have been widely studied in the case of relations with government under the general rubric of "trust in government" (Levi and Stoker 2000). As with inferences about an individual, judgments of institutional trust or distrust are inferences about a group of people or the functioning of an institution that are made based on information about how they have behaved in the past and how they are likely to behave in the future. However, the particular people that a person deals with are only a sample, and not necessarily a random one, of the larger group of people within the institution. For example, most police complaints of excessive force are generated by a few police officers (Adams 1999). A person's experience with one of those officers may have a strong and lasting impact on his or her broader views about the police. However, it is probably not typical of the experience they might expect to have when dealing with police officers in general. Nonetheless, although atypical, those personal experiences are an important source of information about the police.

    In the case of institutional trust, people also rely heavily on indirect information about authorities or institutions in forming their inferences. People typically have limited personal experience with the police or the courts and use their personal experience as only one of several sources of information that they must combine with the experiences of family, friends, neighbors, and so on. They may also draw upon mass media reports. All of these sources of information are combined to form judgments about the police and the courts as institutions and about the general behavior of police officers and judges.

5. Consistent with the low alpha, the obligation to obey scale is skewed, with most people indicating high levels of obligation. Similar skewedness and a low reliability were also found in Tyler (1990).

6. The mean for pride or identification in being an American is 1.69 (standard deviation = 0.67). The mean for pride or identification with one's city is 1.97 (standard deviation = 0.71). The mean for respect from others in America and one's city is 1.67 (standard deviation = 0.55). The correlation between the two indices of pride is r = 0.39. The correlation between pride in the United States and respect is 0.33, and between pride in one's city and respect is 0.28.

Chapter 9

1. There has been a recent resurgence of interest in social capital, based on the assumption that social capital has important and valuable effects on the functioning of society (Coleman 1990). Social capital is the set of public beliefs that facilitate behaviors that are beneficial to institutions and to society. For example, if citizens vote in national elections because they feel a civic duty to vote, civic duty is an important source of desired civic behavior and feelings of civic duty constitute a valued type of social capital.

Social capital theory has obvious implications for process-based approaches to regulation.

We can also connect process-based approaches to the ideas of Habermas (1999) on community participation. Philosophers have argued on normative grounds for the value of participation in communities. These findings make the same point empirically. When people feel that they are involved in deliberations with legal authorities during personal discussions about how to solve community problems and deal with individual behaviors in the community, they are more likely to accept the solutions determined by those authorities. They are also more willing to view the law as legitimate and to engage themselves in the community. Of course, we do not want to push this comparison too far. Much of the philosophical discussion has been based on the idea of distributive fairness, that is, that decisions reached through deliberation will be fair decisions. Here our concern is with the acceptance of such decisions in ways that people will view as fairer, so that the decisions will be more easily accepted.

Part IV

1. Throughout part IV we refer to African Americans, Hispanics, and whites as belonging to different "ethnic" groups. We use this term as a convenient way to describe the broad cultural and racial boundaries commonly acknowledged in American society. There is certainly ethnic (cultural) diversity within each of these groups, and some individuals may regard themselves as members of more than one of these ethnic groups, or none at all. We made no attempt, however, to classify the ethnicity of respondents in the California study more narrowly than beyond their self-reported identification with one of these three groups.

Chapter 11

1. We adopted this approach for simplicity of presentation. However, we also conducted the analysis treating each of the four indices of outcomes as a separate observed indicator, and the results are similar to those presented here.

Chapter 12

1. For a more detailed discussion of the role of subgroup identification in shaping reactions to personal experiences with legal authorities, see Huo and Tyler (2000).

2. In this analysis each ethnic group was compared to whites. We did not examine the issue of, for example, a Hispanic police officer and an African American community resident. The number of minority police officers

was small, and this type of analysis would be difficult to perform. Instead, we examined Hispanic-white encounters and then, separately, African American–white encounters.

Chapter 13

1. The Hearst National Survey on the Courts was designed and conducted by the National Center for State Courts and funded by the Hearst Corporation. The interviews were conducted by the Indiana University Public Opinion Laboratory.

2. In public presentations of the findings of this study, these special samples are weighted so that the results of the study are equivalent to the proportion of those groups in the American population. However, we do not use those weightings in our analysis of the data. Thus, the percentages reported here may not correspond to those shown in the final report on this survey.

3. In this study 98 percent of those interviewed expressed an opinion.

4. The sample contained 1,284 whites, 215 African Americans, 203 Hispanics, and 124 respondents who either identified themselves as "other" or declined to give a race.

Chapter 14

1. Of course, the gains accrue not only to legal authorities but to society and individuals as well. Community residents often end up injured, and even dead, when a spiral of conflict escalates beyond the intentions of both parties.

Chapter 16

1. Psychological jurisprudence can also involve questions of human cognition. For example, judges often tell jury members to put aside their prejudices when making legal decisions. The framework of legal decision making is based on the belief that people can consciously control the issues they take into account when making decisions. However, psychological research raises questions about whether people are actually able to recognize and remove the influence of their biases and prejudices on their decision making. Awareness of this aspect of human psychology suggests a need to design a procedure that accounts for that human limitation. As one example, it is sometimes suggested that trials be videotaped and inappropriate remarks subsequently removed from the tape. Jury members would thus not hear any remarks that they needed to be able to disregard.

References

Abrams, Dominic, Kaori Ando, and Steve Hinkle. 1998. "Psychological Attachment to the Group." *Personality and Social Psychology Bulletin* 24: 1027–39.

Adams, J. Stacy. 1965. "Inequity in Social Exchange." In *Advances in Experimental Social Psychology*, edited by L. Berkowitz, vol. 2. New York: Academic Press.

Adams, Kenneth. 1999. "What We Know About the Police Use of Force." In *The Use of Force by Police: Overview of National and Local Data*. Washington: Office of Justice Programs, National Institute of Justice, U.S. Department of Justice.

Anderson, Eli. 1994. "The Code of the Streets." *Atlantic Monthly* (May): 81–94.

———. 1999. *Code of the Streets: Decency, Violence, and the Moral Life of the Inner City*. New York: Norton.

Axelrod, Robert. 1984. *The Evolution of Cooperation*. New York: Basic Books.

Ayres, Ian, and John Braithwaite. 1992. *Responsive Regulation: Transcending the Deregulation Debate*. Oxford: Oxford University Press.

Baier, Annette. 1986. "Trust and Antitrust." *Ethics* 96: 231–60.

Barber, Benjamin. 1983. *The Logic and Limits of Trust*. New Brunswick, N.J.: Rutgers University Press.

Baumeister, Roy F., and Mark R. Leary. 1995. "The Need to Belong." *Psychological Bulletin* 117: 497–529.

Beetham, David. 1991. *The Legitimation of Power*. Atlantic Highlands, N.J.: Humanities Press International.

Berry, John W. 1991. "Understanding and Managing Multiculturalism." *Psychology and Developing Societies* 3: 17–49.

Blumstein, Albert, Jacqueline Cohen, and Daniel Nagin. 1978. *Deterrence and Incapacitation*. Washington, D.C.: National Academy of Sciences.

Boeckmann, Robert J., and Tom R. Tyler. 1997. "Commonsense Justice and Inclusion Within the Moral Community." *Psychology, Public Policy, and Law* 3: 362–80.

Bok, Sissela. 1978. *Lying: Moral Choice in Public and Private Life*. New York: Pantheon.

Bourgois, Philip. 1996. *In Search of Respect: Selling Crack in El Barrio*. Cambridge: Cambridge University Press.

Boydstun, John. 1975. *The San Diego Field Interrogation Experiment*. Washington, D.C.: Police Foundation.

Bradach, John L., and Robert G. Eccles. 1989. "Price, Authority, and Trust." *Annual Review of Sociology* 15: 97–118.

Braithwaite, John. 1999. "Restorative Justice: Assessing Optimistic and Pessimistic Accounts." In *Crime and Justice: A Review of Research*, edited by M. Tonry. Chicago: University of Chicago Press.

Bratton, William J. 2000. "Why Lowering Crime Didn't Raise Trust." *New York Times*, February 25.

Brehm, John, and Wendy Rahn. 1997. "Individual-Level Evidence for the Causes and Consequences of Social Capital." *American Journal of Political Science* 41: 999–1023.

Brewer, Marilyn B. 1991. "The Social Self: On Being the Same and Different at the Same Time." *Personality and Social Psychology Bulletin* 17: 475–82.

Brewer, Marilyn B., and Roderick M. Kramer. 1986. "Choice Behavior in Social Dilemmas." *Journal of Personality and Social Psychology* 50: 543–49.

Bursik, Robert J., and Harold Grasmick. 1993. *Neighborhoods and Crime: The Dimensions of Effective Community Control*. New York: Lexington.

Burt, Ronald S., and Marc Knez. 1996. "Trust and Third-party Gossip." In *Trust in Organizations*, edited by Roderick Kramer and Tom R. Tyler. Thousand Oaks, Calif.: Sage.

Casper, Jonathan D., Tom R. Tyler, and Bonnie Fisher. 1988. "Procedural Justice in Felony Cases." *Law and Society Review* 22: 483–507.

Citrin, Jack, and Christopher Muste. 1999. "Trust in Government." In *Measures of Political Attitudes*, edited by John P. Robinson, Philip R. Shaver, and Lawrence S. Wrightsman. New York: Academic Press.

Cole, David. 1999. *No Equal Justice: Race and Class in the American Criminal Justice System*. New York: Norton.

Coleman, John. 1990. *Foundations of Social Theory*. Cambridge, Mass.: Harvard University Press.

Daubenmier, Jennifer J., Heather J. Smith, and Tom R. Tyler. 1997. "Status and Cooperation in a Communal Setting." New York University. Unpublished paper.

Dawes, Robyn. 1994. *House of Cards: Psychology and Psychotherapy Built on Myth.* New York: Free Press.

Dupont, Robert T. 2000. "Evaluation Strategies and Outcome Data: Memphis Crisis Intervention Team Model." Paper presented at the annual Conference on Criminal Justice Research and Evaluation, Department of Justice, Washington (July).

Easton, David. 1965. *A Systems Analysis of Political Life.* Chicago: University of Chicago Press.

Easton, David, and Jack Dennis. 1969. *Children in the Political System.* Chicago: University of Chicago Press.

Eck, John E., and Dennis Rosenbaum. 1994. "The New Police Order: Effectiveness, Equity, and Efficiency in Community Policing." In *The Challenge of Community Policing*, edited by Dennis Rosenbaum. Thousand Oaks, Calif.: Sage.

Emler, Nicholas P., and Nicholas Hopkins. 1990. "Reputation, Social Identity, and the Self." *In Social Identity Theory: Constructive and Critical Advances*, edited by Dominic Abrams and Michael A. Hogg. London: Harvester Wheatsheaf and Springer.

Emler, Nicholas, and Stephen Reicher. 1995. *Adolescence and Delinquency.* Cambridge, Mass.: Blackwell.

Engstrom, Richard L., and Michael W. Giles. 1972. "Expectations and Images: A Note on Diffuse Support for Legal Institutions." *Law and Society Review* 6: 631–36.

Ewick, Patrick, and Susan S. Silbey. 1998. *The Common Place of Law.* Chicago: University of Chicago Press.

Felson, Marcus. 1994. *Crime and Everyday Life.* Thousand Oaks, Calif.: Pine Forge Books.

Finkel, Norman J. 1995. *Commonsense Justice: Jurors' Notions of the Law.* Cambridge, Mass.: Harvard University Press.

Fiske, Susan T., and Shelley E. Taylor. 1991. *Social Cognition,* 2nd ed. New York: McGraw-Hill.

Flanagan, Timothy J. 1996. "Reform or Punish: Americans' Views of the Correctional System." In *Americans View Crime and Justice: A National Public Opinion Survey,* edited by Timothy J. Flanagan and Dennis R. Longmire. Thousand Oaks, Calif.: Sage.

Flanagan, Timothy J., and Dennis R. Longmire. 1996. *Americans View Crime and Justice: A National Public Opinion Survey.* Thousand Oaks, Calif.: Sage.

French, John R. P., and Bertrand Raven. 1959. "The Bases of Social Power." In *Studies in Social Power,* edited by D. Cartwright. Ann Arbor: University of Michigan Press.

Frey, Bruno S. 1997. *Not Just for the Money.* Cheltenham, Eng.: Edward Elgar.

Friedmann, Robert R. 1992. *Community Policing.* New York: Harvester Wheatsheaf.

Gaertner, Samuel L., Mary C. Rust, John F. Dovidio, Betty A. Bachman, and Patricia A. Anastasio. 1994. "The Contact Hypothesis: The Role of a Common Ingroup Identity on Reducing Intergroup Bias." *Small Group Research* 22: 267–77.

Garofalo, James. 1977. *Public Opinion About Crime: The Attitudes of Victims and Nonvictims in Selected Cities.* National Institute of Justice, Washington: U.S. Government Printing Office.

Gold, Marty. 1999. *The Complete Social Scientist: A Kurt Lewin Reader.* Washington, D.C.: American Psychological Association.

Gottfredson, M., and T. Hirschi. 1990. *A General Theory of Crime.* Stanford, Calif.: Stanford University Press.

Habermas, Jürgen. 1999. *Between Facts and Norms.* Cambridge, Mass.: M.I.T. Press.

Hagan, John, and Celeste Albonetti. 1982. "Race, Class, and the Perception of Criminal Injustice in America." *American Journal of Sociology* 88: 329–55.

Hamilton, V. Lee, and Joseph Sanders. 1992. *Everyday Justice.* New Haven, Conn.: Yale University Press.

Haney, Craig, and Philip Zimbardo. 1998. "The Past and Future of U.S. Prison Policy: Twenty-five Years After the Stanford Prison Experiment." *American Psychologist* 53: 709–27.

Hardin, Russell. 2002. *Trust and Trustworthiness.* New York: Russell Sage Foundation.

Haslam, S. Alex. 2001. *Psychology in Organizations: The Social Identity Approach.* Thousand Oaks, Calif.: Sage.

Heider, Fritz. 1958. *The Psychology of Interpersonal Relations*. New York: Wiley.

Heimer, Carol. 2001. "Solving the Problem of Trust." In *Trust in Society*, edited by Karen Cook. New York: Russell Sage Foundation.

Hindelang, Michael J. 1974. "Public Opinion Regarding Crime, Criminal Justice, and Related Topics." *Journal of Research in Crime and Delinquency*, 11: 101–16.

Hoffman, Marty. 1977. "Moral Internalization: Current Theory and Research." In *Advances in Experimental Social Psychology*, edited by Leonard Berkowitz, vol. 10. New York: Academic Press.

Hornsey, Matthew J., and Michael A. Hogg. 2000. "Subgroup Relations: A Comparison of Mutual Intergroup Differentiation and Common Ingroup Identity Models of Prejudice Reduction." *Personality and Social Psychology Bulletin*, 26: 242–56.

Huang, W. S. Wilson, and Michael S. Vaughn. 1996. "Support and Confidence: Public Attitudes Toward the Police." In *Americans View Crime and Justice: A National Public Opinion Survey*, edited by T. J. Flanagan and D. R. Longmire. Thousand Oaks, Calif.: Sage.

Huo, Yuen J., Heather J. Smith, Tom R. Tyler, and E. Allan Lind. 1996. "Superordinate Identification, Subgroup Identification, and Justice Concerns: Is Separatism the Problem, Is Assimilation the Answer?" *Psychological Science* 7: 40–45.

Huo, Yuen J., and Tom R. Tyler. 2000. *How Different Ethnic Groups React to Legal Authority*. San Francisco: Public Policy Institute of California (February).

———. 2001. "Procedural Justice, Identity, and Social Regulation Across Group Boundaries: Does Subgroup Loyalty Undermine Relationship-Based Governance?" Department of Psychology, University of California at Los Angeles. Unpublished paper.

Jacob, Herbert. 1971. "Black and White Perceptions of Justice in the City." *Law and Society Review* 6: 69–89.

Jacobson, Michael P. 2000. "From the 'back' to the 'front': The Changing Character of Punishment in New York City." Paper presented at the CUNY Conference Center, New York (June).

Kanouse, David E., and L. Reid Hanson Jr. 1972. "Negativity in Evaluations." In *Attribution*, edited by E. E. Jones et al. Morristown, N.J.: General Learning Press.

Katz, Daniel, Barbara A. Gutek, R. L. Kahn, and Eugene Barton. 1975. "Bureaucratic Encounters." Ann Arbor, Mich.: Survey Research Center.

Kelling, George L. 1988. "Community Policing." Paper presented to the executive sessions on the police, John F. Kennedy School of Government, Harvard University.

Kelling, George L., and Catherine M. Coles. 1996. *Fixing Broken Windows: Restoring Order and Reducing Crime in Our Communities*. New York: Free Press.

Kelman, Herbert C., and V. Lee Hamilton. 1989. *Crimes of Obedience*. New Haven, Conn.: Yale University Press.

Kennedy, L. W., and D. R. Forde. 1999. *When Push Comes to Shove*. Albany: State University of New York Press.

Kennedy, Randall. 1997. *Race, Crime, and the Law*. New York: Pantheon.

Kim, W. Chan, and Renee A. Mauborgne. 1993. "Procedural Justice, Attitudes, and Subsidiary Top Management Compliance with Multinationals' Corporate Strategic Decisions." *Academy of Management Journal* 36: 502–26.

Kitzmann, Katherine M., and Robert E. Emery. 1993. "Procedural Justice and Parents' Satisfaction in a Field Study of Child Custody Dispute Resolution." *Law and Human Behavior* 17: 553–67.

Komorita, Samuel S., Darins K. S. Chan, and Craig D. Parks. 1993. "The Effects of Reward Structure and Reciprocity in Social Dilemmas." *Journal of Experimental Social Psychology* 29: 252–67.

Komorita, Samuel S., and Craig D. Parks. 1994. *Social Dilemmas*. Madison, Wisc.: Brown and Benchmark.

Kramer, Roderick M. 1991. "Intergroup Relations and Organizational Dilemmas." *Research in Organizational Behavior* 13: 191–228.

———. 1999. "Trust and Distrust in Organizations." *Annual Review of Psychology* 50: 569–98.

Kramer, Roderick M., Charles G. McClintock, and David M. Messick. 1986. "Social Values and Cooperative Response to a Simulated Security Dilemma." *Journal of Psychology* 54: 576–92.

LaFree, Gary. 1998. *Losing Legitimacy: Street Crime and the Fall of Social Institutions in America*. Boulder, Colo.: Westview Press.

Lanza-Kaduce, Lonn, and Richard G. Greenleaf. 1994. "Police-Citizen Encounters." *Justice Quarterly* 11: 605–24.

Lasley, J. R. 1994. "The Impact of the Rodney King Incident on Citizen Attitudes Toward Police." *Policing and Society* 3: 245–55.

Levi, Margaret. 1988. *Of Rule and Revenue*. Cambridge: Cambridge University Press.

———. 1997. *Consent, Dissent, and Patriotism*. Cambridge: Cambridge University Press.

Levi, Margaret, and Laura Stoker. 2000. "Political Trust and Trustworthiness." *Annual Review of Political Science* 3: 475–507.

Lewin, Kurt. 1997. "Resolving Social Conflicts and Field Theory in Social Science." Washington, D.C.: American Psychological Association.

Lind, E. Allan, Jerald Greenberg, Kimberly S. Scott, and Thomas D. Welchans. 2000. "The Winding Road from Employee to Complainant." *Administrative Science Quarterly* 45: 557–90.

Lind, E. Allan, Carol T. Kulik, Maureen Ambrose, and Maria de Vera Park. 1993. "Individual and Corporate Dispute Resolution." *Administrative Science Quarterly* 38: 224–51.

Lind, E. Allan, and Tom R. Tyler. 1988. *The Social Psychology of Procedural Justice*. New York: Plenum.

Lind, E. Allan, Tom R. Tyler, and Yuen J. Huo. 1997. "Procedural Context and Conflict: Variation in the Antecedents of Procedural Justice Judgments." *Journal of Personality and Social Psychology* 73: 767–80.

Lipsky, Martin. 1980. *Street-level Bureaucracy: Dilemmas of the Individual in Public Services*. New York: Russell Sage Foundation.

Locke, Hubert G. 1995. "The Color of Law and the Issue of Color: Race and the Abuse of Police Power." In *And Justice for All: Understanding and Controlling*

Police Abuse of Force, edited by William A. Geller and Hans Toch. Washington, D.C.: Police Executive Research Forum.

Luhmann, Nicholas. 1979. *Trust and Power.* New York: Wiley.

MacCoun, Robert J. 1993. "Drugs and the Law: A Psychological Analysis of Drug Prohibition." *Psychological Bulletin* 113: 497–512.

MacCoun, Robert J., E. Allan Lind, Deborah R. Hensler, D. L. Bryant, and Patricia A. Ebener. 1988. "Alternative Adjudication: An Evaluation of the New Jersey Automobile Arbitration Program." Santa Monica, Calif.: Institute for Civil Justice, RAND.

Mael, Fred A., and Blake E. Ashforth. 1992. "Alumni and Their Alma Mater." *Journal of Organizational Behavior* 13: 103–23.

Makkai, Toni, and John Braithwaite. 1996. "Procedural Justice and Regulatory Compliance." *Law and Human Behavior* 20: 83–98.

Mastrofski, Stephen D., R. B. Parks, C. DeJong, and R. E. Worden. 1998. "Race and Everyday Policing: A Research Perspective." Paper prepared for delivery at the Twelfth International Congress on Criminology, Seoul, Korea (August).

Mastrofski, Stephen D., Jeffrey B. Snipes, and Anne E. Supina. 1996. "Compliance on Demand: The Public's Response to Specific Police Requests." *Journal of Research in Crime and Delinquency* 33: 269–305.

McCluskey, J. D., Stephen D. Mastrofski, and R. B. Parks. 1998. "To Acquiesce or Rebel: Predicting Citizen Compliance with Police Requests." Unpublished manuscript. Administration of Justice Program, George Mason University, Manassas, Virginia.

McEwen, Craig A., and Richard J. Maiman. 1984. "Mediation in Small Claims Court: Achieving Compliance Through Consent." *Law and Society Review* 18: 11–49.

Merelman, R. J. 1966. "Learning and Legitimacy." *American Political Science Review* 60: 548–61.

Merry, Sally E. 1990. *Getting Justice and Getting Even: Legal Consciousness Among Working-class Americans.* Chicago: University of Chicago Press.

Messick, David M., Suzanne Bloom, Janet P. Boldizar, and Charles D. Samuelson. 1985. "Why We Are Fairer Than Others." *Journal of Personality and Social Psychology* 21: 480–500.

Messick, David M., and Roderick M. Kramer. 2001. "Trust as a Form of Shallow Morality." In *Trust in Society,* edited by Karen Cook. New York: Russell Sage Foundation.

Meyerson, Debra, Karl Weick, and Roderick M. Kramer. 1996. "Swift Trust and Temporary Groups." In *Trust in Organizations,* edited by Roderick M. Kramer and Tom R. Tyler. Thousand Oaks, Calif.: Sage.

Mikula, Gerald, Birgit Petri, and Norbert Tanzer. 1990. "What People Regard as Unjust: Types and Structures of Everyday Experiences of Injustice." *European Journal of Social Psychology* 22: 133–49.

Miller, Dale T., and Rebecca K. Ratner. 1996. "The Power of the Myth of Self-Interest." *In Current Societal Concerns About Justice,* edited by Leo Montada and Melvin J. Lerner. New York: Plenum.

———. 1998. "The Disparity Between the Actual and Assumed Power of Self-Interest." *Journal of Personality and Social Psychology* 74: 53–62.

Miller, David. 1999. *Principles of Social Justice.* Cambridge, Mass.: Harvard University Press.

Mitchell, Lawrence E. 1995. "Trust, Contract, Process." In *Progressive Corporate Law: New Perspectives on Law, Culture, Society,* edited by Lawrence E. Mitchell. Boulder, Colo.: Westview.

Moore, Mark H. 1997. "Legitimizing Criminal Justice Policies and Practices." *FBI Law Enforcement Bulletin* (October): 14–21.

Moore, Mark H., and Darrel W. Stephens. 1991. *Beyond Command and Control: The Strategic Management of Police Departments.* Washington, D.C.: Police Executive Research Forum.

Moss, Lonis, and Harvey Goldstein. 1979. *The Recall Method in Social Surveys.* London: University of London Institute of Education.

Muir, William K. 1977. *Police: Street Corner Politicians.* Chicago: University of Chicago Press.

Myers, Laura B. 1996. "Bringing the Offender to Heel: Views of the Criminal Courts." In *Americans View Crime and Justice: A National Public Opinion Survey,* edited by Timothy J. Flanagan and Dennis R. Longmire. Thousand Oaks, Calif.: Sage.

Nagin, Daniel S. 1998. "Criminal Deterrence at the Onset of the Twenty-first Century." In *Crime and Justice: A Review of Research,* vol. 23, edited by Michael Tonry. Chicago: University of Chicago Press.

Nagin, Daniel S., and Raymond Paternoster. 1991. "The Preventive Effects of the Perceived Risk of Arrest." *Criminology* 29: 561–85.

Olson, Susan M., and David A. Huth. 1998. "Explaining Public Attitudes Toward Local Courts." *Justice System Journal* 20: 41–61.

Packer, Herbert L. 1968. *The Limits of the Criminal Sanction.* Stanford, Calif.: Stanford University Press.

Pate, Anthony M., and Lorie A. Fridell. 1993. *Police Use of Force: Official Reports, Citizen Complaints, and Legal Consequences.* Washington, D.C.: Police Foundation.

Paternoster, Raymond. 1987. "The Deterrent Effect of the Perceived Certainty and Severity of Punishment." *Justice Quarterly* 4: 173–217.

———. 1989. "Decisions to Participate in and Desist from Four Types of Common Delinquency." *Law and Society Review* 23: 7–40.

Paternoster, Raymond, Ronet Bachman, Robert Brame, and Lawrence W. Sherman. 1997. "Do Fair Procedures Matter?: The Effect of Procedural Justice on Spouse Assault." *Law and Society Review* 31: 163–204.

Paternoster, Raymond, and Leeann Iovanni. 1986. "The Deterrent Effect of Perceived Severity." *Social Forces* 64: 751–77.

Paternoster, Raymond, Linda E. Saltzman, Gordon P. Waldo, and Theodore G. Chiricos. 1983. "Perceived Risk and Social Control: Do Sanctions Really Deter?" *Law and Society Review* 17: 457–79.

Peek, Charles W., George D. Lowe, and Jon P. Alston. 1981. "Race and Attitudes Toward Local Police." *Journal of Black Studies* 11: 361–74.

Penick, Bettye K., and Maurice B. Owens. 1976. *Surveying Crime*. Washington, D.C.: National Academy of Sciences.

Pommerehne, Werner W., and Hannelore Weck-Hannemann. 1996. "Tax Rates, Tax Administration, and Income Tax Evasion in Switzerland." *Public Choice* 88: 161–70.

Pruitt, Dean G., and Peter J. Carnevale. 1993. *Negotiation in Social Conflict*. Pacific Grove, Calif.: Brooks/Cole.

Pruitt, Dean G., Robert S. Peirce, Neil B. McGillicuddy, Gary L. Welton, and Lynn M. Castrianno. 1993. "Long-term Success in Mediation." *Law and Human Behavior* 17: 313–30.

Pruitt, Dean G., Robert S. Peirce, Jo M. Zubek, Gary L. Welton, and Thomas H. Nochajski. 1990. "Goal Achievement, Procedural Justice, and the Success of Mediation." *International Journal of Conflict Management* 1: 33–45.

Pruitt, Dean G., and Jeff Z. Rubin. 1986. *Social Conflict: Escalation, Stalemate, and Settlement*. New York: McGraw-Hill.

Putnam, Robert D. 1993. *Making Democracy Work*. Princeton, N.J.: Princeton University Press.

———. 1995a. "Bowling Alone: America's Declining Social Capital." *Journal of Democracy* 6: 65–78.

———. 1995b. "Tuning In, Tuning Out: The Strange Disappearance of Social Capital in America." *PS: Political Science and Politics* 28(4): 664–83.

Rawls, John. 1971. *A Theory of Justice*. Cambridge, Mass.: Harvard University Press.

———. 1999. *The Law of Peoples*. Cambridge, Mass.: Harvard University Press.

———. 2000. *Lectures on the History of Moral Philosophy*. Cambridge, Mass.: Harvard University Press.

———. 2001. *Justice as Fairness*. Cambridge, Mass.: Harvard University Press.

Reiss, Albert J., Jr. 1971. *The Police and the Public*. New Haven, Conn.: Yale University Press.

———. 1985. *Policing a City's Central District: The Oakland Story*. Washington, D.C.: National Institute of Justice.

Roach, Kenneth. 1999. "Four Models of the Criminal Process." *Journal of Criminal Law and Criminology* 89: 671–716.

Robinson, P. H., and J. Darley. 1995. *Justice, Liability, and Blame*. Boulder, Colo.: Westview Press.

———. 1997. "The Utility of Desert." *Northwestern University Law Review* 91: 453–99.

Rosenbaum, Dennis P. 1994. *The Challenge of Community Policing*. Thousand Oaks, Calif.: Sage.

Ross, H. Lawrence. 1982. *Deterring the Drinking Driver: Legal Policy and Social Control*. Lexington, Mass.: Heath.

Rusbult, Caryl E., and Paul Van Lange. 1996. "Interdependence Processes." In *Social Psychology: Handbook of Basic Principles*, edited by E. T. Higgins and A. W. Kruglanski. New York: Guilford Press.

Sampson, Robert, Stephen Raudenbush, and Feltan Earls. 1997. "Neighborhoods and Violent Crime." *Science* 277: 918–24.

Sarat, Austin. 1977. "Studying American Legal Culture: An Assessment of Survey Evidence." *Law and Society Review* 11: 427–88.

Schlesinger, Arthur M., Jr. 1992. *The Disuniting of America: Reflections of a Multicultural Society*. New York: W. W. Norton and Company.

Scholz, John T. 1998. "Trusting Government." In *Trust and Governance*, edited by Valerie Braithwaite and Margaret Levi. New York: Russell Sage Foundation.

Scholz, John T., and Mark Lubell. 1998. "Trust and Taxpaying." *American Journal of Political Science* 42: 398–417.

Scholz, John T., and Neil Pinney. 1995. "Duty, Fear, and Tax Compliance: The Heuristic Basis of Citizenship Behavior." *American Journal of Political Science* 39: 490–512.

Schuman, Howard, Charlotte Steeh, Lawrence Bobo, and Maria Krysan. 1997. *Racial Attitudes in America*. Cambridge, Mass.: Harvard University Press.

Sherman, Lawrence W. 1992. *Policing Domestic Violence: Experiments and Dilemmas*. New York: Free Press.

———. 1993. "Defiance, Deterrence, and Irrelevance: A Theory of the Criminal Sanction." *Journal of Research in Crime and Delinquency* 30: 445–73.

———. 1998. "Alternative Prevention Strategies and the Role of Policing." Paper presented at the conference "Beyond Incarceration: The Economics of Crime," Harvard Trade Union Program, Cambridge, Mass. (November).

———. 1999. "Consent of the Governed: Police, Democracy, and Diversity." Keynote address at the conference in honor of Professor Menachem Amir, Institute of Criminology, Hebrew University, Jerusalem, Israel (January).

Sherman, Lawrence W., Denise Gottfredson, Doris MacKenzie, John Eck, Peter Reuter, and Shawn Bushway. 1997. "Preventing Crime: What Works, What Doesn't, What's Promising." Washington, D.C.: National Institute of Justice, Office of Justice Programs.

Skarlicki, Daniel P., and Gary P. Latham. 1996. "Increasing Citizenship Behavior Within a Labor Union: A Test of Organizational Justice Theory." *Journal of Applied Psychology* 81: 161–69.

———. 1997. "Leadership Training in Organizational Justice to Increase Citizenship Behavior Within a Labor Union: A Replication." *Personnel Psychology* 50: 617–33.

Skogan, Wesley. 1990a. "Fear of Crime and Neighborhood Change." In *Crime and Justice: A Review of Research*, edited by Albert J. Reiss Jr. and Michael Tonry, vol. 8. Chicago: University of Chicago Press.

———. 1990b. *Disorder and Decline: Crime and the Spiral of Decay in American Neighborhoods*. New York: Free Press.

———. 1994. "The Impact of Community Policing on Neighborhood Residents: A Cross-site Analysis." In *The Challenge of Community Policing*, edited by Dennis Rosenbaum. Thousand Oaks, Calif.: Sage.

Skogan, Wesley G., and Susan M. Hartnett. 1997. *Community Policing, Chicago Style*. Oxford: Oxford University Press.

Skogan, Wesley, and Michael G. Maxfield. 1981. *Coping with Crime*. Beverly Hills, Calif.: Sage.

Smith, Heather J., and Tom R. Tyler. 1996. "Justice and Power: When Will Justice Concerns Encourage the Advantaged to Support Economic Policies Which Redistribute Economic Resources and the Disadvantaged to Willingly Obey the Law?" *European Journal of Social Psychology* 26: 171–200.

———. 1997. "Choosing the Right Pond: The Influence of the Status of One's Group and One's Status in That Group on Self-esteem and Group-Oriented Behaviors." *Journal of Experimental Social Psychology* 33: 146–70.

Smith, Heather J., Tom R. Tyler, Yuen J. Huo, Daniel J. Ortiz, and E. Allan Lind. 1998. "The Self-relevant Implications of the Group-Value Model." *Journal of Experimental Social Psychology* 34: 470–93.

Sobol, William J., James P. Lynch, and M. Planty. 1999. *Crime, Coercion and Community: The Effects of Arrest Policies on Informal Social Control in Neighborhoods.* Washington, D.C.: Urban Institute (July).

Sparks, Richard, Anthony Bottoms, and Will Hay. 1996. *Prisons and the Problem of Order.* Cambridge: Cambridge University Press.

Sparks, Richard, H. G. Genn, and D. J. Dodd. 1977. *Surveying Victims.* New York: Wiley.

Stokes, Donald E. 1962. "Popular Evaluations of Government." In *Ethics and Bigness: Scientific, Academic, Religious, Political, and Military,* edited by Harlan Cleveland and Harold D. Laswell. Cambridge: Cambridge University Press.

Suchman, Mark C. 1995. "Managing Legitimacy: Strategic and Institutional Approaches." *Academy of Management Review* 20: 571–610.

Sykes, Greshawn. 1958. *Society of Captives.* Princeton, N.J.: Princeton University Press.

Tajfel, Henri. 1972. "La categorisation sociale." In *Introduction a la psychologie sociale,* edited by S. Moscovici. Vol. 1. Paris: Larousse.

Tajfel, Henri, and John C. Turner. 1979. "An Integrative Theory of Intergroup Conflict." In *The Social Psychology of Intergroup Relations,* edited by W. G. Austin and S. Worchel. Monterey, Calif.: Brooks/Cole.

———. 1986. "The Social Identity Theory of Intergroup Behavior." In *The Psychology of Intergroup Relations,* edited by S. Worchel. Chicago: Nelson-Hall.

Tedeschi, James T., and Richard B. Felson. 1994. *Violence, Aggression, and Coercive Actions.* Washington, D.C.: American Psychological Association.

Thibaut, John, and Laurens Walker. 1975. *Procedural Justice.* Hillsdale, N.J.: Erlbaum.

Turner, John C., Michael A. Hogg, Pennelope J. Oakes, Stephen D. Reicher, and Michael S. Wetherell. 1987. *Rediscovering the Social Self.* Oxford: Basil Blackwell.

Tyler, Tom R. 1988. "Client Perceptions in Litigation." *Trial* 24: 40–45.

———. 1989. "The Quality of Dispute Resolution Processes and Outcomes." *Denver University Law Review* 66: 419–36.

———. 1990. *Why People Obey the Law.* New Haven, Conn.: Yale University Press.

———. 1994. "Governing Amid Diversity: The Effect of Fair Decisionmaking Procedures on the Legitimacy of Government." *Law and Society Review* 28: 809–31.

———. 1997a. "Citizen Discontent with Legal Procedures." *American Journal of Comparative Law* 45: 869–902.

———. 1997b. "Procedural Fairness and Compliance with the Law." *Swiss Journal of Economics and Statistics* 133: 219–40.

———. 1997c. "Compliance with Intellectual Property Laws: A Psychological Perspective." *Journal of International Law and Politics* 28: 101–15.

———. 1998. "Public Mistrust of the Law: A Political Perspective." *University of Cincinnati Law Review* 66: 847–76.

———. 1999a. "The Psychology of Legitimacy." *Personality and Social Psychology Review* 1: 323–44.

———. 1999b. "Why Do People Help Organizations?: Social Identity and Pro-organizational Behavior." In *Research on Organizational Behavior*, edited by Barry Staw and Robert Sutton, vol. 21. Greenwich, Conn.: JAI Press.

———. 2000. "Social Justice: Psychological Contributions to International Negotiations, Conflict Resolution, and World Peace." *International Journal of Psychology* 35: 117–25.

———. 2001a. "Social Justice." In *Blackwell Handbook of Social Psychology*, vol. 4, *Intergroup Processes*, edited by Rupert Brown and Samuel Gaertner. London: Blackwell.

———. 2001b. "The Psychology of Legitimacy." In *The Psychology of Legitimacy*, edited by J. Jost and B. Major. Cambridge: Cambridge University Press.

———. 2001c. "The Psychology of Public Dissatisfaction with Government." In *Trust in Government*, edited by Elizabeth Theiss-Morse and John Hibbing. Lincoln: University of Nebraska Press.

———. 2001d. "Cooperation in Organizations." In *Social Identity Processes in Organizational Contexts*, edited by Michael A. Hogg and Deborah J. Terry. Thousand Oaks, Calif.: Sage.

———. 2001e. "Trust and Law-abidingness: A Proactive Model of Social Regulation." *Boston University Law Review* 81: 361–406.

———. 2001f. "Public Trust and Confidence in Legal Authorities." *Behavioral Sciences and the Law* 19: 215–35.

———. 2001g. "Understanding How Citizens View Police Behavior." Paper presented at the meeting of the American Psychological Association, San Francisco (August).

Tyler, Tom R., and Stephen Blader. 2000. *Cooperation in Groups: Procedural Justice, Social Identity, and Behavioral Engagement.* London: Psychology Press.

Tyler, Tom R., Robert Boeckmann, Heather J. Smith, and Yuen J. Huo. 1997. *Social Justice in a Diverse Society.* Boulder, Colo.: Westview Press.

Tyler, Tom R., and Jose Canelo-Cocho. 1999. "Report on the Oakland Evaluation of Police Tactics." University of California at Berkeley. Unpublished paper.

Tyler, Tom R., Jonathan Casper, and Bonnie Fisher. 1989. "Maintaining Allegiance Toward Political Authorities." *American Journal of Political Science* 33: 629–52.

Tyler, Tom R., and John M. Darley. 2000. "Building a Law-abiding Society: Taking Public Views About Morality and the Legitimacy of Legal Authorities into Account When Formulating Substantive Law." *Hofstra Law Review* 28: 707–39.

Tyler, Tom R., and Peter Degoey. 1995. "Collective Restraint in Social Dilemmas." *Journal of Personality and Social Psychology* 69: 482–97.

————. 1996. "Trust in Organizational Authorities." In *Trust in Organizations,* edited by Roderick Kramer and Tom R. Tyler. Thousand Oaks, Calif.: Sage.

Tyler, Tom R., Peter Degoey, and Heather J. Smith. 1996. "Understanding Why the Justice of Group Procedures Matters." *Journal of Personality and Social Psychology* 70: 913–30.

Tyler, Tom R., and E. Allan Lind. 1990. "Intrinsic Versus Community-based Justice Models: When Does Group Membership Matter?" *Journal of Social Issues* 46: 83–94.

————. 1992. "A Relational Model of Authority in Groups." *Advances in Experimental Social Psychology* 25: 115–91.

Tyler, Tom R., E. Allan Lind, Kenichi Ohbuchi, Ikuo Sugawara, and Yuen J. Huo. 1998. "Conflict with Outsiders: Disputes Within and Across Cultural Boundaries." *Personality and Social Psychology Bulletin* 24: 137–46.

Tyler, Tom R., and Gregory Mitchell. 1994. "Legitimacy and the Empowerment of Discretionary Legal Authority: The United States Supreme Court and Abortion Rights." *Duke Law Journal* 43: 703–815.

Tyler, Tom R., and Heather Smith. 1997. "Social Justice and Social Movements." In *Handbook of Social Psychology,* edited by Daniel Gilbert, Susan Fiske, and Gardner Lindzey, 4th ed., vol. 2. New York: McGraw-Hill.

————. 1999. "Justice, Social Identity, and Group Processes." In *The Psychology of the Social Self,* edited by Tom R. Tyler, Roderick M. Kramer, and Oliver P. John. Mahwah, N.J.: Erlbaum.

Unz, Ron. 1999. "California and the End of White America." *Commentary* (November): 17–28.

Van Maanen, John. 1974. "Working the Street: A Developmental View of Police Behavior." In *The Potential for Reform of Criminal Justice,* edited by Herbert Jacob. Beverly Hills, Calif.: Sage.

Waddington, P. A. J., and Quinton Braddock. 1991. "Guardians or Bullies?: Perceptions of the Police Amongst Adolescent Black, White, and Asian Boys." *Policing and Society* 2: 31–45.

Walker, Ian, and Heather J. Smith. 2002. *Relative Deprivation: Specification, Development, and Integration.* Cambridge: Cambridge University Press.

Weber, Max. 1968. *Economy and Society,* edited by G. Roth and C. Wittich. Berkeley: University of California Press.

Williamson, Oliver. 1993. "Calculativeness, Trust, and Economic Regulation." *Journal of Law and Economics* 34: 453–502.

Wilson, James Q., and Barbara Boland. 1978. "The Effect of the Police on Crime." *Law and Society Review* 12: 367–90.

Wilson, James Q., and George L. Kelling. 1982. "Broken Windows: The Police and Neighborhood Safety." *Atlantic Monthly* (March): 29–38.

Wissler, Roselle L. 1995. "Mediation and Adjudication in the Small Claims Court: The Effects of Process and Case Characteristics." *Law and Society Review* 29: 323–58.

Worden, Robert E. 1995. "The 'Causes' of Police Brutality: Theory and Evidence on Police Use of Force." In *And Justice for All: Understanding and Controlling*

Police Abuse of Force, edited by William A. Geller and Hans Toch. Washington, D.C.: Police Executive Research Forum.

Wortley, Soot, John Hagan, and Ross MacMillan. 1997. "Just Des(s)ert?: The Racial Polarization of Perceptions of Criminal Injustice." *Law and Society Review* 31: 637–76.

Yankelovich, Skelly, and White, Inc. 1978. "Highlights of a National Survey of the General Public, Judges, Lawyers, and Community Leaders." In *State Courts: A Blueprint for the Future,* edited by T. J. Fetter. Williamsburg, Calif.: National Center for State Courts.

Index

Numbers in **boldface** refer to figures or tables.